工　　　　春　　川菜

錦江春色
鳳鳳大拼
樟茶烤鴨
川蝎龍蝦

(endpapers) The menu for a traditional Sichuan-style evening banquet. Reading from top to bottom and left to right, the courses are: Spring in Jin Jiang – cold plates; the Phoenix Shark's Fin; Duck Smoked over Camphor Wood and Tea Leaves; Pan-fried Lobster; Vegetables with Almonds; Steamed Fillet of Fish; Sichuan Noodles; Lotus Seed Soup – a dessert flavored with fungus and osmanthus blossoms.

AUTHENTIC RECIPES FROM THE CULINARY AUTHORITIES OF BEIJING, SHANGHAI, GUANGDONG AND SICHUAN

China
THE BEAUTIFUL
COOKBOOK

中國名菜集錦節本

"No one can understand the culture of a country without first experiencing its food and drink."

FISHERMAN ON RHONGU LAKE IN GUILIN, GUANGXI PROVINCE

ADAM WOOLFITT

SHREDDED CHICKEN AND TENDER CELERY *(see page 54)*

AUTHENTIC RECIPES FROM THE CULINARY AUTHORITIES OF BEIJING, SHANGHAI, GUANGDONG AND SICHUAN

China
THE BEAUTIFUL
COOKBOOK

中國名菜集錦節本

This edition produced by
Intercontinental Publishing Corporation Limited,
6th Floor 69 Wyndham Street, Hong Kong
A member of the Weldon/Hardie Group of Companies
Sydney · Auckland · Hong Kong · London
for
The Knapp Press, 5900 Wilshire Boulevard,
Los Angeles, California 90036.

Fourth Printing 1987

The recipes in this book provided by the following authorities:

Beijing Friendship Commercial Service Corporation
Shanghai Municipal Meal and Service Corporation
Guangdong Provincial Meal and Service Corporation
Sichuan Provincial Meal, Vegetable and Service Corporation

Text: Kevin Sinclair

Editorial Director: Elaine Russell
Managing Editor: Julia Roles

Recipe Translators: Frances Ting Chiu Ling
                    Chen We Yei, Cai You Qing
                    Kung Sen Wei De

Recipe Editors: Tan Lee Leng
                Jacki Passmore

Picture Editor (China Landscapes): Mary-Dawn Earley
Calligraphy: Ethna Gallacher, Wong Chiu Tung
Map Illustrator: Dee Huxley
Illustrator: Linda Love
Jacket Illustrator: Sumiko Davies

Designer: John Bull, Bull's Graphics

Library of Congress Cataloging-in-Publication Data
Sinclair, Kevin, 1942-
    China the beautiful cookbook – Chung-kuo ming ts'ai chi
chin chieh pen.
    1. Cookery, Chinese. I. Title. II. Title: Chung-kuo ming
ts'ai chi chin chieh pen.
TX724.5.C5S595   1986   641.5951   86-7300
ISBN 0-89535-176-5

Typeset by Deblaere Typesetting Pty Ltd, Sydney, Australia
Printed and bound in Hong Kong

All recipes have been created to serve six people

THE GREAT WALL SNAKES
THROUGH MOUNTAINOUS NORTHERN CHINA

KEN DUNCAN

(following page) TERRACED HILLSIDES IN
THE LIPING VALLEY, GUIZHOU PROVINCE

GEORG GERSTER

APPETIZERS IN A LACQUER BOX (*see page 142*)

Contents

TIBETAN NOMADS IN SICHUAN PROVINCE

LEO MEIER

The Culinary Heritage

CHINA is more than just a country. It is a culture, a civilization, a way of life that has developed through five thousand years of recorded history. It began when the Han people, forebears of the modern Chinese nation, started their long march to destiny from their ancient homeland near the modern city of Xian. Even before these fifty chronicled centuries of settled society, food played a vital role in the developing Chinese culture.

In the misty era before the Han tribes coalesced into the beginnings of the Chinese race, the first mythical hero to emerge was Fu Hsi. The main activities of this god-like fabled figure were hunting and fishing, and to him is attributed the invention of the kitchen and cooking. The next legendary figure in early Chinese mythology was Shen Nung, the Divine Husbandman. To him goes credit for the plow, the hoe and the care of farm animals. Huang Ti, the Yellow Emperor and the patron saint of Taoism, is worshipped still for the conception of planting grain and the invention of the pestle and mortar to crush it to make flour.

The hunter, the husbandman and the farmer — it is no accident that the first three objects of worship of the ancient Chinese should all have to do with food. Emperor Yu, the founder of the Xia Dynasty (twenty-first to sixteenth century BC), the first to unify the early Chinese, has been honored over the centuries not so much for his political role as the earliest emperor but for his development of water control. This worthy step helped to stop the floods that ruined crops and encouraged the use of irrigation to improve yields. Since the days of the Great Yu, the overwhelming priority of every ruler of China has been to fill the rice bowls of the people. So it remains today. The fact that the billion people of China enjoy a healthy, satisfying, substantial diet with no rationing of basic foodstuffs is widely regarded as the single most vital achievement of the modern government in Beijing.

Things have not always been so auspicious. Throughout its long and turbulent history, the vast wealth of China, most of it created on the solid base built by the endless toil of peasants in the fields, has been a magnet for plunderers, adventurers and invaders. Nature, likewise, has taken a savage toll with drought and flood, earthquake and landslide, tidal wave and typhoon destroying the crops and herds so patiently built up at such a cost in sweat and tears. Not for nothing is the Yellow River, once tamed by Huang Ti, referred to as "China's Sorrow." Its floods over the centuries have left generations homeless, beggared whole provinces, destroyed crops over enormous areas and sentenced untold millions to death by famine.

But Chinese ingenuity, grit, vigor and endless toil have overcome all the obstacles. And when the time comes to give thanks to their many gods and beliefs, the

people of China do so while gathered around the dining table. Family feasts, celebratory banquets, birthdays, the summer and winter equinoxes, wedding anniversaries, celebrations of the birthday of Tin Hau, Goddess of Heaven, or of imported faiths like Christianity, Buddhism or Islam, the conclusion of one successful business deal or the agreement on launching a new one; all these and many more occasions call for glasses to be raised and chopsticks to be wielded. Any event can and is used as worthy excuse for a feast. It can be as simple as a home-cooked meal for an unexpected visit by friends, or as lavish as an imperial banquet that takes twenty chefs three weeks to prepare. Whatever the reason, and no matter how humble or splendid the surroundings, the way Chinese traditionally celebrate is by eating.

So food in all its aspects has, since the birth of Chinese civilization, been a cornerstone of the national culture. In no other people has the preparation, preservation, cooking, cultivation and serving of food taken such a dominant and pervasive role. China's very history revolves around the table and the kitchen. The folk heroes of the nation, no matter who rules it, are often in some way or another connected with eating, drinking or making merry. In China today and in the homes of thirty million overseas Chinese scattered around the world, kitchen gods sit in family shrines staring amiably at housewives or chefs preparing the daily meals. Twice a year ancestral graves are swept and incense lit to pay homage to departed ancestors. Roast pork, rice wine and fruit are offered to the dead; food in Chinese culture is important even to those who have passed on.

A DIVERSE CUISINE

Any cuisine is limited by the raw ingredients that are available. In the case of China, the range is virtually boundless. The country is vast, twice as large as Europe excluding Russia, bigger than the United States including Alaska and Hawaii, a quarter as huge again as Australia. Into this gigantic land are crowded more than a billion people. They are unfairly distributed: packed into the rich flatlands along the east and southern coasts; jammed into the great valleys of the Yellow, Yangtze and Pearl rivers; stacked by the millions in the sprawling industrial conurbations; and crammed – no less than one hundred million of them – into the rice-bowl basin of inland Sichuan. But elsewhere they are scattered lightly. The steppes of Mongolia and Xinjiang are still thinly peopled by Kazakh, Uigur and Turkic tribesmen, and the descendants of Genghiz Khan. The ice plateau of Tibet, a land of soaring peaks, precipitous caverns and frigid highland plains, is bigger than Austria, Czechoslovakia, the Netherlands, Switzerland, Belgium, Italy, Portugal, Luxembourg and Hungary combined, and has fewer than two million people. In the jumbled mountains of the southwest, a chaos of races – minority tribes of dozens of nationalities – live in steep river valleys, unaware and uncaring about those who may occupy the next ravine.

This huge landscape has dictated the scores of regional cuisines that have developed in China over the centuries. Although the country produces every delicacy under the sun, much of the grain, vegetables and live-

TIBETAN NOMADS ON HORSE AND YAK, SICHUAN PROVINCE

LEO MEIER

A BAI WAITRESS AT A DALI CITY RESTAURANT, YUNNAN PROVINCE

GREGORY HEISLER

stock is available only in the locality where it is produced. Even today, with vast improvements in communications and transport, what goes into the family pot tends to be that which is grown or raised nearby. The delectable camel hump of Mongolia is a rare and costly luxury in the south. Seafood is understandably scarce in Chengdu, 1,800 miles (3,000 kilometers) upriver from the mouth of the Yangtze. Fresh vegetables are unknown in the frigid Manchurian winter, although the gardens blossom all year round in semitropical Guangdong.

From this immense geographical diversity have developed the manifold varieties of Chinese cuisine. In the past the climate dictated what people ate and, to a lesser extent in this age of efficient artificial preservation, refrigeration and dehydration, it still does today. This is partly because of the inherited and acquired love of the favorite dishes with which people grew up from childhood. While experimentation is encouraged in every Chinese kitchen, the family favorites of childhood tend to hold a tight gastronomic rein throughout life. For Chinese, as for every other people, this is probably because of the international love for the food that mother cooked.

But intertwined with the love of good food is also the ancient basic philosophy of China, the belief in harmony, of the balance of nature, of the duality of existence, of the blending of contrasts. Yin and yang, the two elements, are as significant in the Chinese kitchen as they are in the temple. Yin is soft, yielding, dark, feminine. Yang is hard, bright, masculine, vigorous. In the wok, the hot pot or the steamer, yin and yang combine and complement each other. Sweet contrasts with sour. The two basics of stir-frying — ginger and green onions — are yang and yin. Crunchy sea salt goes with Sichuan peppercorns. Steamed chicken goes with stir-fried fresh greens, the yang of fiery chilies goes with the gentle yin of sugar. The contrast of taste and texture, colors and cooking methods, which results in any balanced Chinese meal is a triumph of the philosophical theory of yin and yang, the world in a happy balance. A Chinese meal, ordered correctly, should be orchestrated like a Mozart symphony: hot and cold, sweet and sour, plain and spicy, meat and pickle, fish and greens, yin and yang.

THE NATIONAL DRINK

Tea is the drink of China and has been so since recorded history began. The preparation and sipping of tea are part of the education of a scholar and the daily life of a manual worker. Learned discussions about how best to make tea, with what implements, the source of the best water, the method of boiling it and the vital question of how long the leaves should be left to steep are matters which for thousands of years have preoccupied writers and artists, generals and merchants, mandarins and emperors. Throughout the land in almost every dialect it is called "cha." The exception is in Fujian, where the word "deh" is used. Because the seafarers of Fujian exported the dried, chopped leaves of the tree, and because it was in the ports of the southeast coast that foreigners loaded it, the beverage is known in the Western world as "tea."

Tea has played a vital role in China throughout recorded history. It has been the reason for polite and learned academic discussions in teahouses; it caused social unrest and riots in China as it once did in Boston;

MARC BERNHEIM

PICKING THE FAMOUS DRAGON WELL TEA, HANGZHOU, ZHEJIANG PROVINCE

THE TEA CEREMONY

When Lu Yu wrote his scholarly but chatty "Classics of Tea" at the time of the early Tang Dynasty (618-907 AD), tea was more than just a drink; it was a symbol and a ceremony. He discoursed on types of water to use, the twenty-four different items of equipment needed to make a cup of tea and the way in which it should be prepared. The best tea leaves, he wrote, "should curl like the dewlap of a bullock, crease like the boot of a Tartar horseman, unfold like the mist rising from a ravine and soften gently like fine earth after it is swept by rain."

Lu Yu, along with similarly minded scholars, helped to inspire centuries of poetry, arts, porcelain manufacture and an enormous range of other academic and industrial activities all concentrating on the best way of making tea. This ostentatious, quasi-religious elevation of the tea ceremony rose to a pinnacle among the idle rich and the literati during the Song Dynasty (960-1279 AD), when fortunes would be paid for a perfectly glazed teacup and officials would sit for hours discussing different brands. This came to an abrupt end with the arrival of the less sophisticated and more direct Mongols of the Yuan Dynasty (1260-1368 AD), for whom a cup of tea was a cup of tea. The tea ceremony still flourished in Japan, to which it had been exported, but in China the ceremony was never again to reach such esoteric heights. However, in modern China the teahouse remains the favored rendezvous.

ALCOHOLIC DRINKS

Loosely translated as wine, the Chinese expression "jiu" means any beverage containing alcohol, of which there are many in China. Like tea, wine is the fountainhead of a thousand legends, most of them affably eccentric. A chef of ancient times is said to have put some rice to soak in a covered jar, which he placed in a corner of his warm kitchen and promptly forgot. A few days later he raised the lid and was engulfed by a strong, unfamiliar aroma. He cautiously dipped in his serving spoon and tasted the contents; and again, and again. Other kitchen staff were attracted by his joyful mirth. They too tried the strange mixture. So was held the first cocktail party in China, and thus was born the Chinese tradition of drinking and making jolly.

The Chinese made a variety of jiu as far back as 2000 BC. Modern vintners would probably not award the ancient beverages any prizes, but ancient tipplers seemed partial to a glass with their meals, and for the past four thousand years Chinese imagination has run enthusiastically riot in distilling alcoholic drinks from almost anything that has come to hand. Today that tradition remains vibrantly alive with a staggering number of wines, beers, spirits and liqueurs being made in every corner of the land. Brewers, winemakers and distillers use as raw materials everything from transplanted French grapes and German hops, to rice, sorghum, wheat, corn, potatoes and fruit of all types. Beverages range from classic German-style wines, to foaming beers, to the explosive sorghum-based Mao Tai, with which Mao Zedong and Richard Nixon toasted ping-pong diplomacy, to sweet but potent tipples such as the Panda brand liqueur made in Sichuan Province and based on the hirsute Chinese gooseberry.

Wine was carried into China in ancient times by Persian traders, and at least a century before Christ vines

and it has been used as a national treasure, a state currency, a government fund-raising monopoly and, in the form of pressed bricks of leaves, as cash. It is also a relaxing, captivating, sacred drink.

There are thousands of varieties of tea. It grows on flat, fertile land but thrives equally well on steep hillsides up to 6,000 feet (2,000 meters) amid eternal mist where other crops fail. In its untended state the tree sprouts to 30 feet (10 meters) or more, but when clipped and pruned for cultivation it is kept to 4 feet (1.2 meters) in height so the strength goes into the leaves. The three leaves on the tip of the bud are used in top-quality teas. There are three main types of tea: red, green and black. Among the most famous of the green varieties is the astringent, pale yellow Dragon Well tea from Hangzhou. The Keemun type grown all over east China, favorite of the British breakfast table, is among the best-known of the red teas. Oolong (Black Dragon) tea includes such leaves as the Iron Goddess of Mercy type from Jiangxi, which when it is pressed into bars is said to be as hard as metal.

Even the most learned scholar cannot say where tea originated. According to legend a forgotten emperor (or a thirsty deity, some versions hold) was sitting contemplatively in his garden sipping a bowl of hot water when a gust of autumn wind blew some leaves off a tree. They landed in the imperial bowl and colored the water. The monarch sipped it and liked what he tasted. Tea was born.

Since then more legends have sprouted from the teacups of China than from almost any other source. Tea is said to soothe the excited and help the restless to sleep. On the other hand, it is held to awaken the senses and rouse the drowsy. It has been used as a medicine and a placebo, to quiet the restless young, relax the tensions of the mature and to ease the discomfort of the old.

were growing around the imperial palace. The grape had a seesaw existence throughout history, often depending on the personal inclination of the emperor. If he drank, vines flourished. If he happened to frown on the pressed and fermented fruit of the vine, imperial decrees went out ordering farmers to rip up the vines and replant their land with food crops. A fillip to the vineyards came at the end of the last century when Europeans in north China, especially missionaries, planted extensive areas of grapes. Today they still exist in vast areas of Shandong and Hebei provinces, and new plantings by French and other joint-venture partners are renewing production of first-class wines in China. With the aid of foreign expertise and modern techniques used in Europe, America and Australia, Chinese wines have won international awards.

Beer also came from foreign influences, many of them unhappy. During the rush to grab parts of China in the last century, Europeans and Japanese brought with them a demand for their native drinks. This dismal episode in China's history had at least one auspicious result because there are thousands of ales and beers in the country today, many of them drawn from brewing techniques introduced into the Treaty Ports. The most famous is the magnificent Tsingtao beer, which originated in the port city of that name (now Qingdao) during German occupation of parts of Shandong Province in the late nineteenth and early twentieth centuries.

Most Chinese drinking is done along with eating; tradition abhors drinking alone or on an empty stomach,

and it is at banquets with family, friends or guests that most Chinese indulge in some of their huge range of drinks. Usually the glasses are filled with one of the countless varieties of rice wines, the most famous of which is Shaoxing wine from Zhejiang Province. This tends to be darkish in color and is poured warm from a vessel like a teapot into small glasses and then drunk with flamboyant gusto. Also favored at banquets, particularly during feasts or when foreigners are present, are some of the strong spirits of China. These include some truly fearsome distilled beverages like the fragrant but potent Mao Tai; the transparent Fen Chiew liquor which is used as a base for Zhu Ye Qing liqueur; and the ferocious Kaoliang of north China, designed to keep out the frigid cold of winter and which, to boot, numbs all other feelings with its 130-proof punch.

Much dinner-table drinking is associated with games. In one, the lazy susan in the middle of the table is spun and the person who ends up staring into the head of the remains of a duck or chicken dish has to swallow his or her drink. Then the host toasts his guests, and the visitors toast the host, and the young raise their glasses to the old, and the aged drink to the more youthful, and everyone drinks to the person sitting next to him. As each glass is raised, everyone calls "kan pei," which in rough translation means good health.

Many of the stories associated with Chinese drinking deal with poets. Historically, poets were regarded as a rather bohemian, happy-go-lucky lot, a large number

SELLING MEDICINAL WINE IN A ZUNYI STREET MARKET, GUIZHOU PROVINCE

MICHAEL YAMASHITA

of them from wealthy or influential families, who spent their lives writing classical couplets, generally while deeply in their cups. Several of them often cited in classical tales came to bad ends because of overindulgence. One is said to have rolled to his death down a steep hill while staggering home from a wine shop. Another of these "drunken dragons," as poets were known, was Li Po, who wrote with enthusiasm of "the rapture of drinking and wine's heady joy." He went everywhere accompanied by two servants whose job was to carry their literary master safely home. Li Po proclaimed during his bouts that he could not write without a drink. His end would seem to bear out this claim; he is said to have clambered into a sampan and pushed himself out on a lake on a still night to admire the reflection of the moon in the calm water. While enthusing about the view, he took another drink. Leaning over the side of the boat trying to embrace the vision of the glorious reflection, he fell into the water and drowned.

Even the stern Confucius liked a drop and noted that "there is no limit to wine drinking." One must not get drunk, he was swift to add, a lesson which was apparently not heeded by Li Po or hundreds of other poets who down the ages have sung the glories of jiu.

THE ART OF PRESERVATION

Entering a Chinese store that sells dried foods, herbs or medicines (and sometimes it is virtually impossible to draw a line between what you take for health and what is for sustenance) is akin to going into a museum of fauna and flora. There will be fungi of incredible sizes and bizarre shapes: tiny button mushrooms from the fields, large drooping fungi from the rain forests of the southern jungles, and the strange monkey brain fungi dug from the frozen soils of Manchuria. Some stores will also have birds' nests from the cliff-side caves of Kalimantan — foul-smelling balls of grass and excrement, but a vital ingredient for the soup of the same name. There will be countless varieties of pasta, fried chilies, a mysterious selection of hundreds of herbs adorning shelf upon shelf, and dangling from the roof will be the rustling skins and skeletal shapes of octopi, jellyfish, squid, fish intestines, seaweeds and other former inhabitants of the deep; just drop them into water for a few hours and they will return to an edible reincarnation. Deers' antlers, horns of rhinoceros, gall bladders of ox and buffalo, and the dried penis of whale are also to be found at awesome prices, because a pinch of the ground powder from such potent items is believed to hold powerful aphrodisiac qualities.

Just how Chinese preserves are used is a secret which many chefs guard closely. And just as only a very fine line can be drawn between the ingredients used for medicine and those for food, so can the doctor's advice merge with the recipes used in a Chinese kitchen. The saying popular among Western food faddists, "You are what you eat," was probably expressed in a score of Chinese dialects several thousand years ago, and the raw material for many of the potions mixed then and commonly in use today can still be found on the shelves of any Chinese dried food store.

A MARKET STALL IN YONGXIN, JIANGXI PROVINCE   ENRICO FERORELLI

THE FIERY CHILI, AN EXPLOSIVE COMPONENT OF SICHUAN CUISINE

MICHAEL YAMASHITA

SELLING MUSHROOMS AT SHIMIAN VILLAGE MARKET, SICHUAN PROVINCE

As with everything to do with the foods of China, preserving techniques were dictated by the climate. In the south, fresh foods were almost always available (just as well, because nothing keeps for long in the torrid, humid summer). In the north, for half the year nature provided natural refrigeration. And in both regions pickling has long been a favored technique, for reasons of taste as well as for preservation.

The average cook in China uses an extensive range of preserves, spices and seasonings every day. Hot chili paste, biting mustard, the inescapable soy sauce, preserved plums, pickled turnips, carrots or cabbage, mushrooms in endless species and black bean sauce are among the most common accompaniments for everyday dishes. And they are the merest tip of a gastronomic iceberg of formidable proportion. Perhaps the most visible preserves in China are the pressed flocks of ducks and the salted schools of fish which hang in the streets outside restaurants throughout the land. They are edible advertisements for what is offered inside.

Nuts of all kinds are an important and often unseen and unsung ingredient of Chinese culinary art. They were prominently mentioned in the gourmet recipe book of Madame Wu, printed in the eleventh century. So were many other preserved foods, which can still be found today in delicatessens or dried food stores in any self-respecting Chinatown.

To preserve meat Madame Wu advised rubbing dry salt into the flesh, putting it in a clay pot with a stone on top and pressing it overnight, then hanging it up to dry in a cool, airy room. The same technique is universally in use today. Fish were kept in times of abundance by grilling them, soaking them in oil and then packing them in jars sealed with damp clay. Similar items, perhaps marketed in more modern containers, can still be bought to be eaten either as snacks or as a course in a feast with other out-of-season foods. Preserved meat and fish and pickled fruit and vegetables are never a meal on their own, but as side dishes and accompaniments to major courses, they are indispensable and valued items in the culinary heritage.

A CULINARY HISTORY

Chinese culinary traditions have adapted freely and changed fluidly with time and circumstances. Five thousand years ago, at the time of the emerging Han tribes, the main crop in their arid, windblown homeland was probably a prehistoric form of millet. But archeological digs in north China show that far before that time, Peking Man had already developed a sophisticated caveman cuisine. Using stone weapons, he hunted down such prey as saber-toothed tigers and roasted them over an open fire.

Steaming, that great basic kitchen technique still in very effective use today, was perfected long before the foundation of the first dynasty. Scientists testing remains outside Xian have ascertained that the inhabitants of a village named Banpo were cooking such delicacies as chicken, carp and elephant three thousand years before the birth of Christ.

Two millennia later the glorious Shang Dynasty flowered (sixteenth to eleventh century BC). In addition to art, commerce, culture and science, cuisine flourished in the rich atmosphere of the court and such delicacies as rhinoceros and elephant were consumed. Religion, closely linked with food, also developed, and as the cooking fires died down the shells of turtles and the thigh bones of oxen were thrown in the embers. From the shapes produced in the flames, soothsayers read omens and foretold the future.

There is no evidence that the prophets of Shang gave warning of the rise of Zhou (1122-256 BC), the dynasty that was to supplant them. The kings of Zhou claimed descent from a ruler of the northwestern plains named Hou Ji, which means Lord Millet, and by the time they imposed their rule over the embryonic northern kingdom that was to grow into the Chinese nation, they had learned how to grow rice, wheat, soybeans, melons, celery and squashes, and on feast days ate roast sheep and boar.

But early gastronomic development was not restricted to the north. As the Han people melded into a great and unified nation on the plains of the Yellow River, a political and culinary evolution was taking place along the fertile banks of the mighty Yangtze. Kingdoms and dukedoms rose and fell and flowered and wilted. But as armies marched, clashed, died and conquered, the peasants of China continued their eternal task of providing food for the ever-increasing population.

Thanks to modern scientific techniques, archeologists and anthropologists can now fit together much fascinating historical evidence. The resulting jigsaw puzzles have many missing pieces, but enough have survived to tell us of a rich gastronomic feast in the vast Yangtze Valley during the ceaseless warring eras of the kingdoms of Wu, Yu and Chu. For three centuries the warriors and lords battled for supremacy. Politically they were stalemated, but on the culinary front, seven hundred years before Christianity, chefs won magnificent victories with such outstanding dishes as noodles sautéed with honey, lamb stewed with sugar cane, braised ox tendons, and bitter melon soup. The soldiers did not beat their swords into plowshares — rather, the farmers used the shoulder blades of their oxen to till the deep, rich soils in which they grew such delicacies as peaches in the hot, damp summers. This gave rise to internal trade. Peaches went north to the sophisticated table of the emperor, and bear paws were dispatched south to the semi-barbarian kings of the warring states.

By the second century BC, the Yangtze Valley was the frontier of Chinese civilization, an Oriental Wild West where the only law was the sword. But China was about to take the gastronomic and geographical shape of today, as the Qin Dynasty (221-206 BC) brought under imperial rule the blooming basin of Sichuan in the upper Yangtze and the broad plains of Guangdong. For the first time the four great branches that were to grow into modern Chinese cuisine – classical Beijing, rich Shanghai, delicate Guangzhou and hearty Sichuan – were all to come under one rule. That rule did not last long, because on a tour of his new lands the man who united China into one realm died. Legend says his body was carried back to the capital Xian amid a load of salted fish (even then a southern delicacy) which disguised the smell of death. He was buried with great honor, guarded by thousands of terracotta soldiers.

Next onto the imperial stage came a commoner from stout farming stock named Liu Bang. In blood and fire he forged the Han Dynasty (206 BC-220 AD), one of the greatest in China's history. Gastronomically the Han

ANCIENT CHINESE BANQUET MENUS

SHUFUNOTOMO

A STREETSIDE BREAKFAST, GUIZHOU PROVINCE

MICHAEL YAMASHITA

period was a vital one. There were staggering culinary achievements — noodles were invented, and so were flour mills. The ancient soybean was made into tofu. Expeditionary forces went into central Asia (then green and fertile, now mostly arid) and brought back treasures like sesame, peas, grapes, coriander and garlic. The culinary delights of the New Territories added Sichuan peppercorn to the imperial banquets. From the tropical south horsemen galloped in relays to speed the exotic lichees of the Pearl River delta to Xian. Today the first lichees of autumn are still rushed north to gourmets, but now they go by express train or jet aircraft.

The Han had pacified, or at least kept at sword's length, the savage Hun horsemen. But when, in the third century AD the Han Dynasty toppled because of internal plots, the barbarians galloped into China and occupied the north. They brought gastronomic disaster with them as well as political terror: their favorite dishes were boiled sheep and smelly cheese. However, the culinary flame was kept burning brightly south of the Yangtze, where the Wu Dynasty (222-280 AD) took what a bountiful climate, fertile soil and dedicated farmers and fishermen had to offer to raise cooking to an art. Oranges went into the cooking pots, as did other southern crops such as lotus seeds and coconuts.

It took three centuries for the Huns to be thrown back from north China to their heartland on the steppes of central Asia, and then the Sui Dynasty was to rule for only four decades (581-618 AD). But what it accomplished in such a tiny span! The Grand Canal was frantically dug by armies of human bulldozers. It linked the two mighty rivers on which China's history had been written, and from Yangzhou on the Yangtze the grains of the south were towed by barge north to the Yellow River plains. Yangzhou became the capital and its chefs labored mightily over charcoal stoves to bring forth miracles of culinary creation that are today some of the most famous manifestations of the Chinese kitchen. The fat, plump Wo noodles that make up rich winter soups came from the Sui Dynasty chefs. So did fried rice and immortal dim sum. It might not have long dominated the political throne of China, but the Sui Dynasty passed on a culinary heritage that today is still renowned.

TRAVELERS' BOUNTIES

And then came the Tang (618-907 AD). Their legacy is both diverse and delectable. They bequeathed us the wok and therefore that most distinctive of Chinese cooking techniques, stir-frying. Distilled spirits came during their three-century rule, during which China was the dominant power on earth. Trade flowered and with the merchants from other lands came nutmeg, saffron, eggplants, spinach and dill. Travelers brought back ideas as well as herbs, and Buddhism, with its vegetarian cuisine, had an immense and lasting influence on Chinese cuisine.

The tides of history washed the Song Dynasty (960-1279 AD) into power, mostly on the shields of barbaric nomads. The Great Wall failed to keep out the savage horsemen, and wave after wave of invaders intent on plunder swarmed into the treasure house that was China. The Song emperors retreated before this storm of uncouth aliens, and once again it was in southern China that food and farming developed. Thwarted from spreading to the north, the Song reached for the sea and their traders brought home exotica from as far afield as

India and Indonesia. More importantly, from what is now Vietnam came seeds for a rice that produced a crop much earlier in the year than existing strains. From these few sacks of seeds can be traced the vast rice-growing tradition of the humid southern provinces.

Most of the barbarians who invaded to plunder, loot and conquer soon fell under the awesome wonder of China's culture, including the cuisine. Over the centuries they were usually lulled into quiet good manners, generally after being liberally plied with gentle wine and strong spirits, soothed with tea and gorged with the incomparable delicacies of the Chinese table. This did not apply, however, to the rude Mongols of the Yuan Dynasty (1206-1368 AD). They gulped down fermented horse's milk and tore at chunks of meat, often raw, which they carried in their sheepskin jackets or stowed under the saddles where, legend has it, the meat was tenderized after being subjected to the pounding of a day's hard riding. Their contribution to culinary history is confined to the one dish that originated from the horseback-broken piece of meat, steak tartare, and an increased appetite for mutton in the north.

It was under the magnificent Ming (1368-1644 AD), the last truly Chinese imperial dynasty, that modern cuisine developed. Their traders roamed the seas to Madagascar and Arabia. Chinese culture was exported and in return foreign ingredients made their way to the kitchens – first in the court, then in the cities, and finally in the peasant homes of the nation. But once again, the

THE TERRACED HILLSIDES OF YUDU COUNTY, JIANGXI PROVINCE

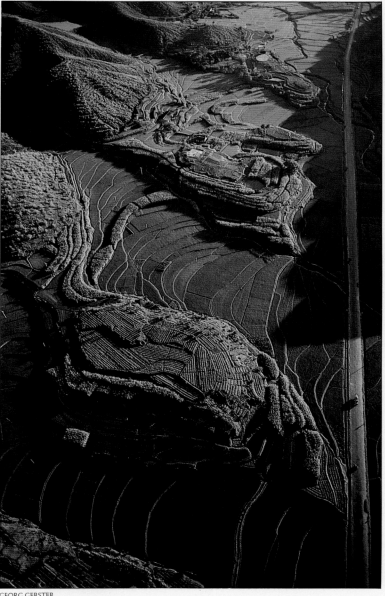

GEORG GERSTER

glory and wealth of China proved a jewel too precious to be ignored by the hungry and fierce barbarians outside the Middle Kingdom. The Ming pleaded with their fearsome neighbors the Manchus for military aid, and they answered this invitation promptly by marching into China. The Manchus threw out the invaders and just as quickly decided that as they had saved China they might as well stay and rule it. Reigning as the Qing Dynasty, the Manchus set up a regime that was to last until the early twentieth century.

The Manchus, though not as crude as the Mongols, brought few gastronomic delights with them from the frozen plains of their homeland. Winter Fire Pot, designed to warm them during the frigid six months of winter, was their major legacy, and it is still enjoyed all over China today. After the initial savage repression of their new realm, designed successfully to terrorize the population into accepting their rule, the Manchus settled down to enjoy life in the graceful civilization that suddenly was theirs. They became, it is said, more Chinese than the Chinese. A couple of generations removed from their horses, the Manchu rulers relaxed in a life of luxury and leisure and spent much of their time concentrating on concubines and the table, while Chinese scholars and civil servants administered the realm.

It was, for two centuries, a time of peace and prosperity. As the Manchus became decadent and feasted on elephants' trunks and larks' tongues in three-day imperial banquets, the food consumed every day by gourmets

was developing into the Chinese cuisine we know and love today. Portuguese traders brought chilies to Macau, from where they traveled up the branches of the Pearl River and into Hunan and Sichuan, creating the basis of the modern spicy dishes of the southwest. Fujian was gaining fame for seafood cooked with imagination. Guangdong dishes were reaching the degree of subtlety and clarity they are now noted for.

Just as important, from the point of view of culinary history, was how Chinese cooking was being taken abroad. Tea went around the world. The Western powers who grasped parts of China during the nineteenth century had little impact on the cuisine. But out of China from the mid-nineteenth century onwards flowed a steady stream of laborers to work the tin mines of Malaya, to dig for gold in Australia, New Zealand and South Africa, to hack railways across the Rocky Mountains and to take their commercial skills to every corner of the Pacific and beyond. This exodus of people, the forebears of today's thirty million overseas Chinese, came mostly from the great southern provinces of Guangdong and Fujian and with them they took Chinese cooking to every country of the world.

But the greatest Chinese cuisine on earth is still found today in the land where it developed. A combination of many centuries of love of good food, a tradition of hospitality and endless experimentation with the fruits of the good earth has gone into making the rich and vibrant feast that is the culinary heritage of China the Beautiful.

DRYING MAIZE IN THE ERLANG MOUNTAINS, SICHUAN PROVINCE   HARALD SUND

北京
Beijing

北京

Beijing

CLASSICAL CUISINE

THE cuisine of Beijing is a contradiction. It is a combination of two very different legacies, the magnificence of classical court cooking forming a splendid but thin veneer over the honest, solid food prepared by farmers' wives in the countless tiny hamlets that dot the dusty plains of northern China.

What the world regards as Beijing food is very different from the daily diet of the peasants of Hebei, Shandong, Henan and Shanxi provinces. For this is poor country, infertile and often arid, a land where living has for centuries been precarious, balanced delicately between persuading the cruel land and bitter climate to provide sufficient millet, wheat, lentils, corn and sweet potatoes to feed the village, and all too often the threat of famine. For the peasant farmers on their tiny plots nature was as often an enemy as a friend. In November, almost overnight it seems, a chill wind begins blowing from the icy wastes of Manchuria and Siberia. The next morning the village ponds are frozen. Over the next few weeks the ground itself is gripped and for five solid months the land is one vast block of unyielding ice.

Through this austere winter, grain, turnips and cabbage provide the basis for the peasant kitchen. Often in the past there has been too little of even these basics. Before the great irrigation works began three decades ago, another unpredictable and savage enemy was that sleeping dragon which curls in bizarre muddy loops across the plains: the Huang Ho, the Yellow River, China's Sorrow. The river that brought the water to give life to the fields also brought floods that ruined crops and signaled famine. So did the many other waterways that meander over the flats towards the Gulf of Bohai or the Yellow Sea.

After the thaw turns the roads to mud and the fields suddenly awaken, the heat of summer comes like a blast from hell itself. The heat sears the plains, bringing a dry wind that in autumn causes almost instant dehydration to a million ducks hanging from every home to provide the main ingredient in the most famous dish of the north, Beijing Duck. But if the heavy rains of summer

THE FORBIDDEN CITY IN BEIJING
THOMAS HOPKER

ONE OF BEIJING'S BUSY INDOOR MARKETS

have not come, the winds from the west bring dust clouds and add to the misery of drought. Little wonder that after a wet summer when the crops are in and the cold winds begin to blow, a time when the farmers of the northern plains have sufficient food to last themselves and their families through the icy months, they bring out the explosive Mao Tai spirits and celebrate in hearty feasts and banquets.

In Beijing the glittering banquets in the Great Hall of the People present the world with a glimpse of the pinnacle of modern Chinese feasts. The capital's business community, the diplomats, the foreign journalists, all have their favorite restaurants featuring gastronomic riches unknown to the millions of peasants of the plains. The capital has people from every province in China and, in addition to the northern dishes, offers a wide range of regional restaurants providing homely provincial favorites for those in the army, government or bureaucracy who serve in Beijing, as well as for local gourmets and adventurous visitors to the capital.

As in every other region, the common food of north China, away from the state banquets, is a mixture of tradition, imported outside influences and restrictions imposed on agriculture by the savage climate. During the brief hot summer the cities of north China are almost choked with a flood of vegetables. Huge tomatoes, immense zucchini, giant cauliflowers, juicy melons, succulent squashes, plump eggplants and enormous pumpkins fill the markets. Alas, it is all too brief. Soon the summer vegetables are gone and the hardy dry staples of winter make for a long and dull gastronomic season until, weather permitting, the bounty of another grow-

ing season is harvested. Despite the harsh environment, the genius of Chinese chefs over the centuries has developed a cuisine out of necessity. A rich culinary stew takes a few local ingredients (millet or wheat), adds a dash of imported Muslim custom (mutton), a hardy staple that thrives in the summer and keeps well throughout the long winter (white turnip or that superb standby of the north, Tianjin cabbage), and from such simple components comes up with a succulent, filling meal like a delicious sliced lamb hot pot.

Muslim cooking has had a strong influence on northern cuisine. Horsemen who surged over the Great Wall into the flatlands were often Muslims. They came to conquer and stayed to settle, and today the countless millions of Chinese with the family name Ma (Horse) can often trace their ancestry to the Muslim raiders. Today, however, it is only in name and culinary tastes that their heritage shows. Mongol, Manchu, Muslim – all have merged in the common Chinese sea to bring influences to modern northern food.

The influence of the Mongols lingers still, although the Yuan Dynasty held sway for less than a century (1206-1368 AD) before the "Devil's Horsemen" retreated to their wide steppes. In no other area of China have the Mongols left any notable culinary legacy.

The Manchu influence, however, is pervasive in the north, particularly around Beijing itself. Over the three centuries of the Qing Dynasty (1644-1911 AD) intermarriage was so common that many residents of the capital today, knowingly or not, carry Manchu genes. After their initial conquest of China the Manchus sat back to enjoy three hundred years of the good life. They caroused with gusto, drank with enthusiasm, had large harems and armies of concubines, and although they may not have made much of a contribution as chefs, they certainly encouraged fine cooking by their conspicuous consumption of the better things of life.

There were up to two thousand chefs at any one time in the kitchens of the Forbidden City, cooking delicacies for the emperor and his court; officials such as the army of advisors, mandarins, and generals; foreign dignitaries seeking audiences with the occupant of the Dragon Throne; the hordes of concubines, eunuchs, members of the royal family, and the rest of the imperial court. The Manchus may have ruled the empire through their corps of fast-riding Bannermen, but in the kitchens of Beijing the Chinese reigned supreme. A standing joke was that the Manchus had invaded China to get a decent meal.

Hated and scorned though they were by many Chinese in the dying decades of their long dynasty, the Manchus enthusiastically assimilated Chinese culture. They became, it is said, more Chinese than the Chinese, and in no way was this more obvious than at the dining table. They had a lust for life. One reason for the strong Muslim influence in modern Beijing is often attributed to the Manchu Emperor Qian Long. Of all his hundreds of concubines, recruited from throughout the empire, he was obsessed above all with a Muslim girl he named the Fragrant One. To humor her the Emperor decreed that a town for her co-religionists be erected in the Forbidden City. From this love affair can be traced the large Muslim presence in Beijing today, as well as items on menus throughout the northern provinces such as lamb, kid and horse meat. Inland in Shanxi, donkey meat is also a legacy of the Muslim presence.

OUTSIDE A HOME IN SUBURBAN BEIJING   THOMAS HOPKER

EARLY MORNING BARGAINING AT A STREET MARKET

LEONG KA TAI

Despite the Yellow River slicing through the northern plain, freshwater fish does not play an important role in the diet. Some say the turgid, muddy waters that carry heavy loads of silt are too thick for a fish to breathe. In winter shallow ponds freeze solid, making fish farming a practical impossibility. Northern chefs hold that only when the golden carp was vigorous enough to fight the flow of the Yellow River and reach as far upstream as the town of Dragon Gate in Henan Province was it fit to eat. By reaching so far upriver the fish was held to have exhibited great courage and stamina. It was classed as a dragon and therefore became worthy of the wok. Shandong is the exception in the north as far as seafood is concerned. It produces notable seafood from both coasts bordering the Gulf of Bohai and the Yellow Sea. The giant prawns of the gulf are sent by train and truck to Beijing, where they have won fame in top gourmet kitchens and restaurants.

Shandong has other special claims to gastronomic fame. For thirty-five years until 1914 the area around the town of Tsingtao (Qingdao) was leased to Imperial Germany, and this brief spell gave a Teutonic flavor to the cuisine as well as to the architecture. One bequest was Tsingtao beer, made according to an old German recipe and now the most famous beer in all China.

CITY DWELLERS BICYCLE TO WORK   LEONG KA TAI

A CHINESE OPERA CHORUS

G. MONRO

Europeans planted large areas of grapes in Shandong, and these vines are now producing wine of international standing. Riesling, Chardonnay and other varieties are now helping Chinese vignerons and their partners from France, Germany, America and Australia to produce top quality table wines. The whites, in particular, have won awards in several international arenas. Many of the varieties of wine being produced from the grapes of Shandong are specially blended and balanced to accompany Chinese food.

Shandong cuisine is formed by combining a bountiful sea harvest with the richest agricultural production in northern China. The population has strong links with the outside world, and this has infused into their cuisine many culinary notions from other regions of China and overseas. It is the most vigorous of the cuisines of the north, but unfortunately it is also one of the least known.

Just as wealth, power and influence flowed inexorably towards the seat of power during Beijing's years as capital of the nation, so too did many of the most talented chefs gravitate to the political center of the Middle Kingdom. Here a young chef could make a name for himself, and with a lot of hard work and a bit of luck, catch the eye of a wealthy gourmet who would set him up in his own establishment – much the same as young French chefs head for Paris today. From all over the nation such ambitious cooks took their knowledge of China's various regional cuisines with them to Beijing.

A wide variety of imported foods, like the sweet potatoes of Shandong, play a vital role in what are now regarded as purely local dishes. In the hard years of this century it was common for Shandong peasants, if they were fortunate, to have three meals a day of sweet potatoes: one potato per meal. This vegetable has become such an integral part of the northern cuisine that it is easily overlooked that sweet potatoes only reached coastal China, via the Philippines from America, in the sixteenth century, about the same time as the potato reached Europe. Today, as it has been for a couple of centuries, the sweet potato is to Shandong what the spud is to Ireland. And it has played just as vital a political role.

Within the sweep of the provinces of the northern plains there is variety upon variety in the way commonplace ingredients are prepared. From one village to the next a tiny but subtle change may be made to the staple kitchen fare so that the food at one side of a province may be very different from that at the other. But everywhere such delicacies as salty soybean sauces, green onions and strong garlic give a distinctive tang to the taste of the north.

A FAMILY OUTING

LEO MEIER

(following page) SUBURBAN BEIJING

Poultry

家禽及野味

YOUNG BOYS TEND THEIR FLOCK OF GEESE

ENRICO FERORELLI

Poultry

家禽及野味

"FIRST, steal a chicken" is the immortal first line of the recipe for Beggar's Chicken. Nobody knows the origin of the dish, but one version often repeated in ancient Chinese texts holds that a humble peasant was sitting by a cooking fire at the side of a lake in Anhui Province when a feudal lord approached. When the poor man saw the nobleman and his armed entourage, he quickly scooped out mud from the lakeside, plastering it around a chicken he had just stolen, and threw the bird onto the coals. The nobleman stopped and got off his horse to warm himself by the fire. By the time he remounted and rode on, the chicken was encased in a brick-hard ball of fired clay. Frustrated, the peasant hurled a stone at the clay, which promptly broke, releasing the delicious aroma still enjoyed by modern diners who order this piquant dish.

POULTRY SELLERS AT A FARM MARKET, JIANGXI PROVINCE

YANG SHAOMING

Every regional kitchen has its own distinctive poultry favorite. Indeed, virtually every town in China has a special way of cooking local birds. The visitor can go into a restaurant in any corner of the country and ask for chicken confident of getting a tasty, satisfying dish. Ask how it has been cooked and the answer is likely to be, "Our way." That way differs throughout the land. In Shandong, it could mean chicken legs steamed, seasoned and then fried. If the chef is from Yunnan, the chicken might be double-steamed in a sealed container. The bird may have been cooked in oyster sauce in Guangdong; brushed with honey in Hebei; smeared with hot red bean paste in Hunan; simmered with anise in Gansu; inflamed with hot chilies in Guangxi or barbecued with white pepper in Mongolia.

Poultry of every description was a favored dish before the first recipe was ever written. Game was always popular at imperial courts and is still eagerly sought today by keen huntsmen. Eagles, owls and other rare creatures once shot for the pot are now totally protected under international agreements honored by China; but ducks, swans, pheasants, quail, geese and a myriad of other birds are the targets of enthusiastic shooters and archers. A prized dish in certain specialty restaurants is made from tiny rice birds caught in nets strung above the ripening grain, salted or preserved in honey and eaten whole — bones, innards and all.

In the capital, of course, pride of place goes to the glory of Beijing Duck, dried in the arid northern winds, then crisply roasted and served with classical grace. But the residents of Nanjing will by no means bow to the duck of the northern plains. Their award goes to the famed pressed duck of the central Yangtze. Further up the river, the proud chefs of the Sichuan kitchen haughtily concede nothing to any poultry dish other than their own smoked duck; while in Guangdong, the subtle delicacy of steamed chicken is the most honored.

Then there is the magnificent goose of the Chiu Chow kitchen, with its spectacular accompaniment of plum sauce; the Yellow Chicken of Hainan Island; the plump roasted pigeons of Fujian; the wild birds of prey shot by archers in the pine forests of the remote Black Dragon River in far northern Manchuria; and the young fowls cooked in coconut juice that are a specialty of the tribal people of the steamy tropical coasts of Guangxi. In Guizhou, a pepper-blasted diced chicken is named Guardian of the Palace after the title of the Ming Dynasty mandarin who invented the dish.

Throughout the country, and even in Beijing where duck is the dish for celebrations, chicken is the daily king of every kitchen. The bird appears in thousands of guises. Sometimes, as in a famous Guangdong recipe, the chicken is not a bird at all. A fowl is skinned and the meat cooked. The chef or housewife puts away the skin for another day, when it will be stuffed with glutinous rice, mushrooms, ham, bacon, sweet wine and seasonings. With the holes sewn, baked and put on the table, it looks like a plump bird. Only when the diners try to eat it is the joke discovered — but it still tastes magnificent.

The humble chicken eaten in China is usually a more mature fowl than that cooked in the Western kitchen. Most Chinese chefs prefer a bird of about 3-4lb (1½-2kg) because of the richer flavor. Important medicinal values are attributed to the fowl: it is said to keep the five vital internal organs – heart, liver, kidneys, lungs and spleen – active, to stimulate the stomach, to strengthen muscles and bones and improve the circulation of the blood. The stock from a boiled bird is invariably kept to make one of a million varieties of chicken soup, held by Chinese grandmothers to be the cure-all for every ailment.

WHITE GEESE ON A VILLAGE POND

LEO MEIER

39

CHICKEN BALL AND PEA SOUP

Beijing 北京

CHICKEN BALL AND PEA SOUP

5 oz (155 g) chicken breast meat
1 egg white, lightly beaten
1 tablespoon cornstarch
ice water, salt
2 cups (16 oz) lard or oil for deep-frying
4 cups (1 l) chicken stock
2 teaspoons rice wine or dry sherry
1 cup (5 oz) fresh peas, cooked
1 tablespoon rendered chicken fat, melted (optional)

Reduce the chicken meat to a paste with a cleaver or in a food processor. Add the egg white, cornstarch and ½ cup ice water and season with ½ teaspoon salt. Stir in one direction only. The mixture should be so smooth and moist that the chicken paste falls from a chopstick in large droplets.

Heat the lard or oil in a wok. Pour the chicken paste into a funnel and allow it to drip into the hot fat in drops about the size of peas. Fry until just white and cooked through, then lift out with a slotted spoon and drain.

Heat the chicken stock and add the rice wine, then add the drained peas and the chicken balls and heat through. Season with salt to taste and thicken, if desired, with 1½ tablespoons cornstarch mixed with a little cold water. Add the chicken fat, if used, and serve.

Sichuan 四川

STEAMED WHOLE CHICKEN WITH GLUTINOUS RICE AND DELICACIES

Chicken cooked according to this recipe is one of the most delectable of the traditional Sichuan dishes. It requires skillful preparation, but the result is well worth the effort involved. The dried "eight delicacies" used are sold in packages and simply need to be soaked before adding the rice to make this unique stuffing.

1 2½-lb (1¼-kg) chicken
1 carrot (garnish)
1 small cucumber (garnish)
2 eggs, separated (garnish)
1 tomato (garnish)

STUFFING

4 oz (125 g) glutinous rice
20 fresh or dried lotus seeds
2 tablespoons barley
¼ cup (1 oz) fox nuts or gingko nuts (white nuts)
1 tablespoon dried shrimp
4 dried black mushrooms, soaked for 25 minutes
2½ oz (75 g) salted ham or bacon
1 tablespoon fresh peas
1½ teaspoons salt (or to taste)
OR use 1 pack of "eight delicacies" and glutinous rice for
the stuffing

SAUCE

½ cup (4 oz) chicken stock
1 tablespoon arrowroot or cornstarch
½ teaspoon salt
few drops sesame oil
pinch of pepper

Bone the chicken, leaving the skin intact; use a sharp knife with a long narrow blade to work around the carcass until it can be completely removed. Sever the wing and leg bones from the carcass, leaving the skin and meat in place.

To prepare the stuffing, soak the rice in water to cover for 1 hour, then place on a rack in a wok or steamer, cover and steam for about 25 minutes or until almost cooked through. Drain.

Wash fresh lotus seeds or soak dried ones with the barley and fox nuts for 2-3 hours to soften. Shell gingko nuts and soak in hot water for about 25 minutes. Use a toothpick to push out the bitter core and discard. Soak the shrimp to soften, then drain and chop coarsely. Squeeze water from the mushrooms, remove the stems and dice the caps. Dice the ham.

If using packaged "eight delicacies," soak for 1 hour and steam for 10 minutes.

Mix these ingredients with the peas, salt, steamed rice and barley and stuff into the chicken, molding it into its original shape. Sew up the opening, then place breast down in a heat-proof dish on a rack in a wok or steamer. Steam, covered, over gentle heat for 50-60 minutes or until completely tender.

Prepare garnishes by carving the carrot and cucumber into attractive shapes. Beat the egg whites and yolks separately, pour into separate dishes and steam until firm. Slice and cut into diamond-shaped pieces. Drop the tomato into boiling water, remove and peel. Cut into wedges, then trim away the pulp and seeds leaving petal shapes. Set the garnishes aside.

When the chicken is done, lift out and place breast up on a serving plate.

Pour about ½ cup of the liquid from the steaming dish into a wok and add the sauce ingredients. Bring to boil and simmer, stirring, until the mixture thickens. Adjust seasoning.

Add the garnishes and simmer for a few moments, then pour over the chicken and serve.

STEAMED WHOLE CHICKEN WITH GLUTINOUS RICE AND DELICACIES

BRAISED CHICKEN WITH LEMON

CHICKEN AND GINGKO NUTS

Shanghai 上海

BRAISED CHICKEN WITH LEMON

1 2-lb (1-kg) chicken
2 tablespoons light soy sauce
1 tablespoon rice wine or dry sherry
2 tablespoons lemon juice
1 cup (8 oz) peanut oil
1 lemon, sliced

SAUCE

2 cups (16 oz) chicken stock or water
3 green onions, chopped
6 slices young fresh ginger, shredded
1 tablespoon tomato ketchup
3 tablespoons lemon juice
1 tablespoon sugar
½ teaspoon salt

Clean the chicken and wash well. Dry with paper towels, then place in a dish. Mix the soy sauce, rice wine and lemon juice together and rub over the chicken, pouring the remainder inside the cavity. Cover and let stand for 1 hour, turning once; then drain, reserving the marinade, and leave to dry on a rack.

※ Heat the peanut oil in a wok and fry the chicken over moderate heat on all sides until golden, then transfer to a casserole.

※ Pour the remaining marinade over the chicken and add the sauce ingredients. Cover and bring to the boil, then reduce the heat and simmer very gently for about 1 hour or until the chicken is completely tender.

※ Remove the chicken, drain and cut straight through the bones into serving portions. Arrange on a plate and place the sliced lemon in a line down the center of the back.

※ Rapidly boil the sauce until well reduced, then pour over the chicken and serve.

Sichuan 四川

CHICKEN AND GINGKO NUTS

There are groves of gingko trees on Mount Ching Chen in Kuan Shian County. They are a popular tourist attraction, and many believe that the age-old trees will bless them with longevity.

In ancient China, people regarded the gingko as a fruit. Yang Wan Li, a famous poet in the Bei Song Dynasty (960-1127 AD), wrote: "Silver gingko might well keep the golden peach company."

The core of the gingko nut must be removed before the nut is used, as it is very bitter and is said to cause stomach pain.

12 oz (375 g) fresh or canned gingko nuts
1 2½-lb (1¼-kg) chicken
3 green onions
6 slices fresh ginger
2 tablespoons rice wine or dry sherry
1 teaspoon salt
pinch of white pepper

Soak fresh gingko nuts in boiling water, then drain and scrape off the skin. Pick off the two ends, push the bitter core through with a toothpick, then soak again.

※ Blanch the chicken in boiling water, then hold under cold running water to rinse. Drain and place breast upwards in a casserole.

※ Add the remaining ingredients, except the gingko nuts. Cover with water, bring to boil, reduce the heat and simmer for 15 minutes. Turn the chicken over, add the gingko nuts and continue to simmer until the chicken is completely tender.

※ Remove the chicken and cut in half lengthwise, then cut the meat diagonally from the center into slices. Arrange in its original shape on a serving plate. Lift the gingko nuts from the stock with a slotted spoon, arrange around the chicken and serve at once.

Beijing 北京

CHICKEN IN A LANTERN

The presentation of this dish is impressive. Lightly cooked chicken pieces and selected vegetables are placed in a square of clear cellophane and tied with ribbon. The parcel is held over a wok of hot oil and the oil is quickly ladled over the bag. The heat causes the air inside the bag to expand, blowing it up like a lantern.

8 oz (250 g) chicken breast meat
2 teaspoons light soy sauce
1 egg white, lightly beaten
1 tablespoon cornstarch
1 green onion
2 slices fresh ginger
1 clove garlic
3 dried black mushrooms, soaked for 25 minutes
4 canned water chestnuts, drained
2 tablespoons fresh peas
1 tablespoon blanched almonds
6 cups (1½ l) oil for deep-frying
3 oz (90 g) rice vermicelli
1 tablespoon oil for stir-frying

SEASONING

1 tablespoon rice wine or dry sherry
1 tablespoon chili sauce (or to taste)
2 teaspoons sugar
1 teaspoon salt

Cut the chicken into small cubes and place in a dish with the soy sauce, egg white and cornstarch. Mix well and let stand for 20 minutes.

❀ Trim the green onion and cut into short lengths. Shred the ginger and chop the garlic. Drain the mushrooms, squeezing out all water; cut off the stems and dice the caps. Dice the water chestnuts. Parboil the peas and halve the almonds.

❀ Heat the 6 cups oil in a large wok over medium heat and deep-fry the chicken in a wire ladle or frying basket for about 2 minutes, shaking frequently to cook evenly. Lift out and drain well. Deep-fry the almonds briefly and drain on paper towels.

❀ Increase the heat under the oil, and when very hot deep-fry the vermicelli quickly. They will expand to several times their original volume and turn white. Lift out and drain – do not allow them to color. Place on a serving plate.

❀ In another wok heat about 1 tablespoon oil and briefly stir-fry the green onion, garlic, ginger and mushrooms. Add the seasoning ingredients and stir-fry briefly, then add the chicken, water chestnuts, peas and almonds. Mix together thoroughly.

❀ Spoon the mixture into the center of a square of clear cellophane, bring the corners together to enclose it and tie a ribbon round the center. Reheat the oil, hold the parcel over the wok and quickly ladle oil over until it expands. Drain and place in the center of a serving dish. Untie the bag at the table and tip the contents over the vermicelli.

CHICKEN IN A LANTERN

PHOENIX BREAST WITH SOUR SAUCE

Sichuan 四川

PHOENIX BREAST WITH SOUR SAUCE

According to legend, the phoenix is the king of birds, symbolizing nobility, respect and glory. The Emperor's residence used to be called the phoenix residence, the Emperor's carriage the phoenix carriage and the queen's headdress the phoenix crown. Chicken breast, being the best part of the chicken, is known as phoenix breast in China, and in this dish is deliciously sour and tasty.

6 oz (185 g) chicken breast meat
1 tablespoon rice wine or dry sherry
½ teaspoon salt
1 egg white, well beaten
2 tablespoons soy flour or cornstarch
12 oz (375 g) lard or oil for frying

SAUCE

2 slices fresh ginger, finely chopped
2 cloves garlic, finely chopped
1 pickled red chili, finely chopped
1 green onion, minced
1 oz (30 g) fresh or canned bamboo shoots, very finely
   chopped
1½ tablespoons red vinegar
1 tablespoon sugar
1 tablespoon light soy sauce

Cut the chicken into very small dice and place in a dish with the wine, salt, egg white and soy flour or cornstarch. Mix well and let stand for 20 minutes. Heat the lard or oil in a wok to the smoking point, then lower the heat and fry the chicken, stirring with chopsticks to separate the pieces. When it turns white, lift out and drain well on paper towels.

※ Drain the wok and wipe out. Return 1 tablespoon of the lard or oil to the wok and stir-fry the chopped sauce ingredients for 1 minute, then add the remaining ingredients and return the chicken. Toss together over high heat until well mixed and the sugar is dissolved, then serve immediately.

Shanghai 上海

FRIED CHICKEN LEGS

The drumsticks can also be served straight from the steamer, omitting the crisp-frying, and are excellent with a plain bowl of rice and a little of the sauce.

8 chicken drumsticks, about 1½ lb (750 g)
2 pieces pork caul fat, cut into triangles
1 egg, well beaten
1 cup (4 oz) dry breadcrumbs
oil for deep-frying
hot soy sauce and tomato or chili sauce

SEASONING

1 tablespoon rice wine or dry sherry
2 tablespoons light soy sauce
3 tablespoons water
1 tablespoon finely chopped cilantro
1 tablespoon finely chopped green onion
¾ teaspoon finely chopped fresh ginger
1 cinnamon stick
1 piece dried orange peel
1 teaspoon Sichuan peppercorns (Fagara or Sansho)
1 star anise
½ teaspoon salt
1 tablespoon sugar

Mix the seasoning ingredients in a large, shallow heatproof dish and add the chicken drumsticks. Cover with plastic wrap and leave for 3 hours, turning several times. Then uncover and place the dish on a rack in a wok or steamer, cover and steam over gently simmering water for about 30 minutes. Remove and leave to drain.

※ Wrap each drumstick in a triangle of the pork caul fat, then dip into beaten egg. Coat with dry breadcrumbs. Refrigerate for about 30 minutes for the breadcrumbs to set.

※ Heat the oil in a wok to the smoking point and deep-fry the drumsticks until crisp and golden. Drain and arrange on a serving plate. Serve with small dipping bowls of hot soy sauce and tomato or chili sauce.

FRIED CHICKEN LEGS

Shanghai 上海

BRAISED CHICKEN LEGS IN A LOTUS SHAPE

12 chicken drumsticks
3 tomatoes
1 cup (8 oz) milk
1 egg
1 egg white
lard or vegetable oil
12 vegetable hearts (miniature Chinese white cabbage) or bok choy
pinch of salt
grated lemon rind (optional)

SEASONING/STOCK

2 cups (16 oz) chicken stock
2 tablespoons dark soy sauce
1 tablespoon sugar
3 slices fresh ginger
2 tablespoons vegetable oil

Use a sharp knife to cut around the chicken bones to where the meat begins to be fleshy. Scrape the skin completely away from the lower part of the bone, leaving it exposed.

Arrange the chicken drumsticks in a wide flat saucepan. Mix the seasoning/stock ingredients together and pour over the drumsticks. Bring almost to the boil, then simmer gently for about 45 minutes or until the drumsticks are very tender and the sauce is reduced to a syrupy glaze.

Blanch the tomatoes in boiling water, then skin. Cut each into large wedges and trim away the pulp and seeds to leave pointed petal shapes. Set aside.

Lightly beat the milk, egg and egg white together. Stir-fry in a wok in a little lard or vegetable oil over gentle heat until thickened. Set aside, keeping warm.

In another wok, stir-fry the vegetable hearts in a little oil or lard, adding a pinch of salt. Pour in 1 tablespoon water, cover and steam until tender. Lift out and arrange on a round serving plate, alternating the drumsticks with the vegetables.

Mound the fried egg in the center of the platter, and then arrange the tomato "petals" in a lotus flower shape in the egg and sprinkle the center of the "flower" with a little grated lemon rind.

Spoon any remaining sauce over the drumsticks and serve.

CHICKEN ROLLS WITH SESAME SEEDS

MANDARIN DICED CHICKEN

Beijing 北京

CHICKEN ROLLS WITH SESAME SEEDS

The best chicken for this dish is a special breed of Beijing chicken that is large and strong and said to have high nutritional value. The coating of sesame seeds gives it a delightfully nutty taste.

12 oz (375 g) chicken meat, cooked
1 green onion
2 slices fresh ginger
4 oz (125 g) canned bamboo shoots, drained
1 tablespoon rice wine or dry sherry
1 teaspoon salt
4 eggs
oil for deep-frying
2 oz (60 g) white sesame seeds

GLAZE

1 egg, beaten
2 tablespoons all purpose flour

Finely chop the chicken, green onion, ginger and bamboo shoots, add the rice wine and salt and mix well.
❋ Beat the eggs with a pinch of salt. Rub out a wok with an oiled cloth and pour in one-sixth of the beaten eggs. Tilt and slowly move the pan so that the egg spreads out into a thin round omelet. Fry gently on both sides. Cook the remaining egg to give 6 omelets.
❋ Divide the filling among the omelets, spreading one-sixth across the center of each. Fold 3 sides over and roll up.
❋ Coat each roll with the pre-mixed glaze, then roll in sesame seeds.
❋ Heat the oil and fry the rolls over moderate heat until golden brown. Drain well and serve.

Sichuan 四川

MANDARIN DICED CHICKEN

This is one of the most famous traditional Sichuan dishes and its creation is connected with an interesting anecdote.

A few years before the downfall of the Qing Dynasty (1644-1911 AD), a new governor, Ting Pao Ts'en, was assigned to Sichuan. Upon his arrival a banquet was given in his honor. The cooks created a special dish for this old mandarin using spring chicken cut into tiny pieces and flavored with local spices. They named it "Kung Pao," or "Mandarin Diced Chicken."

"Kung Pao" has since become a technical term in Sichuan cooking, referring to a dish containing dried chilies and Sichuan pepper (the seed of the prickly ash tree), with a tart, hot, slightly vinegary taste.

10 oz (315 g) chicken breasts
2-3 dried red chilies
1 teaspoon Sichuan peppercorns (Fagara or Sansho)
3 oz (90 g) peanuts, preferably raw
2 green onions
3-4 slices fresh ginger
2 cloves garlic
2 cups (16 oz) oil for deep-frying

MARINADE

1 tablespoon rice wine or dry sherry
1 tablespoon light soy sauce
½ teaspoon salt
1½ teaspoons cornstarch

SEASONING/SAUCE

⅔ cup (5 oz) chicken stock
1 tablespoon light soy sauce
1 teaspoon sugar
1 teaspoon brown vinegar
1½ teaspoons cornstarch

Cut the chicken into small dice, place in a dish with the marinade ingredients, mix well and let stand for 20 minutes.
❋ Chop the chilies into short lengths and lightly crush the peppercorns. Skin the peanuts. Cut the green onion and ginger into shreds and thinly slice the garlic.
❋ Heat the oil in a wok to the smoking point. Deep-fry the chilies and peppercorns in a frying basket or wire strainer until crisp, remove and set aside. Add the chicken to the wok and fry until it turns white and firm. Remove, then fry the peanuts until lightly colored, lift out and drain on paper towels.
❋ Pour off all but about 2½ tablespoons of the oil, then reheat and stir-fry the green onions, ginger and garlic briefly. Return the chicken with the chilies and peppercorns and stir-fry together briefly over high heat. Add the pre-mixed seasoning/sauce ingredients and bring to boil. Simmer, stirring, for about 1 minute, then stir in the peanuts and serve.

SLICED CHICKEN AND SEASONAL VEGETABLES

Sichuan 四川

SLICED CHICKEN AND SEASONAL VEGETABLES

This simple dish is typical of home-style Sichuan cooking — light and delicate ingredients contrasted by a hint of hot spice.

8 oz (250 g) chicken breasts
1-3 pickled red chilies
2 green onions
3 oz (90 g) chayote or other squash
2½ tablespoons oil for frying
2 teaspoons brown vinegar

SEASONING/SAUCE

1 clove garlic, crushed
½ teaspoon grated fresh ginger
3 tablespoons chicken stock
1 tablespoon light soy sauce
2 teaspoons rice wine or dry sherry
1 teaspoon sugar
1 teaspoon cornstarch
pinch each of salt and Sichuan pepper (Fagara or Sansho)

Skin and slice the chicken very thinly, then stack the slices and cut them into fine shreds. Shred the pickled chilies and green onions. Peel the squash, slice thinly, then cut into matchstick pieces and set aside.

Heat the oil in a wok and stir-fry the chicken until it turns white; remove and set aside. Add the chili, green onions and squash sticks and stir-fry over moderate heat for about 2 minutes. Add the garlic and ginger from the seasoning/sauce ingredients and stir-fry briefly, then return the chicken and add the vinegar. Stir-fry together for 1 minute over moderate heat, then add the remaining pre-mixed seasoning/sauce ingredients, simmer until thickened and serve.

STEAMED WHOLE LANTERN-SHAPED CHICKEN

Sichuan 四川

STEAMED WHOLE LANTERN-SHAPED CHICKEN

Lanterns are used on many occasions to symbolize happiness. This particular dish is meant to bring that happiness to the table. The chicken is bright red and looks like an elegant lantern on the plate.

The red color is obtained from chili powder, so the chicken is quite hot, aromatic and very tasty. Only a tender young chicken will give good results.

1 2½-lb (1¼-kg) chicken
1 teaspoon chili powder
carrot slices (garnish)
lemon peel (garnish)
steamed carrot (garnish)
pickled or salted cabbage (garnish)

MARINADE/SEASONING

2 tablespoons rice wine or dry sherry
1 tablespoon grated fresh ginger
1 tablespoon minced green onion
1½ teaspoons salt
1 teaspoon Sichuan peppercorns (Fagara or Sansho)*

Rinse the chicken, then wipe dry inside and out.

Mix the marinade/seasoning ingredients together, rub into the chicken both inside and out, and pour any remaining liquid into the cavity. Place on a rack and leave for at least 12 hours.

Place the chicken in a pot and cover with cold water. Remove the chicken and bring the water to the boil, then return the chicken, reduce the heat, cover and simmer gently for about 30 minutes, turning once.

Lift out, drain, retain the stock and put the chicken on a rack to dry, then rub the chili powder into the skin to make it bright red. Set the rack in a wok or steamer over simmering water, cover and steam for 30 minutes.

In the meantime briskly boil the retained stock until reduced to about 1 cup. Adjust the seasoning.

When the chicken is done, add the liquid from the cavity of the chicken to the stock and simmer briskly until well reduced. Spoon over the chicken and serve.

The simple but effective garnish in this picture comprises carrot slices carved into Chinese characters and symbols. The two lanterns are carved from lemon peel with tassels of shredded steamed carrot, and the cord is made from shreds of salted cabbage.

Dry-fry the peppercorns to bring out their full flavor, then grind to a powder.

DICED TOMATO AMIDST CHICKEN SNOW

CHICKEN SHREDS AND GARLIC CHIVES

Sichuan 四川

DICED TOMATO AMIDST CHICKEN SNOW

The chicken paste cooked according to this recipe is as white and soft as snow. The chef adds contrasting taste, color and texture with diced tomato. A typical Sichuanese dish to serve in early spring.

1 large ripe tomato
8 oz (250 g) chicken breasts
¾ cup (6 oz) chicken stock
2 egg whites
¾ teaspoon salt
1 tablespoon soy flour or cornstarch
pinch of white pepper
1½ tablespoons lard

Place the tomato in a pot of boiling water, leave for 8 seconds, then remove on a slotted spoon and peel. Cut the flesh into dice, discarding the seeds.
※ Use either two cleavers simultaneously or a food processor to pound the chicken to a smooth paste. Pull away any tough tendons. Mix with one-third of the stock, the lightly beaten egg whites, salt, soy flour or cornstarch and pepper, and stir until the mixture is smooth and creamy.
※ Heat the lard in a wok and stir-fry the chicken gently over moderate heat until it turns white and is cooked through. Pour in the remaining stock and simmer for 1½ minutes.
※ Spoon onto a serving plate, carefully stir in the diced tomato and serve at once.

Sichuan 四川

CHICKEN SHREDS AND GARLIC CHIVES

Bright green, tender and aromatic, garlic chives are one of the vege-tables of early spring. They have a subtle flavor of onion and garlic, and are often cooked with pork and chicken.

12-18 garlic chives or small green onions
6 oz (185 g) chicken breasts
2 tablespoons oil for frying

SEASONING

1 egg white, lightly beaten
1 tablespoon cornstarch
½ teaspoon salt
pinch of white pepper

SAUCE

½ cup (4 oz) chicken stock
2 tablespoons rice wine or dry sherry
pinch of salt
1½ teaspoons soy flour or cornstarch

Rinse the garlic chives in cold water, shake well, then cut into 2-in (5-cm) lengths and set aside.
※ Slice the chicken very thinly, discarding skin and any bone fragments. Stack the slices and cut into fine shreds. Place in a dish, add the pre-mixed seasoning ingredients and set aside for 20 minutes.
※ Heat the oil in a wok and stir-fry the chicken over moderate heat until white. Push to one side of the pan and add the chives. Stir-fry over higher heat for about 1 minute.
※ Pour in the pre-mixed sauce ingredients, mix with the chicken and chives and simmer until thickened and clear, stir-ring occasionally. Serve immediately.

Shanghai 上海

CHRYSANTHEMUM FIRE POT

Chrysanthemum dishes are a specialty of Chinese cuisine. Over two thousand years ago poets wrote of the beauty and edibility of the chrysanthemum flower. The great medicinal expert Le She Zhen of the Ming Dynasty (1368-1644 AD) praised chrysanthemums for their ability to brighten the eyes and relieve internal heat, and today they are still used as a medicine and served as tea.
   Chrysanthemum Fire Pot is a famous dish, served in autumn and winter. The uncooked ingredients are arranged in an attractive design on plates around a burner on the table and cooked by the diners.

24 prawns or shrimp
1 10-oz (315-g) carp or other meaty white fish, filleted
2 duck gizzards or duck or chicken hearts
6 oz (185 g) chicken breasts
8 oz (250 g) spinach leaves
6 eggs
oil for deep-frying
4 oz (125 g) dried bean thread vermicelli
4 oz (125 g) dried egg noodles
assorted meat*

STOCK

6 cups (1½ l) chicken stock
2-3 slices fresh ginger
2 green onions
2 teaspoons salt
½ teaspoon white pepper
1 white chrysanthemum flower

DIP

1 cup (8 oz) light soy sauce
1/2 cup (4 oz) sesame oil
1-2 tablespoons toasted white sesame seeds (optional)

Peel and devein the prawns, leaving the tail section intact. Thinly slice the fish, duck gizzards and chicken breasts and arrange on small plates.

✻Wash the spinach under cold running water and trim, discarding stems. In a wok, heat the oil to the smoking point, then reduce the heat slightly. Deep-fry the vermicelli for a few seconds. They will expand dramatically, but should not be allowed to color. Drain on paper towels, then place on a large serving plate. Soak the egg noodles to soften, then drain and place in a dish.

✻Combine the dip ingredients and divide among 6 small bowls. Beat one egg in each of 6 rice or soup bowls.

✻Place all the stock ingredients except the flower in a hot pot or large saucepan over a portable burner in the center of the table, and bring to boil. When gently bubbling, pull the chrysanthemum flower apart and scatter the petals over the stock.

✻Each diner can choose the ingredients he likes, hold them in the hot stock until lightly poached, and then dip into the beaten egg and the dip before eating. Take care to use wooden or bamboo chopsticks and not plastic ones.

✻The noodles and fried vermicelli are cooked after the other ingredients have been eaten, and consumed with the rich stock at the end of the meal.

Additional plates of very thinly sliced lean pork, ham, pork liver, beef, squid or tripe can be added to the above assortment.

CHRYSANTHEMUM FIRE POT

CHICKEN BRAISED IN SOY SAUCE WITH TWO KINDS OF MEATBALLS

Guangzhou 广州

CHICKEN BRAISED IN SOY SAUCE WITH TWO KINDS OF MEATBALLS

The soy sauce used in this recipe is a special product of Guangdong's Pu Ling county. It is smooth, strong and golden colored, with a distinct local flavor not to be found in other soy sauces. The prawn balls and meatballs, which are in fact duck gizzards cut in flower shapes, are optional additions to the basic recipe that transform it into an elegant banquet dish.

1 2-lb (1-kg) spring chicken
2 teaspoons cornstarch

SEASONING

2 tablespoons Pu-Ling or other light soy sauce
2 tablespoons rice wine or dry sherry
1 tablespoon finely chopped green onion
1 tablespoon chopped fresh cilantro
1 teaspoon grated fresh ginger
1 teaspoon sesame oil
1 teaspoon sugar

Rinse the chicken, dry thoroughly inside and out and place in a dish. Mix the seasoning ingredients together and rub over the chicken, pouring the remainder into the cavity. Let stand for at least 2 hours to absorb the flavors.
☒ Prepare the meatballs as described in the following recipes.
☒ Place the chicken in a heatproof dish on a rack in a wok or steamer, cover and steam over rapidly boiling water for at least 30 minutes or until tender. Remove and let cool.
☒ Chop the chicken into serving slices, cutting straight through the bones in the Chinese style. Arrange on a serving plate.
☒ Pour the sauce from the dish in which the chicken was steamed into a wok and add the cornstarch mixed with a little cold water. Bring to boil and simmer, stirring, until thickened. Pour over the chicken, arrange the meatballs on the side and serve.

PRAWN BALLS

6 oz (185 g) fresh prawn or shrimp meat
2 oz (60 g) ground pork fat
salt and pepper
1 cup (4 oz) all purpose flour, seasoned with salt and pepper
1 egg, well beaten
dry breadcrumbs
oil for deep-frying

Place the prawn meat on a board and mash with the side of a cleaver until reduced to a pulp, or grind in a food processor. Mix to a smooth paste with the pork fat, season with salt and pepper and roll into balls. Coat lightly with the seasoned flour, dip into the beaten egg, then coat with breadcrumbs.
☒ Heat the oil in a wok to the smoking point, lower the heat slightly and deep-fry the balls for about 2 minutes or until cooked through and golden brown. Remove, drain well and keep warm.

DUCK GIZZARD "FLOWERS"

3 duck gizzards or duck or chicken hearts
1 tablespoon Pu-Ling or other light soy sauce
1 teaspoon sugar
salt and pepper
oil for deep-frying

Score the duck gizzards very deeply from the inside, cutting almost through them in a criss-cross pattern so that the finished gizzard has the appearance of a chrysanthemum. Cut each into several pieces. Place in a dish with the soy sauce, sugar, salt and pepper and let stand for 5-6 minutes.
☒ Heat the oil in a wok to the smoking point and deep-fry the duck gizzards for about 45 seconds in a frying basket or until they curl up and change color. Drain well and serve.

Shanghai 上海

ASSORTED EARTHEN POT DISH

This recipe is a delicious way to use leftover roast chicken and duck. Including the typical Chinese ingredients of simmered sea cucumber, fried pork rind and fresh bamboo shoots, it has a wonderfully rich flavor.

6 oz (185 g) pork rind (from the belly or leg)
1 cooked dried or fresh sea cucumber*
oil for deep-frying
8 oz (250 g) roast chicken
8 oz (250 g) roast duck
4-8 oz (125-250 g) lean cooked ham
6 oz (185 g) canned or cooked fresh bamboo shoots
12 fresh or canned straw mushrooms
2 tablespoons rice wine or dry sherry
6 cups (1½ l) chicken stock or Superior Stock (*see page 124*)
1¾ teaspoons salt
2 tablespoons lard
2 freshwater prawns or crayfish

Deep-fry the pork rind in a wok in heated oil until bubbles appear on the surface, then place in water or stock and simmer for several hours until tender.
☒ Cut the sea cucumber, pork rind, chicken, duck, ham, bamboo shoots and mushrooms into thin slices and arrange separately in a wide shallow casserole. Sprinkle with the wine and add the stock and salt.
☒ Set the pot on a rack in a wok or steamer, cover and steam over simmering water for at least 30 minutes or until the flavors are well mingled and the stock is full of flavor. Add the lard and place the prawns, still in their shells, on top. Return to the steamer for another 5-10 minutes. Serve in the pot.

To cook the sea cucumber, soak in cold water until softened, then drain, cut open and clean. Simmer in water with green onion, ginger, salt and wine for several hours or until completely tender.

ASSORTED EARTHEN POT DISH

WENCHANG CHICKEN, GUANGZHOU STYLE

SLICED CHICKEN WITH SCALLION OIL

Guangzhou 广州

WENCHANG CHICKEN, GUANGZHOU STYLE

More than forty years ago, the chef of the Guangzhou Restaurant heard that chickens reared in Wenchang County on Hainan Island were particularly plump and tender. Journeying there to investigate, he found it was indeed true, the only setback being that the bones were rather hard, making it difficult to serve the chicken in the traditional ways. After much experimenting, he perfected this recipe.

1 2-lb (1-kg) chicken
2 teaspoons salt
6 slices salted ham
4 chicken livers
1 luffa, or 10 stalks kale or broccoli
1 tablespoon vegetable oil (if using luffa)
1 teaspoon sesame oil

SAUCE

1½ cups (12 oz) chicken stock
1 tablespoon light soy sauce
½ teaspoon salt
pinch of white pepper
1½ tablespoons cornstarch

Rinse the chicken, wipe dry and rub inside and out with the salt. Set aside for 30 minutes.
Cut the ham and chicken livers into pieces about 2½ x 1½ in (6 x 4cm).
Using a sharp knife or vegetable peeler, remove the sharp ridges of the luffa, but do not peel the sections in between unless they are tough. Cut into pieces the same size as the ham. Plunge into boiling water with the vegetable oil and simmer until tender, then refresh under cold water. If using broccoli or kale, cut into short lengths and blanch for 3-4 minutes in lightly salted water, refresh and drain.
Oil a large heatproof plate, cut the chicken in half down the back and spread out on the plate. Place on a rack in a wok or steamer and steam over briskly simmering water for about 25 minutes. Brush with sesame oil and let cool. Pour off the liquid to use in the sauce.
Bone the chicken and cut the meat into slices. Place a slice of chicken liver on each piece of chicken and top with a piece of ham. Arrange on a heatproof plate in a chicken shape with the head, wings and drumsticks. Return to the steamer and steam until the ham and chicken livers are tender and the dish is hot and moist, about 6 minutes. Surround with the vegetables and heat through briefly in the steam.
Pour the sauce ingredients into a wok and boil until the sauce clears. Pour over the chicken and serve at once.

Guangzhou 广州

SLICED CHICKEN WITH SCALLION OIL

In Guangdong this dish features frequently in family meals and feasts. It is simple to prepare and has a pleasant, distinctive flavor.

1 2-lb (1-kg) spring chicken
1 tablespoon grated fresh ginger
1 teaspoon salt
3 tablespoons peanut oil
4 green onions
cucumber slices (garnish)
carrot (garnish)

Rinse the chicken, drain well and dry with a paper towel. Rub thoroughly inside and out with the ginger and salt and let stand for 1 hour to absorb the flavors.
Heat the peanut oil in a wok and add the coarsely chopped green onions. Fry until light brown, then remove the onions with a slotted spoon and pour the scallion oil into a dish.
In a large saucepan, boil enough water to cover the chicken, adding a pinch of salt. Put in the chicken, then reduce the heat and simmer gently for about 25 minutes. Remove the chicken and cover with cold water. This shrinks the skin and gives it a better texture.
Return the chicken to the boiling water and simmer gently for another 10-15 minutes.
Lift out and drain well. Brush with the scallion oil and let cool. Cut into slices and arrange on a plate with a garnish of cucumber slices and carrot.

Guangzhou 广州

DONG JIANG SALT-BAKED CHICKEN

Historical records of the area of Dong Jiang in Guangdong state that cooked chickens wrapped in tissue paper were preserved in salt mounds in local salt fields. Their golden color and moist, delicious taste were much appreciated by businessmen and bureaucrats of the area.

In the late Qing Dynasty (1644-1911 AD) the area became the collection and distribution center for salt merchants who often served their guests the Dong Jiang style of salt-preserved chicken. Eventually they turned to baking fresh chickens in coarse salt for immediate consumption, thus retaining the unique salty flavor, while making the chickens even more tender and tasty.

DONG JIANG SALT-BAKED CHICKEN

BONED CHICKEN WINGS WITH CRAB ROE

1 3-lb (1½-kg) chicken
1 teaspoon salt
¼ teaspoon ground star anise
6 slices fresh ginger
2 green onions
3-4 large sheets of parchment paper
8-10 lb (4-5 kg) rock or coarse salt
sesame oil (optional)

DIPPING SAUCE

1 tablespoon grated fresh ginger or powdered galangal
1 tablespoon table salt
3 tablespoons melted lard or vegetable oil

Rinse the chicken with boiling water and hang in an airy place for several hours to allow the skin to dry.

※ Using a sharp knife or cleaver, slash through the skin on either side of the wings and legs to allow the flavors to penetrate the meat more thoroughly. Dust the cavity with the salt mixed with the star anise and place the ginger slices and green onions inside. Brush the chicken skin sparingly with lard to keep the paper from sticking, then wrap the chicken with the paper.

※ In a very large wok heat the rock salt until almost smoking. Stir with a ladle, then make a large well in the center. Put in the chicken and mound the hot salt evenly over it.

※ Maintain a steady moderate temperature under the wok and cook for about 25 minutes, then turn the chicken and cook the other side for about 30 minutes or until cooked through. It should be slightly pink around the bones but the juices should be clear when the bird is pierced near the thigh. Remove from the salt, unwrap carefully and discard the paper.

※ Skin and bone the chicken, then cut the meat into strips. Place the head, wings and drumsticks in position on the serving plate and pile the bones in the center. Mound the chicken over the bones to resemble its original shape. Brush sparingly with sesame oil if desired.

※ Divide the ginger or galangal powder between 3 or 4 small dishes and add the table salt. Cover each dish with the melted lard, stir lightly and serve with the chicken.

Guangzhou 广州

BONED CHICKEN WINGS WITH CRAB ROE

This recipe is a good example of the Chinese approach to the balance of flavor, presentation and aroma in cooking.

Chicken wings are selected as the smoothest, most tender part of the chicken, especially when deep-fried. The bones are removed to enhance the diners' pleasure, and the chicken is complemented by a bright green vegetable, the coral red of crab roe with its unique flavor and texture, and the fresh tang of ginger and green onions. The result is a unique dish with the colors of jade, coral and pearl.

8 chicken wings, central sections only
2 tablespoons light soy sauce
1 lb (500 g) choy sum or other Chinese green vegetable
3 small dried black mushrooms, soaked for 25 minutes
2 cloves garlic
2 slices fresh ginger
5 slices canned or cooked fresh bamboo shoots
1 green onion
oil for deep-frying
3 oz (90 g) crab roe

SAUCE

¾ cup (6 oz) chicken stock
1 tablespoon light soy sauce
¼ teaspoon dark soy sauce
¼ teaspoon sesame oil
¼ teaspoon salt
¼ teaspoon sugar

Using a sharp knife with a long thin blade, remove the bones from the wings. Place in a dish and add the soy sauce. Rub well into the chicken and let stand for 20 minutes.

※ Trim the choy sum, cutting off the thick ends of the stems; rinse and drain well. Squeeze the mushrooms dry. Finely chop the garlic and shred the ginger. Cut the bamboo shoot slices into decorative shapes and the green onion into 1-in (2.5-cm) diagonal slices.

※ Heat the oil until quite hot. Place the choy sum in a wire sieve and lower into the oil. As soon as it changes color, remove and place under cold running water, then set aside.

※ Reheat the oil and deep-fry the chicken wings until lightly colored; remove and drain on a paper towel.

※ Drain off the oil, reserving about 3 tablespoons. Stir-fry the garlic briefly. Add the mushrooms, ginger and bamboo shoots and stir-fry for 1 minute, then pour in the sauce ingredients and bring to boil, stirring constantly.

※ Push a stalk of choy sum into the cavity of each chicken wing. Place in the sauce and simmer gently until the wings and vegetables are tender.

※ Place the crab roe on a plate over a saucepan or wok of gently simmering water and steam until bright red and firm.

※ Arrange the wings and vegetables on a plate and top with the roe. Serve at once.

STEAMED CHICKEN WINGS WITH FILLING

Shanghai 上海

STEAMED CHICKEN WINGS WITH FILLING

12-15 chicken wings, central sections only
2½ oz (75 g) lean ham
2½ oz (75 g) fresh or canned bamboo shoots
3 dried black mushrooms, soaked for 25 minutes
2-3 fresh Chinese long-leaf lettuces
pinch of salt
1 tablespoon vegetable oil
1 egg
oil for frying
1 tablespoon chopped ham

SAUCE

1 cup (8 oz) stock*
1 tablespoon rice wine or dry sherry
2 teaspoons light soy sauce
2 teaspoons vegetable oil
2 teaspoons cornstarch
1 teaspoon dark soy sauce
½ teaspoon salt

Use a long, thin-bladed knife to remove the bones from the chicken wings.

Cut the ham, bamboo shoots and drained mushrooms into matchstick lengths and insert several of each into the cavities in the chicken wings.

Lightly oil a heatproof plate and arrange the stuffed chicken wings on it. Set on a rack in a wok or steamer and steam, covered, over simmering water for about 30 minutes.

Cut the lettuces in half lengthwise and drop into a saucepan of boiling water to which a pinch of salt and 1 tablespoon vegetable oil have been added. Blanch for 2 minutes, then remove and drain well. Arrange around the chicken wings.

Beat the egg lightly. Heat the frying oil in a wok and stir-fry the egg, breaking it up with a fork into fine drops (or fry the egg in a thin flat sheet without stirring, and cut into fine shreds). Arrange over the chicken.

In another wok, bring the pre-mixed sauce ingredients to boil and stir until thickened. Pour over the dish and serve at once.

An excellent stock can be made with the water in which the mushrooms were soaked and the wing tips removed from the chicken wings. Simmer for 20 minutes.

Sichuan 四川

SHREDDED CHICKEN AND TENDER CELERY

Celery is said to strengthen vigor, calm the nerves and release summer heat. In this dish, tender stems of celery are cooked with shredded chicken. The contrasting greenish yellow of the celery, white of the chicken and deep red of the pickled chili complement each other perfectly.

8 oz (250 g) young celery stalks
6 oz (185 g) chicken breasts
1 egg white
1 tablespoon cornstarch
4 oz (125 g) lard
2 green onions, shredded
3 slices fresh ginger, shredded
1 pickled red chili, shredded

SEASONING

3 tablespoons chicken stock
2 teaspoons rice wine or dry sherry
½ teaspoon sesame oil
½ teaspoon salt

Cut the celery into 3-in (7.5-cm) lengths. Very thinly slice the chicken breast, cut into narrow strips, place in a dish and mix with the lightly beaten egg white and cornstarch.

Heat the lard in a wok and stir-fry the chicken over moderate heat until it turns white, then remove. Drain off all but 1½ tablespoons lard and stir-fry the celery over higher heat with the green onions, ginger and chili until the celery begins to soften.

Return the chicken and add the pre-mixed seasoning ingredients. Stir-fry together over high heat for 1 minute, then serve at once.

SHREDDED CHICKEN AND TENDER CELERY

STEWED CHICKEN, LI KOU FU STYLE

Guangzhou 广州

STEWED CHICKEN, LI KOU FU STYLE

During the 1930s, all restaurants in Guangzhou competed with each other in creating their own chicken specialties. When the Li Kou Fu Restaurant was newly established, the owner devised this chicken dish which he named after his restaurant, and only he and his wife knew the seasoning ingredients. The distinctive flavor is now known to come mainly from Zhu Hou soy sauce and mellow Mei Gui Lu wine. Both are famous for their exquisite fragrance.

1 1½-lb (750-g) chicken
4 green onions
cilantro (garnish)

SEASONING

⅔ cup (5 oz) Zhu Hou or other dark/mushroom soy sauce
⅓ cup (2½ oz) Mei Gui Lu wine (rose-scented Chinese rice wine)
2 teaspoons sugar
2 teaspoons sesame oil
pinch of salt

Rinse the chicken and wipe dry. Place the green onions in the cavity and put into a deep, small casserole. Mix the seasoning ingredients together. Pour a little into the cavity, then pour the remainder over the chicken.

※ Cover the pot tightly and place in a water bath to prevent the chicken from coming into direct contact with the heat and burning. Simmer the chicken very gently until tender, about 1¼ hours, turning once or twice.

※ Lift out the chicken, cut into serving pieces and arrange on a plate. Pour the sauce over and garnish with cilantro.

STEAMED SPRING CHICKEN WITH STRAW MUSHROOMS

Beijing 北京

STEAMED SPRING CHICKEN WITH STRAW MUSHROOMS

12-18 dried or canned small straw mushrooms
1 2-lb (1-kg) spring chicken
2 green onions
2 slices fresh ginger
2 teaspoons cornstarch

SEASONING

2 tablespoons light soy sauce
2 tablespoons rendered chicken fat
2 teaspoons rice wine or dry sherry
1 teaspoon sugar
1/4 teaspoon salt

Cover dried straw mushrooms with lukewarm water and soak for about 30 minutes. Drain, reserving the liquid, then trim the mushrooms, removing the stems. Wash the caps thoroughly in clean cold water, squeeze dry and set aside.

❀ Cut the chicken into cubes, discarding all bones. Dice the green onions and shred the ginger.

❀ Arrange the chicken in a heatproof dish with the mushroom caps and place the green onion and ginger on top. Pour on the reserved mushroom water (or use the liquid from the can if using canned mushrooms). Add pre-mixed seasoning ingredients and place on a rack in a wok or steamer. Cover and steam over gently simmering water for at least 15 minutes or until the chicken is tender and the dish very aromatic.

❀ Discard the green onion and ginger, pour the liquid into a wok and thicken with cornstarch mixed with a little cold water. Simmer, stirring, until the sauce clears, then pour over the chicken and serve at once.

Shanghai 上海

DICED CHICKEN STIR-FRIED WITH SESAME SAUCE

This style of cooking was originally the specialty of Sichuan Province, but the chef in the Green Willow Village Restaurant in Shanghai modified the original recipe and added a local product — wine-pickled egg yolk.

12 oz (375 g) chicken breasts
3 oz (90 g) peanuts, preferably raw
oil for frying
2 green onions, chopped
1/2 cup (4 oz) chicken stock

DICED CHICKEN STIR-FRIED WITH SESAME SAUCE

SEASONING/SAUCE

3 tablespoons light soy sauce
2 tablespoons sesame seed paste (tahini)
1 tablespoon brown vinegar
1 tablespoon sugar
1-3 teaspoons chili oil or chili sauce
1 teaspoon grated fresh ginger
1 teaspoon crushed garlic
1/2 teaspoon Sichuan peppercorns (Fagara or Sansho), ground
1 wine-pickled egg yolk, mashed

Cut the chicken into small cubes, discarding any skin and slivers of bone. Drop the peanuts into boiling water to loosen the skins, then drain and peel.

❀ Mix the seasoning/sauce ingredients together, mix with the chicken meat and let stand for 20 minutes.

❀ Heat about 2 1/2 tablespoons oil in a wok and stir-fry the peanuts for about 1 minute. Add the chicken and green onions and stir-fry over fairly high heat until the chicken is cooked through. Pour in the stock and simmer for about 1 1/2 minutes or until absorbed.

❀ Spoon into a serving dish and serve at once.

Guangzhou 广州

SAUTÉED CHICKEN BREASTS WITH TOMATO SAUCE

12 oz (375 g) chicken breasts
1 tablespoon light soy sauce
2 egg whites
1/2 cup (2 oz) cornstarch
12-18 dried shrimp chips
oil for deep-frying

SEASONING/SAUCE

2 tablespoons sugar
2 tablespoons tomato ketchup
1 1/2 tablespoons vinegar
1 tablespoon rice wine or dry sherry
1/2 teaspoon grated fresh ginger
1/2 teaspoon salt

Skin the chicken breasts and cut into thin slices, cutting diagonally across the grain to improve tenderness. Place in a dish, add the soy sauce and let stand for 20 minutes.

❀ Beat the egg whites lightly and mix into a thick batter with the cornstarch. Heat the oil to quite hot and fry the shrimp chips until well puffed and crisp. Drain and set aside.

❀ Dip the chicken pieces one by one into the batter, then place in the oil. Fry, turning twice, until cooked through and golden. Remove and drain well.

SAUTÉED CHICKEN BREASTS WITH TOMATO SAUCE

※ Pour off the oil, reserving about 1 tablespoon. Add the sauce ingredients and bring to boil, stirring. Put in the chicken pieces and cook gently, stirring carefully from time to time, until the liquid has been absorbed.

※ Arrange the chicken in the center of a serving plate, pour a little of the hot frying oil over the chicken to give it a gloss and surround with the shrimp chips. Serve immediately.

Beijing 北京

WHITE DEW CHICKEN

8 oz (250 g) chicken breast meat, steamed
all purpose flour
6 oz (185 g) white fish fillets
5 egg whites
2 tablespoons rendered chicken fat, melted
red bell pepper or carrot shreds
cilantro

SEASONING

½ cup (4 oz) milk
1½ tablespoons cornstarch
2 teaspoons rice wine or dry sherry
1 teaspoon ginger juice
¾ teaspoon salt

SAUCE

¾ cup (6 oz) chicken stock
1½ teaspoons cornstarch
1 teaspoon rice wine or dry sherry
1 teaspoon ginger juice
½ teaspoon salt

Cut the chicken into thin slices and arrange evenly in the

WHITE DEW CHICKEN

bottom of a shallow casserole. Sprinkle lightly with flour.

※ Grind the fish and mix with the pre-mixed seasoning ingredients. Beat the egg whites until fluffy but not stiff and fold into the fish with the chicken fat.

※ Spread over the chicken slices and garnish with the shredded bell pepper or carrot and the cilantro.

※ Place on a rack in a wok or steamer, cover and steam for about 18 minutes or until just firm.

※ Mix the sauce ingredients together and boil them in a small saucepan, stirring until the sauce thickens and clears. Pour over the dish and serve.

STEAMED CHICKEN WITH EGG WHITE

Shanghai 上海

STEAMED CHICKEN WITH EGG WHITE

This is a meticulously prepared dish. The three layers of ingredients are subjected to three separate steaming procedures. The lower layer consists of very thinly sliced chicken breast; the central layer of minced prawn and pork fat mixed with wine; and the upper layer of whipped egg white. When the dish is completely assembled and cooked for the second time, it is cut into diamond-shaped sections and garnished with pea leaves and ham before its final steaming.

The elegant appearance of this dish enhances its delicious flavor.

4 oz (125 g) chicken breasts
8 oz (250 g) peeled fresh prawns or shrimp
3 oz (90 g) pork fat
1 tablespoon cornstarch
2 teaspoons rice wine or dry sherry
1 teaspoon salt
4 egg whites, well beaten
fresh pea or young spinach leaves (garnish)
1 slice salted ham (garnish)
1 tablespoon rendered chicken fat, melted

Very thinly slice the boned and skinned chicken breasts and arrange in the bottom of an oiled baking pan, 8-in (20-cm) square.

※ Grind the prawns and pork fat and mix with the cornstarch, wine and salt. Spread over the chicken. Place on a rack in a wok or steamer and steam, covered, over high heat for about 20 minutes, or until cooked through.

※ While the pan is still hot, pour on the beaten egg whites, cover and steam gently until just set. Remove from the steamer and let cool.

※ Cut into diamond-shaped pieces and place a double pea leaf and a tiny piece of ham, cut into the shape of a flower, on each piece. Transfer them to a flat heatproof plate, then return to the steamer for about 5 minutes until heated through. Sprinkle with chicken fat just before serving to give the dish a gloss.

QUICK-FRIED CHICKEN CUBES IN BROWN BEAN SAUCE

Beijing 北京

QUICK-FRIED CHICKEN CUBES IN BROWN BEAN SAUCE

Brown bean sauce is a special sauce from Beijing made from soybeans, flour and salt. It is light brown, very fine and smooth, and has a sweet and salty aroma. It is used for quick-frying and to season stuffings.

This well-known Shandong dish is rated as one of the best quick-fried dishes seasoned with brown bean sauce. The sauce should adhere to the chicken pieces when cooked, and not remain in the bottom of the wok.

10 oz (315 g) chicken breast meat
1 egg white, lightly beaten
2 tablespoons cornstarch
1/2 cup (125 g) lard
1 teaspoon sesame oil

SEASONING

1 tablespoon brown bean sauce
2 teaspoons sugar
2 teaspoons rice wine or dry sherry
1 teaspoon ginger juice

Cut the chicken breast into small cubes and dip into a mixture of beaten egg white and cornstarch, coating evenly.
❋ Heat the lard in a wok and quick-fry the chicken until white and almost cooked through. Remove and pour off all but 1½ tablespoons of the lard. Add the sesame oil and heat well, then fry the brown bean sauce briefly before adding the remaining seasoning ingredients. Mix well, then return the chicken and stir-fry until the seasoning ingredients coat the chicken cubes. Transfer to a serving plate and serve immediately.

CHICKEN WING AND FROG LEG TAPESTRY

Guangzhou 广州

CHICKEN WING AND FROG LEG TAPESTRY

The wings are golden yellow, the frogs' legs are pale, the ham is pink and the vegetables green. This dish is as colorful as a tapestry, hence its name.

12 chicken wings, central sections only
3 slices lean ham
12 frogs' legs
6 stems choy sum or other Chinese green vegetable
oil for deep-frying
3/4 cup (6 oz) chicken stock
2 teaspoons cornstarch

SEASONING A

1 tablespoon rice wine or dry sherry
1/2 teaspoon sesame oil
1/4 teaspoon salt
pinch of white pepper

SEASONING B

1 tablespoon rice wine or dry sherry
2 teaspoons cornstarch
1/2 teaspoon salt
pinch of white pepper

Cut the wings in half and use a sharp knife to remove the small bones. Cut the ham into shreds the length of the chicken pieces, and place several ham shreds in the cavity of each chicken wing. Arrange side by side in a dish, add the seasoning A ingredients and set aside for 20 minutes.
❋ Bone the frogs' legs. Cut the vegetable stems in half and place a portion in the cavity of each frog's leg. Arrange in a heatproof dish, add the seasoning B ingredients and set aside for 20 minutes.
❋ Set the dish of chicken wings on a rack in a wok or steamer over simmering water. Cover tightly and steam for about 35 minutes or until tender.
❋ Heat the oil and deep-fry the frogs' legs until golden and cooked through. Drain well.
❋ Pour the liquid from the wings into a wok, add the stock mixed with the cornstarch and bring to boil. Simmer, stirring, until the sauce clears.
❋ Pile the chicken wings in the center of a serving plate and surround with the frogs' legs. Pour the sauce over and serve.

Beijing 北京

VELVET CHICKEN WITH SHARKS' FINS

This classic dish is often served as the first course of an elaborate ten-course dinner banquet.

2 oz (60 g) dried shredded sharks' fins
5 cups (1¼ l) Superior Stock (*see page 124*)
10 oz (315 g) chicken breasts
3 tablespoons ice water
4 egg whites, well beaten
1½ tablespoons cornstarch
2 teaspoons rice wine or dry sherry
¾ teaspoon salt
3 cups (24 oz) chicken stock
½ cup (4 oz) milk
2 green onions
3 slices fresh ginger

Prepare the sharks' fins by soaking for 1 hour in cold water, then bring to boil, simmer for 10 minutes and drain. Soak again in cold water for about 30 minutes, then bring to boil and simmer for 30 minutes. Repeat the second soaking and boiling process, then drain well and cover with the Superior Stock. Simmer for about 1 hour or until the fins are tender.

Very finely grind the chicken, mixing in the ice water. Add the egg whites and cornstarch and season with wine and salt.

Set aside a small portion of the sharks' fins for decoration and stir the remainder into the chicken paste. Form this mixture into lotus-petal shapes and arrange on a bamboo rack. Place the rack in a wok and pour in the chicken stock and milk. Add the whole green onions and the sliced ginger. Cover and simmer over very low heat until most of the stock has evaporated or been absorbed. Lift out, transfer to a serving plate and garnish with the remaining sharks' fins shreds before serving.

VELVET CHICKEN WITH SHARKS' FINS

SWEET AND SOUR CHICKEN SHREDS

Shanghai 上海

SWEET AND SOUR CHICKEN SHREDS

This is the Shanghai version of a traditional Sichuan dish. Tender chicken breasts are cut into fine shreds, stir-fried and then flavored with a spicy, sweet and sour mixture of condiments and seasonings.

8 oz (250 g) chicken breasts, skinned
1 tablespoon rice wine or dry sherry
1 small egg white, lightly beaten
2 teaspoons cornstarch
1 teaspoon salt
2 slices fresh ginger
½ red bell pepper
1 green onion
8 oz (250 g) fresh spinach leaves
oil for frying

SEASONING

2 teaspoons chili oil or chili sauce
1 teaspoon black bean paste
1 teaspoon sugar

Very thinly slice the chicken breasts, then cut into shreds. Place in a dish and add the wine, egg white, cornstarch and salt. Mix well and let stand for 20 minutes to marinate.

Shred the ginger and the trimmed bell pepper. Cut the green onion into 2-in (4-cm) lengths, then lengthwise into shreds. Rinse the spinach leaves thoroughly, remove stems and drain well.

Heat 2 tablespoons of the oil in a wok and stir-fry the spinach over high heat until wilted. Transfer to a serving plate.

Add about 2 tablespoons oil to the wok and stir-fry the ginger briefly, then add the bell pepper and onion shreds and stir-fry for about 1 minute, adding the pre-mixed seasoning ingredients. Push to one side of the wok and add the chicken shreds. Stir-fry over high heat until cooked through and white, then mix thoroughly with the pepper, onion and the sauce.

Spoon onto the serving plate beside the spinach and serve.

DICED QUAIL STIR-FRIED IN CHICKEN FAT

Guangzhou 广州

DICED QUAIL STIR-FRIED IN CHICKEN FAT

Wild quail breed in northeast China and migrate to the southeast in winter. A type of turtledove, they eat grains and grass seeds, which give them a plump and tender breast. Nowadays they are bred commercially all over China for their delicious meat and tiny eggs, the latter a favorite in Guangdong. This dish is traditionally served sandwich-style, wrapped in fresh lettuce leaves.

4 quail, 6 oz (185 g) each
1 tablespoon light soy sauce
1 egg white, well beaten
3 tablespoons cornstarch
2 oz (60 g) fresh or canned winter bamboo shoots
3 dried black mushrooms, soaked for 25 minutes
peanut oil
3 tablespoons rendered chicken fat

SEASONING/SAUCE

1 clove garlic, finely chopped
2 slices fresh ginger, finely chopped
2 green onions, finely chopped
2 teaspoons rice wine or dry sherry
2 teaspoons oyster sauce
1 teaspoon sugar
1/2 teaspoon salt
pinch of white pepper

Cut the heads, necks, wings and legs off the quail. Reserve one pair each of wings and legs and marinate in the soy sauce in a small bowl.
❊ Remove the meat from the quail carcasses and cut into very fine dice. Mix with the egg white and 2 tablespoons cornstarch.
❊ Drop the fresh bamboo shoots into a saucepan of boiling water, simmer for 2 minutes, then drain well. Drain and trim the mushrooms, then dice them and the bamboo shoots finely.
❊ Coat the marinated quail's wings and legs thickly with the remaining cornstarch. Heat the peanut oil in a wok and deep-fry these parts until crisp and golden, then arrange on a serving plate.
❊ Drain the wok, reheat it with the chicken fat and stir-fry the mushrooms and bamboo shoots for 1 1/2 minutes. Push to one side and add the diced quail meat. Stir-fry until just cooked, about 2 minutes, then add the garlic, ginger and green onions. Stir in the bamboo shoots and mushrooms and add the remaining seasoning/sauce ingredients, tossing together over high heat until well mixed. Place the mixture on the plate with the fried wings and legs, then serve.

FRIED GOOSE LIVERS WRAPPED IN PORK CAUL FAT

Shanghai 上海

FRIED GOOSE LIVERS WRAPPED IN PORK CAUL FAT

This delicate dish is a specialty of the Ningbo area in Zhejiang Province, where the wrap-and-fry method of cooking is often used. Goose livers are said to be better than those of other poultry because they are large, soft and flavorful. Wrapping the livers in pork caul fat, and then frying, preserves the tasty juices of the liver.

10 oz (315 g) fresh goose or duck livers
1 piece pork caul fat
1 small egg
1/2 cup (2 oz) all purpose flour
salt and pepper
2 tablespoons cornstarch
oil for deep-frying

SEASONING

2 1/2 tablespoons finely chopped green onions
1 tablespoon rice wine or dry sherry
pepper

HOT SOY SAUCE DIP

3 tablespoons dark soy sauce
1 fresh red chili, finely chopped

SICHUAN PEPPER-SALT DIP

1 tablespoon Sichuan peppercorns (Fagara or Sansho)
3 tablespoons fine table salt

Trim the livers and cut into slices. Place in a dish and add the seasoning ingredients, mix well and let stand for 30 minutes.
❊ Rinse the caul fat and dry well; place on a dry paper towel.
❊ Beat the egg and flour to make a smooth batter, adding salt and pepper. Cut the caul into long wide strips and brush with batter. Place liver mixture in a thick line down the center and roll up in a sausage shape, tucking the ends in. Repeat with the remaining caul fat and liver.
❊ Grease a heatproof plate and place the liver rolls on it. Set on a rack in a wok or steamer, cover and steam for about 25 minutes or until cooked. Remove and let cool.
❊ When cool, brush the outside with the remaining batter and coat lightly with cornstarch. Heat the oil in a wok and deep-fry until golden and crisp on the surface. Drain well and arrange on a serving plate.
❊ Mix the soy sauce dip ingredients and divide among several small dishes.
❊ To prepare the pepper-salt dip, dry-fry the peppercorns in a wok for about 1 minute, then remove and grind finely. Heat the salt in the dry wok, stirring constantly, and remove from the heat just before it begins to color. Mix with the pepper powder. Pour into several small dishes.

DICED DUCK MEAT WITH GREEN PEPPERS

SMOKED DUCK WITH TENDER GINGER

Beijing 北京

DICED DUCK MEAT WITH GREEN PEPPERS

The large, dark green bell peppers that grow in and around Beijing are characterized by their thick layer of pulp. Sweet and crisp, they are especially good for frying. In this recipe they are combined with very tender duck meat. For those who like it hot, some chili oil can be added.

12 oz (375 g) boneless duck meat, preferably from the breast
1 egg white, well beaten
2 tablespoons cornstarch
3/4 teaspoon salt
1 large green bell pepper
1 lb (500 g) lard, oil or rendered duck fat for frying
2 teaspoons cornstarch

SEASONING

1/2 cup (4 oz) duck or chicken stock
2 tablespoons light soy sauce
2 teaspoons rice wine or dry sherry
1 1/2 teaspoons sugar
1 teaspoon sesame oil
pinch each of salt and pepper

Cut the duck meat into small cubes and place in a dish with the egg white, cornstarch and salt. Mix well and let stand for 15 minutes.

Cut the green pepper in half, trim away the seed core and inner white ribs and discard the stem. Cut into squares.

Heat the oil or fat in a wok until smoking, then reduce the heat to moderate. Fry the duck for about 3 minutes or until cooked through, then remove and set aside. Add the pepper squares and fry until slightly colored; remove and drain. Pour off all but 2 tablespoons of the oil, add the seasoning ingredients and bring to boil, stirring constantly.

Return the duck and pepper and stir together for a few moments over high heat. Thicken slightly with a thin mixture of cornstarch and cold water and serve.

Sichuan 四川

SMOKED DUCK WITH TENDER GINGER

"Before going to bed take some radish, after getting up take some ginger," is an old Chinese saying derived from the belief that the radish aids digestion, while ginger stimulates the appetite.

Ginger was first brought to China from Indonesia at least two thousand years ago. Poets and herbalists have written in praise of it, and chefs have created many delicious dishes using its fine flavor.

1 whole breast of a camphor and tea smoked duck*
12 slices young fresh ginger
1-2 fresh red chilies
2 green onions or garlic chives
3 cloves garlic
2 tablespoons oil for frying
1 teaspoon brown vinegar

SEASONING

2 tablespoons light soy sauce
1 tablespoon hot bean paste
2 1/2 teaspoons sugar
2 teaspoons rice vinegar

Do not skin the duck, but cut the breast into thin slices, then stack several slices on top of each other and cut into narrow shreds.

Cut the ginger, chilies and green onions or garlic chives into shreds and slice the garlic.

Heat the oil in a wok to the smoking point and stir-fry the duck until crisp on the edges. Remove and set aside.

Stir-fry the vegetables and garlic together for about 1 1/2 minutes, then add the seasoning ingredients and stir-fry together for another 30 seconds.

Return the duck meat and continue to stir-fry over high heat until all ingredients are well mixed. Stir in the brown vinegar and serve.

Duck smoked over chips of camphor wood and Chinese black tea leaves to give a strong, smoky flavor and rich deep color.

FRIED SESAME DUCK LIVER

Beijing 北京

FRIED SESAME DUCK LIVER

Duck livers offer a good source of protein and vitamins. They are said to be good for the liver and eyes, and able to cure night blindness and anemia. Sesame seeds, a major source of rich cooking and flavoring oil, are said to replenish strength and help muscle and brain development. Thus the combination of duck livers and sesame in this recipe makes an extremely beneficial and nutritious dish.

10 duck or chicken livers
2 teaspoons rice wine or dry sherry
½ teaspoon salt
1 cup (4 oz) all purpose flour
2 egg whites
¾ cup white sesame seeds
peanut oil for frying

Blanch the livers in boiling water, drain well, then cut open (without cutting through completely) and flatten out butterfly-style. Place in a dish, season with the rice wine and salt and let stand for 20 minutes.

Pour the flour into a dish. Beat the egg whites in another dish until frothy. Spread sesame seeds on a plate.

Coat each piece of liver with flour, then dip into the beaten egg white. Dip one side of each liver into the sesame seeds, coating thickly. Heat about 1 in (2.5 cm) of oil in a wide pan or wok and gently fry the livers for about 3 minutes or until golden on the surface and tender inside. Serve immediately.

Beijing 北京

BEIJING DUCK

Records of the famed Beijing duck actually date back as far as the Song Dynasty (960-1279 AD), but the dish became a favorite of the imperial kitchen only during the Ming Dynasty (1368-1644 AD). The ducks used then were the small, black-feathered type from the Nanjing lakes, quite different from the plump-breasted white Beijing ducks used today.

At the beginning of the fifteenth century the capital of China was moved from Nanjing to Beijing, and rice had to be transported from Nanjing to Beijing to meet the extravagant demands of the imperial court. Canals were dug to transport the rice, but much was lost in the canals, and subsequently the ducks bred in this area became extremely well fed. A new breed of Beijing duck thus emerged, and duck breeding became a prosperous business.

Beijing ducks are now artificially fed, and sixty to seventy days after hatching their weight can be as much as 7 pounds (3½ kilograms). Their distinctive features are white feathers, short wings, a long back and strong healthy body, with the thin skin that is best for roasting.

There are different ways of roasting the duck, although this is not usually done at home. At the famous Quan Ju De Restaurant in Beijing the ducks are hung inside a special brick oven suspended on steel rods over the fire. Just beyond the front opening is a small platform where aromatic fruit tree wood is burnt, and its specially fragrant smoke penetrates the ducks during the cooking process.

The method used by the equally famous Bian Yi Fang Beijing Duck Restaurant does not allow the flame to touch the ducks directly. The walls of the oven are first heated to the right temperature, then the oven door is tightly closed and the ducks roasted in the heat from glowing charcoal underneath. Gas and electric ovens used in other restaurants also give excellent results. The correct temperature results in minimal loss of oil and juice, a light crisp skin and the characteristic bright color of Beijing duck.

Regardless of the roasting method, the ducks are always given a standard pre-roasting treatment. After the ducks have been killed and plucked, air is pumped beneath the skin to make it balloon. The internal organs are removed and the cavity is washed well. The ducks are then hung on a hook and scalded with boiling water. A syrupy mixture made from diluted malt sugar is poured over the skin and the ducks are left to dry. Finally, before hanging in the oven to roast, the bodies are filled with water, which boils the meat from the inside as it roasts outside. This gives the duck its famed crisp, dry skin and succulent tender meat.

Beijing Duck should be eaten immediately. The duck is taken to the table and the brightly colored skin, resembling brilliantly lacquered wood (giving it the name of 'lacquered duck') is quickly sliced off in squares. While diners enjoy the slivers of skin dipped into sweet bean paste and eaten with thin wheat flour pancakes, sticks of cucumber and fresh green onion, the meat is carved and arranged on a serving plate.

The meat is the second course of Beijing Duck, and it is sometimes served with lotus leaf cakes and sesame buns instead of pancakes. The leftover bones and fragments of meat are boiled with white cabbage and winter melon to make a soup which is brought to the table towards the end of the banquet.

BONED DUCK SIMMERED WITH LEMON JUICE

Guangzhou 广州

BONED DUCK SIMMERED WITH LEMON JUICE

12 oz (375 g) boned duck meat
2 eggs, well beaten
1 cup (4 oz) cornstarch
3 cups (24 oz) oil for deep-frying
1 teaspoon sesame oil
1 tablespoon peanut oil (optional)
fried sliced tomatoes (garnish)

SEASONING

2 tablespoons water
2 tablespoons finely chopped green onion
1 tablespoon rice wine or dry sherry
1 teaspoon grated fresh ginger
1 teaspoon salt
1/3 teaspoon baking soda

SAUCE

1½ cups (12 oz) chicken or duck stock
3 tablespoons lemon juice
2 tablespoons rice wine or dry sherry
1½ tablespoons sugar

Cut the duck meat into finger-sized pieces and place in a dish. Pour on the pre-mixed seasoning ingredients and mix well. Cover and let stand for 1-2 hours.

※ Drain and pat dry. Dip each piece into the beaten egg, then coat thickly with cornstarch. Heat the deep-frying oil in a wok to the smoking point, then reduce the heat slightly and deep-fry the duck pieces, several at a time, until golden on both sides. Lift out, drain well and place in a clay pot or casserole.

※ Add the sauce ingredients and bring just to the boil, then reduce the heat and simmer, partially covered, for about 40 minutes or until the duck is very tender and the liquid almost absorbed.

※ Sprinkle on the sesame oil and peanut oil, transfer to a serving plate and surround with fried sliced tomato.

Beijing 北京

SUNFLOWER DUCK

1 3-lb (1½-kg) duck
16 small dried black mushrooms, soaked for 25 minutes
12 small slices Yunnan or other salted ham
3/4 cup (6 oz) chicken stock
1 tablespoon rendered chicken fat
1 teaspoon sugar
1 tablespoon cornstarch
parboiled carrot sticks (garnish)

SEASONING

2 tablespoons finely chopped green onion
1 tablespoon light soy sauce
2 teaspoons rice wine or dry sherry
½ teaspoon finely chopped fresh ginger
pinch of salt

Rinse and dry the duck inside and out and place in a dish. Mix the seasoning ingredients together, spoon into the cavity and marinate for 1 hour, turning the duck from time to time.

※ Set the duck on a rack in a wok or steamer, cover and steam over gently simmering water for about 1 hour or until tender. Three-quarters of the way through cooking the duck add the mushrooms and ham to the steamer. Remove, allow to cool, then bone and cut off 16 slices of the most tender part of the duck, the breast and upper thighs. Cut off the mushroom stems and arrange the caps, together with the ham and slices of duck, skin downwards, alternately in several rows on a heatproof plate.

※ Mix the chicken stock, chicken fat and sugar together and pour over the dish. Steam for a further 10-12 minutes. Drain the liquid into a wok, then place a plate over the dish and invert so that the duck skin faces upwards.

※ Add the cornstarch mixed with a little cold water to the liquid in the wok. Bring to boil and pour over the dish. Arrange the carrot sticks around the edge and serve at once.

SUNFLOWER DUCK

FLAMED DUCK HEARTS

Beijing 北京

FLAMED DUCK HEARTS

It takes just three seconds to cook this dish! The marinated duck hearts are tossed into a very hot wok where the moisture from the marinade, contacting the hot fat, bursts into flames. This dramatic spectacle illustrates the versatility of the Chinese wok and the creative genius of the Chinese chef.

6 oz (185 g) duck hearts
3 tablespoons rendered duck fat
4 green onions, shredded
8 sprigs cilantro

SEASONING

2 tablespoons light soy sauce
1 tablespoon Mao Tai wine or dry sherry
1 teaspoon sesame oil
1 teaspoon sugar
1/3 teaspoon salt
pinch of pepper

Cut open each heart, place cut side upwards on a cutting board and pound several times with the side of the cleaver to flatten and tenderize. Make criss-cross scores across the cut side of each heart. Place in a dish, add the pre-mixed seasoning ingredients and let stand for 20 minutes to marinate.

In a large wok heat the duck fat to the smoking point. Quickly drop in the hearts and allow the fat to catch fire. Stir the hearts once and remove from the wok in a strainer.

Have the shredded green onion and cilantro spread over a serving plate, pile the hearts onto the plate and serve immediately.

SHREDDED DUCK MEAT WITH BEAN SPROUTS

Beijing 北京

SHREDDED DUCK MEAT WITH BEAN SPROUTS

It is an old Chinese custom to eat spring rolls filled with fresh bean sprouts at the beginning of springtime every year. This dish of shredded duck with bean sprouts is quite similar to a traditional spring roll filling and could be used as such.

10 oz (315 g) roast duck breast meat
4 oz (125 g) fresh mung or soybean sprouts
1 green onion, sliced
3 slices fresh ginger, shredded
2½ tablespoons oil for frying
2 teaspoons Sichuan pepper (Fagara or Sansho) oil*

SEASONING/SAUCE

½ cup (4 oz) chicken or duck stock
2 teaspoons rice wine or dry sherry
1½ teaspoons brown vinegar
3 cloves garlic, finely chopped

Cut the duck into thin slices, then into fine shreds. Blanch the sprouts in boiling water for a few seconds, then drain very well and let cool.

※ Place the green onion and ginger in a wok with the frying oil and heat to the smoking point, then turn off the heat and let stand for 5 minutes. Remove and discard the onion and ginger and reheat the oil.

※ Mix the seasoning/sauce ingredients together.

※ When the oil is at the smoking point, very quickly add the sprouts and stir-fry for a few seconds, then add the duck meat and stir quickly. Pour in the sauce mixture and heat through very quickly. Transfer to a serving plate and sprinkle with the Sichuan pepper oil.

Heat 2-3 tablespoons of peanut or other vegetable oil in a wok to the smoking point. Add 2 teaspoons lightly crushed Sichuan peppercorns and fry for 1 minute, then turn off the heat and let stand in the oil until cool. Drain off the oil and store in a jar.

Beijing 北京

DUCK WING LANTERNS

Colored cellophane frills are used to decorate the bones of these crisp-fried duck wings. If the lighting on the banquet table is correct, the brightly colored paper causes a rainbow of colored lights.

12 duck wings, central section only
¾ cup (3 oz) cornstarch
oil or rendered duck fat for deep-frying
cellophane frills

SEASONING

2 tablespoons finely chopped green onion
1 tablespoon rice wine or dry sherry
1 tablespoon light soy sauce
2 teaspoons dark soy sauce
2 teaspoons sugar
1 teaspoon grated fresh ginger
¼ teaspoon salt
pinch of white pepper

Use a small sharp knife to cut around one end of each wing bone and push the meat along to form a ball at one end. Leave only one bone in each wing. Place in a dish, add the pre-mixed seasoning ingredients and marinate for 1 hour, turning several times.

※ Place the duck wings on a heatproof dish on a rack in a wok or steamer, cover and steam over gently simmering water for 20-25 minutes or until the wings are very tender. Remove and drain well, leave to dry for a few minutes, then coat thickly with cornstarch, shaking off the excess.

※ Heat the oil in a wok and deep-fry the wings over high heat for about 1½ minutes or until the surface is crisp and well colored. Drain well, decorate the tips of the bones with cellophane frills and serve immediately.

DUCK WING LANTERNS

Shanghai 上海

STIR-FRIED PHEASANT MEAT WITH BEAN SPROUTS

Pheasant is sometimes called wild chicken. The texture of its meat is tight and fine grained, as well as very tender and full of flavor, its breast meat being especially delicious and firm.

Bean sprouts picked clean of their seed pods and tapering roots are called silver sprouts. The color of these two ingredients together is subtle and the texture smooth and crisp.

6 oz (185 g) pheasant breast meat, skinned
1 small egg white
2 tablespoons lard
8 oz (250 g) fresh silver sprouts
pinch of salt
2 tablespoons rice wine or dry sherry
¾ cup (6 oz) stock made from the boiled pheasant bones
1 tablespoon cornstarch

Very thinly slice the breast meat, then cut into fine, even shreds. Lightly beat the egg white, mix with the pheasant meat and set aside for 20 minutes.

※ Heat the wok, add half the lard and stir-fry the silver sprouts until softened, adding a pinch of salt. Arrange around the edge of a serving dish.

※ Add the remaining lard and stir-fry the pheasant meat over high heat for 2-3 minutes or until it changes color and is just cooked through.

※ Add the wine and cook briefly. Mix the stock and cornstarch together, add to the wok and boil until the sauce thickens. Check the seasoning, then pile the pheasant shreds in the center of the dish. Serve at once.

SHANGHAI'S LEGENDARY WATERFRONT, THE BUND

LEONG KA TAI

上海
Shanghai

上海
Shanghai
THE GOURMET'S METROPOLIS

WHERE the mighty flood of the Yangtze River rushes 20 miles (32 kilometers) wide into the East China Sea, an astonishing maze of tributaries, creeks, rivers, lakes, ponds and marshlands twist, shimmering, between endless fields of rice and vegetables. On the river itself, and in the countless waterways stretching in all directions, nets are cast to harvest fish such as the Yangtze catfish, which grows up to 6 feet (2 meters) in length. A rich crop of freshwater carp and other table fish is raised to tender plumpness in a million ponds. At sea the sails of junks and sampans spread to the horizon as their crews await the flood tides to help carry them upriver to one of the biggest cities in the world, where the twelve million inhabitants of Shanghai await their daily catch. To the north of the river lies the province of Jiangsu, now the richest in China, where more than sixty million people proudly refer to their lake-studded home as the Land of Fish and Rice. To the south, equally rich and proud of its culinary heritage, is Zhejiang Province, which has made its own vital contribution to China's gastronomic heritage. As the Western world calls an area of bounteous plenty a "land of milk and honey," so to the Chinese a place where generous nature opens its heart and bestows all the good things of life is known as a "land of fish and rice." Hence the reason for joy in the bounteous harvest lands of the Yangtze delta.

And in the middle is the jewel, the immense industrial powerhouse of Shanghai. Sprawling around a river of its own, the Huangpu, with its endless wharves and berths and cranes and ferries, it is a city of superlatives. Shanghai works hard, and to keep its enormous workforce productive and churning out a third of China's industrial wealth, it supports a stunning range of restaurants. Shanghai is a working city and much of the eating is done on the run. The steaming hot buns stuffed with pork and vegetables are the Chinese equivalent of the American hamburger, the Australian meat pie or the British fish and chips. Crowds of thousands cram the hundreds of hot bun shops yelling orders.

THE GRAND CANAL IN WUXI, JIANGSU PROVINCE   TOM NEBBIA

But Shanghai is just one of the cities clustered in the fertile plain and studded on the waterways of the central coast of China. Historic and fabled places such as Suzhou, Wuxi, Hangzhou, Nanjing, Ningbo and a score of other cities all boast their own culinary traditions and local delicacies. And, above all, Yangzhou. Over the centuries this ancient city has given to the national table such dishes as the big, tender meatball known as Lion's Head, as well as fried rice, noodles and many others. In the gastronomic wealth of this region every city has a claim to culinary fame, every district has given some twist to the immense variety of dishes which originate in the Land of Fish and Rice. The busy port city of Ningbo bequeathed salted fish and other preserved foods designed to stock the galleys of its roaming fleet. Hangzhou gave a tradition of juicy carp from its West Lake, the famed Dragon Well tea, and of course its gentle but potent spiced rice wine. Little wonder Marco Polo called it the finest and most splendid city in the world, and for the rest of his life was to speak glowingly of its gastronomic glory. Some of Suzhou's specialties are so famous that gourmets from Shanghai will drive up for the day to sample the local crab, mandarin fish or eel. Spareribs are said to have first been sizzled in Wuxi, and Nanjing claims the best pressed ducks in the land – producing a staggering fifty million birds every year. Zhejiang Province is proud of its vinegar, rightfully claimed to be the best in China and, therefore, the world.

The Shanghai region has one dish that is justifiably acclaimed as being supreme throughout the whole of China. No matter how ardent a culinary nationalist from another area of the country may be, he will concede that nothing can ever equal the freshwater delicacy known as Shanghai hairy crab. The very name of the creature that makes up this dish is misleading, because the most famous hairy crabs do not come from Shanghai but from Yangcheng Lake, halfway up the river to Nanjing. But it is as Shanghai hairy crab that they are known to the world, and the devotees who pay up to a hundred dollars for a 5-inch (13-centimeter)-wide crab are certain that it is money well spent.

Those not familiar with the fame of this crustacean may look askance at such sums being paid for what appears to be an undistinguished creature that glares balefully out of two enraged tiny eyes and is covered with unsightly blackish fur. But come autumn, Yangcheng Lake delivers up its harvest, and gourmets flock from around the world to partake of the delicacy. Every day during the season two express trains leave Shanghai and rumble south to Hong Kong to deliver baskets of fresh crabs to specialist chefs in the city. The crabs are steamed alive and placed in front of eager diners. Those who throng to the tables to eat the delicacies are not only Chinese; in recent years Japanese gourmets have flown to Hong Kong by the hundreds merely to enjoy a meal of the small freshwater crabs.

The four-gilled carp is another freshwater delicacy. In all the world, the tiny fish, which averages about 6 inches (15 centimeters) in length, lives only in one small stretch of one river. The Chinese government permits only a limited number to be caught every year, and because the four-gilled carp is said to have numerous health benefits for those who eat it, the price paid for it is correspondingly high.

CHINA'S MAIN FILMMAKING CENTER, SHANGHAI HAS MANY CINEMAS   LEONG KA TAI

WATERWAYS DISSECT THE CENTRAL COAST OF CHINA

PAUL LAU

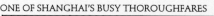
ONE OF SHANGHAI'S BUSY THOROUGHFARES

The lower Yangtze Valley is the area generally considered to be the center of the Shanghai cuisine. Shanghai, however, became a city only in the nineteenth century when China was forced at gunpoint to open the series of coastal and river settlements known as Treaty Ports. So there is no such thing as a historical Shanghai cuisine. The city, as it swelled to its present immense size, first as an international settlement and then as China's premier port and industrial complex, borrowed the cuisines from the surrounding provinces. Into the conurbation on the banks of the Huangpu poured the genius of the people of Jiangsu, Zhejiang, Anhui and Hubei. They went to Shanghai to make their fortunes, and when they had made them they wanted to spend some of their money on eating their native foods. So up sprang thousands of provincial restaurants serving the countless delicacies of the central coast of China and the Yangtze Valley. Over the years these specialties merged into what is now known as the Shanghai kitchen.

What makes Shanghai food distinctive? Gourmets will tell you that it is more oily than that of other regions. Gentle, slow braising rather than vigorous stir-frying is a favored cooking technique, making dishes more succulent and highly flavored. To give balance a pinch of sugar is often added to meat recipes. Many dishes are spiced with the wine of Shaoxing, famous in all China and used so lavishly in dishes from this area that the gourmet will know immediately that he is being served Shanghai delicacies. China's favorite fish and seafood are found here in abundance, and the fish recipes from this eastern region are as good as or better than those of any other part of the country. Meat and poultry are also excellent, the favorite choices being pork and chicken. The region

WELDON TRANNIES

is also famous for its beautifully arranged cold platters. The bountiful supplies of vegetables add color and variety to the diet which, with its heavy reliance on fresh fish and fresh vegetables, is one of the healthiest and most balanced in the world.

The slower braising and stewing, and the natural delta ingredients, make for wonderful dishes in which the bounty of the canals, ponds and gardens combine their varying flavors with wine, soy and vinegar. The combination proved irresistible to one gourmet. The Manchu emperor who reigned under the name Chien Lung was noted for his love of art and literature as well as for his keen palate and enthusiastic eye for the ladies. But he was no idle dilettante. Dressing up in the clothes of a merchant, Chien Lung made it a practice to roam his realm to see for himself how people lived, to discover their problems, to uncover the mysteries of his vast domain. As a devoted student of fine food he took notes on what he ate. During one of these anonymous sojourns along the Yangtze he made lengthy notes on some of the dishes, and after his incognito trip was over he enthusiastically incorporated many of them into the menu of the imperial court.

The range is so extensive and its origins so diverse that it is impossible to generalize about the school of cooking now known as Shanghai cuisine. It has borrowed dishes, techniques, raw materials and traditions from an area as large as western Europe, with a similar population, and combined them all into the specialties of one vast metropolis. The cooking of the lower Yangtze Valley is the splendid result.

THE SERENITY OF THE HUANGSHAN MOUNTAINS, ANHUI PROVINCE   PAUL LAU

THE PORT OF SHANGHAI

LEONG KA TAI

(following page) THE SERENITY OF THE HUANGSHAN MOUNTAINS, ANHUI PROVINCE

PAUL LAU

PINES CLING TO A DRAMATIC GRANITE PEAK IN
THE HUANGSHAN MOUNTAINS, ANHUI PROVINCE

PAUL LAU

海鮮
Seafood

CORMORANT FISHING, WUXI, JIANGSU PROVINCE

PAUL LAU

海鮮 Seafood

IN CHINESE the sound for fish is "yu." Pronounced with a slightly different inflection, "yu" also means abundance. So a whole steamed or baked fish is the traditional final dish at a formal dinner banquet, signifying to the guests that although twelve courses of rich culinary delights have already been consumed, there is plenty more to eat if they are still hungry. Fish are abundant throughout China, in the enormous landlocked interior as well as along its jagged coastline. And in almost every provincial cuisine, fish, crabs, eels, frogs and other food from the rivers, streams, canals, ponds and swamps feature on the menu.

Nature has distributed seafood and freshwater fish generously but unevenly. The fishermen who ply their craft along the banks of the Black Dragon River in the frigid north of Manchuria have a life as harsh as the climate: most of the year the river is frozen. Much easier is the lot of those who sail the warm waters of the Gulf of Tonkin and the South China Sea. If they can avoid the great winds of the typhoons they can reap one of the richest marine harvests that any of the seven seas can offer. In the bitter winter the waters of the Gulf of Bohai freeze into an ice shelf reaching far out from shore. Huddled in their padded clothes, fishermen dangle hooks for their prey through holes cut in the thick ice. Life is much easier for the crab catchers of Suzhou, who can sip tea on the banks of the Yangtze lakes as they await the hairy crabs – worth literally their weight in gold – to scamper up the mud to be trapped. And what an idyllic life for shore-based fishermen in the thousands of southern bays, relaxing under a sunshade as they wait for their catch to swim into the big scoop nets dangling on long bamboo poles from a cliff face.

Chinese chefs have been conducting a love affair with fish for longer than history can record. It is a feeling

NETTING RED CARP   YANG SHAOMING

still ardently expressed in every province of the land. Over 2,000 miles (3,000 kilometers) up the Yangtze fish is a daily feature on Yunnan menus, and fish, albeit salted, is a treasured item even in the remote Gobi. In southern coastal ports dwell the Hoklo people, bound to their junks and frail sampans with emotional ropes as strong as those that hold their nets. The Hoklo are born, grow up, marry, give birth and die on their boats. Some can trace their family back thirty generations on the water. Seldom, except when they are selling their catch, do they venture ashore.

FISHING FOR CARP BY THE GIANT BUDDHA IN LESHAN, SICHUAN PROVINCE

SHUFUNOTOMO

When the catch is landed, from sea, river or pond, it must be cooked immediately. It is vital to catch the freshness of the fish in the wok – a maxim firmly held by chefs from every Chinese kitchen. A visit to a fishmarket anywhere in the country is a memorable experience — fish from sea and river swim and splash; tanks of eels squirm; live crabs, their claws tied to safeguard the customers, crawl in huge rattan baskets; frogs hop; turtles crawl; toads squat; octopi and squid glare; and bucket after bucket holds different types of shellfish from tiny mussels to hulking whelks. If it swims, crawls, scrambles, has gills or lives in the water, it is guaranteed pride of place on the Chinese menu. Even a creature as unattractive as the sea cucumber, difficult to define as animal or vegetable, is considered a delicacy — as indeed is seaweed, packed with vital minerals. Jellyfish is prized because it adds an unusual textural experience to a meal: chewy yet crunchy. The fin of a shark, tough as the horn of an elderly buffalo, and less attractive in appearance, is surely as indigestible an item as can be devised by nature, but it becomes the prime ingredient in one of the most famed dishes in Chinese cooking.

PRAWNS BRAISED IN SAUCE

Shanghai 上海

PRAWNS BRAISED IN SAUCE

Prawns curl when they are cooked, but the chefs at the Dong Feng Restaurant in Shanghai wanted to create something different. The result is this dish, in which seven large prawns are aligned in swimming postures and bathed in a strong, sweet-sour sauce.

7 large fresh prawns or shrimp in their shells, weighing
   about 1½ lb (750 g)
3 tablespoons peanut oil
1 green onion, chopped
3 slices fresh ginger, shredded

SAUCE

2 tablespoons tomato ketchup
1 tablespoon light soy sauce
2 teaspoons rice wine or dry sherry
1½ teaspoons sugar
½ teaspoon brown vinegar
¼ teaspoon salt

Cut the legs and antennae from the prawns and devein. Make several cuts across and along the underside to keep them from curling during cooking.
🦐 Heat the oil in a wok and stir-fry the prawns until they turn pink. Remove and drain off all but 1½ tablespoons of the oil.
🦐 Add the green onion and ginger and stir-fry briefly, then pour in the pre-mixed sauce ingredients. Bring to boil and simmer for 1 minute, then return the prawns and simmer gently in the sauce until well glazed.
🦐 Arrange on a serving plate with all the heads in the same direction, pour the rest of the sauce on and serve immediately.

Guangzhou 广州

FRIED PRAWN OMELET

Like all cuisines, Chinese cooking has evolved and expanded over the years until it is now among the most diverse in the world. This recipe has evolved from two traditional dishes: Smooth Fried Eggs and Oil-fried Fresh Prawns. The former is smooth and highlights the natural taste of egg; the latter is crisp yet tender, with the delicious aroma of fresh prawns.

8 oz (250 g) peeled fresh prawns or shrimp
½ teaspoon salt
1 tablespoon cornstarch
2 green onions
6 eggs
¾ teaspoon salt
pinch of white pepper
⅓ teaspoon sesame oil
8 oz (250 g) lard

Devein the prawns and place in a dish with ½ teaspoon salt and the cornstarch. Add a little cold water and rub the prawns gently to whiten them. Rinse thoroughly, then drain well.
🦐 Finely chop the white parts of the green onions. The green tops may be kept to use as a garnish. Beat the eggs with the salt, pepper and sesame oil.
🦐 Heat the lard in a wok and fry the prawns quickly until they turn bright pink – about 2 minutes. Remove and drain. Pour off all but 2 tablespoons of the lard and fry the green onions briefly, then add the eggs. Cook gently, stirring slowly, until the eggs begin to set. Add the prawns and continue to cook over gentle heat until the eggs are just firm.
🦐 Transfer to a serving plate and serve at once.

SCALDED PRAWNS

Guangzhou 广州

SCALDED PRAWNS

Prawns scalded in their shells retain all their flavor and are easy to prepare. The prawns are eaten by hand, being first shelled and then dipped into an accompanying sauce of soy, chopped chilies and oil.

24 large fresh prawns or shrimp in their shells
3-4 slices fresh ginger
green onions, finely chopped
3 tablespoons light soy sauce
1-2 green chilies, finely chopped
3 tablespoons oil

Rinse the prawns and drain. Boil a large wok or saucepan of lightly salted water and add the ginger. Place the prawns in a basket, lower into the water and simmer for about 5 minutes. When ready the shells will be bright pink and the prawns will feel firm. Test one by removing the segment of shell below the head – the meat should be white and firm, no longer transparent or gelatinous looking. Drain, pile onto a plate and garnish with green onion.

✕ Mix the soy sauce, chilies and oil together and pour into several dishes. Serve immediately.

Beijing 北京

TWO-COLOR PRAWNS

8 large prawns or shrimp in their shells
2 teaspoons rice wine or dry sherry
1 teaspoon grated fresh ginger
1 teaspoon sugar
½ teaspoon salt
1 tablespoon rice wine or dry sherry
oil for deep-frying
2½ tablespoons oil for frying
cornstarch
1 teaspoon black sesame seeds

FILLING

1 oz (30 g) pork fat, finely minced or ground
2 water chestnuts, finely chopped
1 small egg white, lightly beaten
pinch each of salt and pepper

Cut the prawns in half, separating heads and tails. Peel the tail sections, leaving the tail shell in place. Cut deeply down the back without cutting through, then beat with the side of a cleaver to flatten. Pick out the vein. Sprinkle with 2 teaspoons rice wine, salt and pepper and set aside. Cut through the head sections of the prawns just above the eyes. Cut down the center back through the shell and pull away the vein. Place in a dish and marinate with the grated ginger, sugar, salt and rice wine for 20 minutes.

✕ Mix the filling ingredients together, working with your fingers until smooth and sticky. Place a portion of the filling on the cut part of each prawn tail, smoothing with a wet spoon. Sprinkle a few black sesame seeds over each, pressing in lightly, then coat lightly with cornstarch.

✕ Heat a wok with deep-frying oil and when almost at the smoking point heat another wok with about 2½ tablespoons oil.

✕ Place the prawn tails carefully in the deep-frying oil and let cook, meanwhile stir-frying heads in the other wok. Turn the tails at least once to fry evenly. When the heads are bright red and cooked through, remove to the center of a serving plate. Drain the fried tails and arrange around the edge of the dish. Serve at once.

TWO-COLOR PRAWNS

Beijing 北京

LANTERN PRAWNS

This dish is particularly well presented: the bright red prawns are piled in the center of a platter with a tassel of yellow egg shreds, giving the appearance of a traditional red paper lantern trimmed with gold.

10-12 large fresh prawns or shrimp in their shells, weighing about 2 lb (1 kg)
2½ tablespoons lard or vegetable oil
2 eggs
1 strip dried beef (optional)
1 strip dried bean curd or carrot (optional)
1 medium cucumber (optional)
½ teaspoon sesame oil

SEASONING/SAUCE

1½ tablespoons rice wine or dry sherry
½ cup (4 oz) chicken stock
2 tablespoons finely chopped green onions
1½ teaspoons sugar
1 teaspoon grated fresh ginger
½ teaspoon salt
pinch of white pepper

Cut off the tips of the prawn heads, then cut along the center back through the shells and devein. Rinse the prawns under cold running water, then dry well.

❊ Heat the lard in a wok and stir-fry the prawns for about 3 minutes or until they are pink and almost cooked through.

❊ Add the wine and cook for a few seconds before adding the remaining pre-mixed seasoning/sauce ingredients. Simmer until the prawns are coated with a rich red glaze, then pile them onto a serving plate with their heads pointing towards the top of the plate.

❊ Rinse the wok and oil it very lightly. Beat the eggs together and pour half into the wok. Tilt the pan until the egg spreads into a very wide thin omelet. When firm on the underside, turn over and cook the other side, then remove from the pan, cook the other omelet and cool before rolling them up and cutting into shreds to form the tassel of the lantern.

❊ Arrange the dried beef like the branches of a pine tree the lantern is hanging in, and very thinly slice and shape the cucumber to resemble its leaves. Form a handle for the lantern from the bean curd strip or carve a carrot in a chain shape. The decorations should be prepared before cooking the dish so that it can be served piping hot.

❊ Sprinkle the sesame oil over the prawns immediately before serving.

SCALDED PRAWN SLICES

Shanghai 上海

SCALDED PRAWN SLICES

1 lb (500 g) fresh prawns or shrimp in their shells
½ teaspoon salt
2 tablespoons cornstarch
1 egg white, well beaten
1½ tablespoons lard
2 green onions, white part only, chopped
2 slices fresh young ginger, shredded
2 teaspoons rice wine or dry sherry
2 tablespoons chicken stock

Peel and devein the prawns. Cut in half lengthwise, then cut each prawn into several pieces. Rinse well in cold water, rubbing with a little cornstarch and salt to whiten them and remove any fishy smell. Drain and place in a dish with the salt, cornstarch and egg white, mixing well.

❊Heat a wok, add the lard and stir-fry the green onion and ginger until softened, then add the rice wine and stock and bring to boil. Remove from the heat.

❊Boil a saucepan of water, slide in the prawns and cook for about 40 seconds or just until they change color. Lift out and drain well, stir into the wok with the green onions and ginger, spoon onto a serving plate and serve immediately.

Shanghai 上海

PRAWNS SERVED IN TWO WAYS

3 lb (1½ kg) fresh prawns or shrimp in their shells
4 cups (1 l) oil for deep-frying
¾ cup (3 oz) cornstarch
3 oz (90 g) thin rice noodles
2 green onions, chopped
2 slices fresh ginger, shredded

SEASONING

1 tablespoon rice wine or dry sherry
1 teaspoon ginger juice
½ teaspoon salt
pinch of white pepper

SAUCE

2 tablespoons chicken stock
2 tablespoons tomato ketchup
1 tablespoon sugar
2 teaspoons rice wine or dry sherry
2 teaspoons light soy sauce
2 teaspoons white vinegar
2 teaspoons cornstarch
pinch of salt

Peel and devein the prawns. Place two-thirds of the prawns in a dish and add the pre-mixed seasoning ingredients. Heat the oil in a wok. Coat the seasoned prawns with cornstarch and deep-fry in the oil until pink and just cooked through. Remove, drain well and keep warm.

❊Divide the noodles into 6 even portions and cook separately: spread each in a small frying basket or perforated ladle, top with another basket or ladle and fry in the oil until crisp and golden. Remove the "nests" and set aside.

❊Drain the wok, retaining about 1½ tablespoons of the oil, and stir-fry the green onions and ginger. Remove and mix with the stir-fried prawns.

❊Add the uncooked prawns to the wok and stir-fry until they change color, then add the pre-mixed sauce ingredients and simmer until the sauce thickens and clears.

❊Pile the stir-fried prawns in the center of a large serving platter and surround with the "nests." Fill each nest with a portion of the prawns in sauce and serve at once.

PRAWNS SERVED IN TWO WAYS

salt and pepper. Mix well and let stand for 20 minutes.

✻ Shred the green onion and set aside. Trim and rinse the vegetables. Heat half the lard in a wok and stir-fry the drained vegetables for 2 minutes over moderate heat. Splash in 2 tablespoons cold water, cover and cook until the vegetables are tender and the liquid is absorbed. Remove and set aside.

✻ Heat the remaining lard in the wok and stir-fry the prawns over high heat, stirring briskly until they turn white. Push to one side of the pan, add the green onion and ginger and fry for a few moments, then pour in the pre-mixed sauce ingredients and bring to boil until the sauce thickens. Add the vegetables, heat through and serve.

PRAWNS WITH BOK CHOY

Beijing 北京
PRAWNS WITH BOK CHOY

1 lb (500 g) fresh prawns or shrimp in their shells
1 egg white, well beaten
2 tablespoons cornstarch
¼ teaspoon baking soda
¾ teaspoon salt
pinch of white pepper
2 green onions, white parts only
8-10 young hearts of bok choy or other fresh Chinese vegetable
2 tablespoons lard
2 thin slices fresh ginger, shredded

SAUCE

½ cup (4 oz) chicken stock
1 teaspoon rice wine or dry sherry
¾ teaspoon sugar
pinch of salt and pepper
¼ teaspoon sesame oil
1½ teaspoons cornstarch

Peel and devein the prawns, rinse thoroughly in cold water and drain well.

✻ Place in a dish with the egg white, cornstarch, baking soda,

Beijing 北京
ZHUA CHAO YU
FRIED PRAWNS

12 oz (375 g) fresh prawns or shrimp in their shells
¾ cup (3 oz) cornstarch
oil, preferably peanut oil, for deep-frying

SAUCE

1 green onion, white part only
3 slices fresh ginger
2 tablespoons lard
1 tablespoon light soy sauce
2 teaspoons brown vinegar
1 teaspoon rice wine or dry sherry
1 teaspoon sugar
pinch each of salt and pepper

Peel and devein the prawns. Rinse thoroughly and dry on paper towels. Mix the cornstarch with water to make a thin paste. Coat the prawns with the paste, then deep-fry in a wok with the hot peanut oil for about 1½ minutes or until cooked through and golden on the surface. Drain well.

✻ Finely chop the green onion and ginger and stir-fry in the lard in another wok for about 45 seconds. Add the pre-mixed remaining sauce ingredients and bring to boil. Add the prawns, turn carefully in the sauce until it has been completely absorbed and serve.

ZHUA CHAO YU FRIED PRAWNS

YUNLUO PRAWNS

Beijing 北京

YUNLUO PRAWNS

This dish of large golden prawns with their prominent red tails "swimming" through a cloud of white vermicelli makes an attractive appetizer or main course.

12 oz (375 g) fresh prawns or shrimp
4 egg whites
1¼ tablespoons all purpose flour
2 tablespoons cornstarch
oil for deep-frying
1½ oz (45 g) rice vermicelli
fresh cilantro or parsley (garnish)
slivers of colored pickled radish (garnish)

SEASONING

2 teaspoons rice wine or dry sherry
½ teaspoon salt
large pinch of white pepper

Peel and devein the prawns, then rinse under running cold water and drain well. Dry on paper towels. Mix in a dish with the seasoning ingredients and let stand for 10 minutes.
❀ Beat the egg whites until frothy; mix in the flour and cornstarch. Do not overstir, but leave the batter slightly lumpy.
❀ Heat the oil in a wok to smoking point, then reduce the heat slightly and add the vermicelli. They will immediately expand and turn white. Turn and cook the other side briefly without allowing them to color. Lift out and drain well, then place on a serving plate and break up lightly.
❀ Dip the prawns into the batter and deep-fry them in a wok for about 1¼ minutes or until the surface is golden. Remove from the oil and let stand for 5 minutes, then reheat the oil to very hot and deep-fry the prawns briefly for a second time to make the batter very crisp. Drain and arrange over the vermicelli, adding fresh cilantro or parsley and slivers of colored pickled radish to garnish.

Beijing 北京

PHOENIX-TAILED PRAWNS

In Chinese legend the phoenix is portrayed as a five-colored creature with the head of a chicken, neck of a snake, chin of a swallow, back of a turtle and the tail of a fish. It signifies dignity and good luck.

This dish is so named because the tails of the prawns bear some resemblance to the flared tail of the phoenix.

8 large fresh prawns or shrimp
½ teaspoon salt
2 egg whites
½ cup (2 oz) cornstarch
oil for deep-frying

SAUCE

4 tomatoes
1 teaspoon sugar
1 teaspoon sesame oil
½ teaspoon salt

Peel and devein the prawns, leaving the tails in place. Rinse in cold water and dry well. Place them cut side down on a cutting board and beat with the side of a cleaver to flatten. Sprinkle with the salt.
❀ Beat the egg whites until stiff and fold in the cornstarch to make a batter. Add a few drops of water if necessary.
❀ Heat the deep-frying oil in a wok to the smoking point, then lower the heat slightly. Coat each prawn thickly with the batter and deep-fry, in batches of four, for about 1½ minutes each, then remove and drain well.
❀ Drop the tomatoes into boiling water, remove after about 8 seconds and peel, discarding the soft centers and seeds. Finely dice the flesh and stir-fry in another wok with the sugar, sesame oil and salt until tender.
❀ Reheat the deep-frying oil and return all of the prawns to fry briefly for a second time to make the batter very crisp. Drain and arrange in a circle on a serving plate with the tomato sauce placed in the center.

PHOENIX-TAILED PRAWNS

Shanghai 上海

STIR-FRIED PRAWNS WITH LONGJING TEA

Longjing tea is named after the Dragon Well, China's famous tea growing region. After picking, the leaves are processed until they are neat and smooth, flat as a sparrow's tongue and as green as an orchid's stem. The tea's four famous qualities are its green color, fragrant lingering aroma, sweet taste and pleasant appearance.

Prawns of the highest grade must be used for this dish. They are first stir-fried and then covered with the green tea leaves taken from a pot of freshly brewed Longjing tea before serving.

2 tablespoons Longjing or other green tea leaves
2 lb (1 kg) fresh prawns or shrimp in their shells
1 tablespoon rice wine or dry sherry
¾ teaspoon salt
1 egg white, well beaten
1 tablespoon cornstarch
2 tablespoons lard

Brew the tea leaves with 1½ cups (12 oz) boiling water; cover and set aside.

※ Peel and devein the prawns, rinse under cold running water and rub with a little salt and cornstarch to make them very white and remove any fishy smell.

※ Place in a dish and season with the wine and salt, then mix in the egg white and cornstarch and set aside for a few minutes.

※ Heat the wok over high heat and add the lard. Stir-fry the prawns quickly until cooked through and lightly pink in color, then remove and set aside.

※ Rinse the wok and return to the heat. Return the prawns and pour in ½ cup (4 oz) of the tea, plus a spoonful of the brewed leaves. Heat through briefly, mix well and serve.

TOMATO PRAWN CAKES

Beijing 北京

TOMATO PRAWN CAKES

1 lb (500 g) fresh prawns or shrimp
2 egg whites
1 tablespoon cornstarch
1 teaspoon ginger juice
oil for deep-frying

SWEET AND SOUR SAUCE

½ cup (4 oz) chicken stock
½ cup (4 oz) sugar
4 tablespoons vinegar
3 tablespoons tomato ketchup
2 tablespoons rice wine or dry sherry
1 tablespoon cornstarch
¾ teaspoon salt

Peel and devein the prawns. Rinse in cold water, drain and pat dry with a paper towel. Beat to a pulp with the side of a cleaver or grind in a food processor.
❈ Beat the egg whites until frothy and add the cornstarch and ginger juice. Mix with the prawns and stir the mixture in one direction only until thoroughly amalgamated.
❈ Heat the oil in a wok, form spoonfuls of the prawn mixture into coin-shaped pieces and deep-fry over moderate heat until golden. Remove, place in a strainer and drain well.
❈ In another wok or saucepan mix the sauce ingredients and bring to boil, stirring constantly, until thickened, then simmer for another minute.
❈ Arrange the prawn cakes on a plate and pour the sauce over them before serving.

Guangzhou 广州

DEEP-FRIED SNOW-WHITE PRAWNS

8 oz (250 g) peeled fresh prawns or shrimp
2 tablespoons cornstarch
½ teaspoon salt
2 cups (16 oz) milk
6 egg whites
1 slice lean ham, very finely diced
2 tablespoons lard
vegetable flowers and cucumber fans (garnish)

SEASONING

½ teaspoon sesame oil
1 teaspoon salt
pinch of white pepper

DEEP-FRIED SNOW-WHITE PRAWNS

Devein the prawns and rub with half the cornstarch and the salt, then rinse under cold running water. This helps to whiten the prawns and remove any fishy taste.
❈ Pour the milk into a mixing bowl; add the lightly beaten egg whites and the ham. Add the seasoning ingredients and mix well.
❈ Heat the lard in a wok over moderate heat. Fry the prawns gently until they just color, then remove with a slotted spoon and set aside.
❈ Pour the milk batter into the wok and cook gently, stirring until it begins to firm up. Return the prawns and continue to cook, stirring gently, until the milk batter is cooked through and the prawns are tender.
❈ Transfer to a serving plate and garnish with vegetable flowers and cucumber fans. The finished dish is said to resemble "treasures buried beneath the snow."

Guangzhou 广州

STRAW MUSHROOMS WITH PRAWN FILLING TOPPED WITH CRAB ROE

15 fresh or canned straw mushrooms
3 oz (90 g) fresh prawn or shrimp meat
3 oz (90 g) white fish fillets
½ egg white
2 teaspoons rice wine or dry sherry
½ teaspoon salt
pinch of pepper
4 fresh crab claws*

SAUCE

4 oz (125 g) fresh crab roe
vegetable oil
½ cup (4 oz) fish stock
2 teaspoons cornstarch
salt and white pepper
sesame oil

Rinse the fresh mushrooms after trimming the bases off, leaving only the darker rounded tops. Pound the prawn meat and fish on a board with the flat side of a cleaver until thick and pastelike, then add the egg white, wine, salt and pepper, mixing well with the fingers.
❈ Use a wet spoon to mound a portion of the filling over the cut side of each mushroom, smoothing the top. Stand the mushrooms on a heatproof plate and set on a rack in a wok or steamer over simmering water. Cover and steam for about 7 minutes if using canned mushrooms, 8-10 minutes if the mushrooms are fresh. (Canned mushrooms may be smaller than

the fresh variety. If so, simply cut from the top almost through to the bottom, spread open and stuff the slit with the filling.)

🦀 In a wok, sauté the crab roe in very little vegetable oil for 20-30 seconds, then add the remaining sauce ingredients, mixed together. Simmer, stirring, until the sauce thickens and the roe is brightly colored and firm.

🦀 Simmer the crab claws in boiling, lightly salted water for about 5 minutes, then remove, crack the shells and extract the meat.

🦀 Transfer the mushrooms to a serving plate, arrange the crab claw meat around the edge and pour the sauce over.

Fresh crab meat can be substituted, or the claws may be omitted.

STRAW MUSHROOMS WITH PRAWN FILLING TOPPED WITH CRAB ROE

Sichuan 四川

JADEITE PRAWNS

This delicately textured and subtly flavored dish is often served at banquets. "Jadeite" refers to the bright green peas dotted amongst the pearl white of the prawns.

8 oz (250 g) peeled fresh prawns or shrimp
2 egg whites, lightly beaten
1 tablespoon soy flour or cornstarch
pinch of salt
3 tablespoons oil for frying
½ cup (2 oz) frozen peas or parboiled fresh peas
1 green onion, finely chopped
1 pickled red chili, finely chopped

SAUCE

1 cup (8 oz) chicken or fish stock
1 teaspoon rice wine or dry sherry
¾ teaspoon salt
pinch of white pepper
1 tablespoon cornstarch

Devein the prawns. Rinse in cold running water after rubbing with a little cornstarch and salt to whiten. Dry on paper towels and place in a dish, adding the egg whites, soy flour or cornstarch and the pinch of salt. Mix well and let stand for 20 minutes.

🦀 Heat the oil in a wok and stir-fry the prawns over high heat until cooked through, then remove. Add the peas, green onion and chili to the wok and stir-fry for 1 minute, then add the sauce ingredients, except the cornstarch, and a little of the stock. Cover and simmer until the peas are tender, then return the prawns.

🦀 Mix the cornstarch with the remaining stock, pour into the sauce and simmer, stirring, until thickened and clear. Serve at once.

JADEITE PRAWNS

Guangzhou 广州
CRISPY CRAB CLAWS

River crabs are caught throughout the year, but are in greatest quantity during autumn, the season of orange fragrance and blooming chrysanthemums. Some are found in the rivers flowing towards the sea, but they lay their eggs only in shallow water near the river mouths. Fu Zuan of the Song Dynasty (960-1127 AD) described their reproductive pattern and noted that during the change of seasons from autumn to winter, the crabs follow the river currents and swim to the sea. Hence if a net is cast during this period, you are sure of a catch.

The chef of the Ban Xi Restaurant removes the hard shell from the foremost section of the crab claw, extracts the meat in one piece and supplements it with prawn and pork meat before returning it to the shell to be steamed. Alternatively, the tip of the claw can be covered with a ball of prawn and pork meat, as in this recipe. The mock crab claw is then coated with a light crisp batter and deep-fried.

The very large oysters gathered along the coast of this region are also cooked in this way.

12 crab claws
10 oz (315 g) fresh prawn or shrimp meat
2½ oz (75 g) fatty pork
1 teaspoon salt
pinch of white pepper
pinch of sugar
cornstarch
oil for deep-frying
light soy sauce or five-spice salt (*see page 123*)

CRISP BATTER

1 cup (4 oz) all purpose flour
1 teaspoon baking powder
⅓ cup (1½ oz) cornstarch
2 egg whites

Break away the main part of the crab claw shell, leaving just the points attached to the meat.

※ Place the prawns on a cutting board and crush to a smooth paste with the flat side of a cleaver, or in a food processor. Finely mince or grind the pork until smooth and sticky and mix with the prawn, adding the salt, pepper and sugar.

※ Divide the mixture into 12 equal portions. Dust the crab claws lightly with cornstarch and mold a portion of the prawn and pork mixture around each, forming a ball shape. Coat lightly with cornstarch and set aside.

※ Sift the flour and baking powder together and add the cornstarch. Beat the egg whites lightly and fold into the batter, adding enough cold water to give a coating consistency.

※ Heat the oil in a large wok. Dip the crab claws into the batter, holding onto the pincers so that they remain uncoated. Deep-fry over moderate to high heat, turning several times, until golden and crisp – about 5 minutes.

※ Remove, drain well and arrange on a napkin on a serving plate. Serve with soy sauce or five-spice salt.

Beijing 北京
SUANSHAZI CRABS

6 female hairy river crabs or small mud crabs
½ cup (4 oz) rice wine or dry sherry
¼ small green bell pepper
¼ small red bell pepper
2-in (5-cm) piece giant white radish
6-8 slices fresh young ginger

SAUCE

½ cup (4 oz) chicken stock
2 tablespoons rendered chicken fat
1 tablespoon sugar
2-3 teaspoons red vinegar
2 teaspoons cornstarch
½ teaspoon salt

Rinse the crabs well in cold water and remove the undershell. Discard the inedible parts, cut the bodies in half and put the halves back together, placing them in a wide, heatproof dish. Sprinkle with the rice wine and set the dish on a rack in a wok or steamer. Cover and steam for 15 minutes. Transfer to a serving plate.

※ Cut the pepper, radish and ginger into fine shreds. Simmer the radish briefly in the stock for the sauce, then arrange the shredded vegetables in groups over the crabs.

※ Bring the stock and remaining pre-mixed sauce ingredients to boil, stirring until the sauce thickens and clears. Pour over the crabs and serve hot.

CRISPY CRAB CLAWS

STIR-FRIED CRABS AND EGG

Shanghai 上海

STIR-FRIED CRABS AND EGG

The green crab differs in shape and taste from other common crabs found in clear water, its shell being rhombus shaped and its meat very tender. The green crabs from Xiangshan, Zhejiang Province, are known for their rich meat.

This dish, combining green crabs with beaten egg, is a traditional meal from Xiangshan and was introduced to Shanghai by the cooks in the Ningbo Restaurant.

4 medium-size green crabs or sand crabs
1 cup (4 oz) cornstarch
1/3 cup (2 1/2 oz) oil for frying
3 green onions, sliced
5 slices fresh ginger
1 tablespoon rice wine or dry sherry
1 teaspoon salt
3 eggs, well beaten
1 tablespoon lard, melted

Kill the crabs by piercing them through the head and into the stomach with a sharpened chopstick or bamboo stick. Wash well in cold water, cut off the tips of the claws and discard. Remove the pincers and crack the shells with the back of a cleaver. Pull the crab shells away from the bodies, remove the inedible parts and chop each body into quarters. Coat with cornstarch.

✺ Heat a wok over high heat and add the oil. Stir-fry the crab for about 2 minutes, add the green onion and ginger and continue stir-frying for another 2-3 minutes or until the crabs are bright red and cooked through.

✺ Pour off most of the oil and add the rice wine and salt, then pour in the beaten egg and cook gently, stirring only occasionally, until the egg is just set. Pour the lard over and serve.

Shanghai 上海

STEAMED HAIRY CRABS

Freshwater crab is a highly regarded delicacy in China. In all the coastal areas, from Liaoning Province in the north to Guangdong Province in the south, the rivers and lakes yield freshwater crabs, although the best by far come from the hinterland of the city of Shanghai. Here the lakes are inhabited by millions of minute organisms, making the crabs fat and delicious.

The female crab is considered to be at its best during the ninth lunar month when it is full of roe; the male's peak season is during the tenth lunar month. The most delicate part of the crab is the roe, and the most tender part is the flesh inside the two front claws. Crab tastes best when steamed alive. The Chinese of ancient times loved to nibble on chrysanthemum flowers while eating crabs.

As it is cold-blooded, crab is said to be bad for the health if too much is eaten. People with weak stomachs should be particularly careful not to overindulge themselves.

The Shanghai hairy crab is an expensive delicacy which should be served with shreds of young tender ginger, a dip of red vinegar and a glass of wine.

6 Shanghai freshwater hairy crabs or small mud crabs
2 green onions
fresh ginger
red vinegar

Wash the crabs thoroughly, then tie the claws and legs together with string before steaming. This prevents them struggling during cooking, releasing their roe and juices, and making them dry and tasteless. Place the crabs upside down on a bamboo rack in a wok or steamer and place the green onion and several slices of ginger on top. Cover and steam for about 8 minutes or until the crabs are cooked through. Untie before serving.

STEAMED HAIRY CRABS

Beijing 北京

CRABS WITH CHRYSANTHEMUM

6-8 fresh Shanghai river crabs or small mud crabs
1 large chrysanthemum blossom (garnish)

SEASONING

1 tablespoon finely chopped green onion
1 1/2 teaspoons red vinegar
1 teaspoon rice wine or dry sherry
1 teaspoon sugar
3/4 teaspoon salt
1/2 teaspoon finely chopped fresh ginger

Wash the crabs, open them from the underside and remove the inedible parts. Take out as much meat as possible without breaking the shell. Mix the meat with the seasoning ingredients, stuff the mixture into the shells and tie with string to keep the stuffing from falling out during cooking.

✺ Set on a rack in a wok or steamer, cover and steam for about 15 minutes. Arrange in a circle on a serving plate and garnish with a single large chrysanthemum blossom.

Shanghai 上海

FRIED AND BRAISED RIVER CRABS

River crabs captured in June are full of roe, which is therefore called June gold. The shell is bright red after cooking and the sauce prepared according to this recipe is thick and golden, while the crabmeat remains tender and tasty. Only the choicest live crabs should be used for this dish.

3-4 8-oz (250-g) freshwater crabs
3 tablespoons tapioca flour or cornstarch
8 oz (250 g) lard
1 tablespoon finely chopped green onion
2 teaspoons grated fresh ginger

SEASONING/SAUCE

½ cup (4 oz) chicken or fish stock
2 tablespoons light soy sauce
1 tablespoon rice wine or dry sherry
1½ teaspoons sugar
¼ teaspoon salt
1 teaspoon cornstarch

Clean the crabs thoroughly to remove mud and sand, then halve each crab, cutting straight through the center of the shell from head to rear. Remove part of the soft undershell and scrape out the inedible parts. Use a cleaver to cut off the tips of the claws.

※ Dip the cut edges of the crab into the tapioca flour, coating thickly.

※ Heat the lard in a large wok and stir-fry the crabs until they turn bright red. Add the green onion and ginger and stir-fry briefly, then pour in all the pre-mixed seasoning/sauce ingredients except the cornstarch. Cover and braise over moderate heat for about 8 minutes or until the crabs are completely tender. The pan should be tightly covered during braising so that the crab is steamed and braised at the same time and the cooking liquid is not reduced. If it begins to dry up, add a little extra stock or water.

※ Mix the cornstarch with a little cold water, stir into the sauce and boil gently until the sauce clears. Serve at once.

Beijing 北京

ABALONE SLICES WITH DUCK MEAT

Connoisseurs of Chinese cooking are traditionally rather partial to abalone, an expensive mollusk. In this recipe the duck meat is used as a filling between two slices of abalone, and the sandwich is topped with green peas. It is then steamed to perfection.

1 13½-oz (425-g) can abalone
8 oz (250 g) duck breast meat
8 water chestnuts
2 green onions, white parts only
2 slices fresh ginger
1½ teaspoons rice wine or dry sherry
½ teaspoon salt
½ teaspoon sesame oil
1 tablespoon green peas

SAUCE

¾ cup (6 oz) duck stock
1½ tablespoons rendered duck fat
2 teaspoons rice wine or dry sherry
¾ teaspoon salt
1 tablespoon cornstarch

Drain the abalone and cut each piece into thin horizontal slices, discarding the frilly outer edges.

✺ Very finely mince or grind the duck meat with the water chestnuts, green onions and ginger. Add the rice wine, salt and sesame oil and mix to a smooth paste.

✺ Spread half of the abalone slices with the duck paste and top with the remaining abalone slices, pressing them gently together. Arrange on a wide heatproof plate and place on a rack in a wok or steamer. Cover and steam for about 20 minutes over gently simmering water.

✺ Bring the sauce ingredients to boil, omitting the cornstarch; add the peas and simmer until tender. Mix the cornstarch with a little cold water and stir into the sauce. Simmer until thickened, then remove the abalone slices from the steamer and drain the plate.

✺ Pour on the sauce and serve at once.

RAZOR CLAMS BOILED WITH SALT

Shanghai 上海

RAZOR CLAMS BOILED WITH SALT

20 razor clams in their shells
1 cup (8 oz) water
1 teaspoon salt
1 green onion, roughly chopped
2 slices fresh ginger, chopped
1 tablespoon rice wine or dry sherry
2 tablespoons vinegar
curls of green onion or sprigs of cilantro (garnish)

Wash the clams thoroughly with cold water, then put them in a pot of lightly salted water for several hours so they will disgorge any grit. Wash thoroughly in cold water again and trim away the black tendon on the back of each clam.

✺ In a wok, bring the water to boil, adding salt, onion, ginger and wine. Put in the clams, cover and shake the pan over high heat until the shells open, then remove immediately from the heat. Do not overcook or they will become tough. Use a slotted spoon to transfer them to a serving plate.

✺ Boil up the cooking liquid, add the vinegar and spoon over the clams. Decorate the dish with curls of green onion or cilantro and serve.

ABALONE SLICES WITH DUCK MEAT

BOILED CLAMS WITH SOY SAUCE AND SESAME OIL

STEAMED DRIED SCALLOPS

Shanghai 上海

BOILED CLAMS WITH SOY SAUCE AND SESAME OIL

1¼ lb (625 g) clams in their shells
1 teaspoon salt
2 tablespoons finely chopped fresh ginger
2 tablespoons finely chopped chives or green onions

DIP

3 tablespoons dark soy sauce
2 tablespoons sesame oil

Wash the clams thoroughly, brushing off all grit and mud. Soak for 20 minutes in cold salted water, then drain.
❀ Boil a large pot of water and add the clams, stirring for about 2 minutes or until they open.
❀ Drain and remove the top shells. Arrange clams in a serving dish and sprinkle with the chopped ginger and chives.
❀ Mix the soy sauce and sesame oil and divide among several small dishes. Serve as a dip with the clams.

Beijing 北京

STEAMED DRIED SCALLOPS

Scallops are an expensive seafood found all along the coast of China, although the best come from Shandong Province. The scallops used in the following recipe are sun-dried, which preserves them as well as intensifying their flavor. Good-quality dried scallops are large, reddish yellow, fine-grained and aromatic.

10-12 large dried scallops
½ cup (4 oz) chicken stock
1-2 teaspoons chili oil or chili sauce
1 tablespoon cornstarch

SEASONING

1 cup (8 oz) chicken stock
2 tablespoons rice wine or dry sherry
1 teaspoon ginger juice

Rinse the scallops and soak in cold water for about 1 hour or until they swell up and become pliable.
❀ Place in a heatproof dish and add the seasoning ingredients. Set the dish on a rack in a wok or steamer and steam, covered, over gently simmering water for about 1 hour.
❀ Strain, reserving the seasoning liquid, and arrange on a serving plate. Set aside to keep warm. Mix about ½ cup (4 oz) of the reserved liquid with the chicken stock, chili oil and cornstarch. Simmer for 1 minute, stirring, until thickened. Adjust the seasoning and pour over the scallops before serving.

Beijing 北京

STIR-FRIED DRIED SCALLOPS WITH CELERY

There are many ways to cook dried scallops, but when they are combined with crisp young celery the result is outstanding.
In ancient China there are detailed records about the medicinal and dietary values of celery. In particular it is suggested that it may help to reduce high blood pressure.
This dish must be eaten hot or its subtle flavors will be lost.

8 oz (250 g) young celery stalks
12 dried scallops, soaked for 25 minutes
¾ cup (6 oz) chicken stock
2 tablespoons oil for frying
1 green onion, sliced
2 slices fresh ginger
2 teaspoons rice wine or dry sherry
½ teaspoon salt

Rinse the celery, drain well and cut into 3-in (7.5-cm) lengths.
❀ Place the scallops in a wok or saucepan with the stock and bring to boil. Cover and steam for about 40 minutes over moderately high heat until the scallops are tender and the stock is flavorful. Set aside.
❀ Heat the oil in a wok and stir-fry the celery, green onion and ginger for about 3 minutes or until tender. Add the scallops in their liquid, the rice wine and salt. Simmer together very briefly and serve immediately.

STIR-FRIED DRIED SCALLOPS WITH CELERY

HERO'S THREE-IN-ONE FISH

Beijing 北京

Hero's Three-in-one Fish

This innovative Chinese dish is spectacular enough to impress a returning hero. One large fish is cut across into three pieces, which are prepared in three different ways and then arranged on a serving platter with the head and tail to resemble two fish side by side. Fresh carp is the fish favored for this dish, but sea bass gives excellent results.

1 3-lb (1½-kg) fresh carp or sea bass
2 oz (60 g) salted ham, finely shredded
5-6 slices white radish, finely shredded
1 tablespoon rice wine or dry sherry
1 green onion
3 slices fresh ginger
1 tablespoon lard

2 tablespoons peanut oil
1 tablespoon lard
1 green onion, chopped
2 slices fresh ginger, chopped
1 clove garlic, chopped
1 tablespoon hot bean paste
2 teaspoons rice wine or dry sherry
1 tablespoon brown vinegar
2 teaspoons dark soy sauce
1 tablespoon sugar
½ cup (4 oz) fish or chicken stock

oil for deep-frying
2 tablespoons rice wine or dry sherry
¾ cup (3 oz) cornstarch
1 egg white, well beaten

Clean and scale the fish, rinse in cold water and dry well. Cut off the head, slice in half and set aside. Cut the body of the fish across into three portions, leaving the tail on the lower part.

Make shallow cuts across the central section on both sides, place on a lightly oiled heatproof plate and top with the ham and radish. Add the rice wine and place the green onion and ginger on top. Melt the lard and pour over, then set the plate on a rack in a wok or steamer, cover and steam for about 20 minutes or until completely tender. Keep warm.

Score diagonally across the upper part of the fish on both sides. Heat the wok and add the peanut oil and lard. Fry on both sides until cooked through and lightly colored on the surface, then set aside. Add the green onion, ginger, garlic and bean paste to the wok and stir-fry for 2 minutes, then add the wine, vinegar, soy sauce, sugar and stock and bring to boil. Reduce heat, return the fish and simmer until the flavors have been absorbed. Remove and set aside, keeping warm.

In a clean wok, heat the deep-frying oil of the third part of the ingredients list. Cut the tail end of the fish in half lengthwise; sprinkle with the rice wine. Coat with cornstarch, then dip into the beaten egg and coat thickly with the cornstarch again, shaking off excess. Slide into the oil and deep-fry until cooked through and golden. Lift out and drain well.

Coat the head halves with cornstarch and deep-fry in the hot oil until crisp and well colored. Place the heads at one end of a large platter and tails at the other, and the braised and steamed parts side by side between the heads and tails. Serve a dish of spiced salt (1 tablespoon warmed salt mixed with 1½ teaspoons five-spice powder) to accompany the crisp-fried section of the fish.

STIR-FRIED FISH AND PINE NUTS

Shanghai 上海

STIR-FRIED FISH AND PINE NUTS

8 oz (250 g) fillet of rock carp or other meaty white fish
3 tablespoons peanut or vegetable oil
½ cup pine nuts
1 tablespoon finely chopped red bell pepper
1 tablespoon finely chopped green bell pepper
1 tablespoon finely chopped green onion

SEASONING

1 tablespoon cornstarch
2 teaspoons rice wine or dry sherry
1 teaspoon ginger juice
½ teaspoon salt

Skin the fish and cut it into very small dice. Place in a dish with the pre-mixed seasoning ingredients and mix well. Let stand for about 10 minutes.
❈ Heat the oil in a wok and fry the pine nuts until lightly golden, then lift out and drain well.
❈ Stir-fry the bell peppers and onion in the wok over high heat until just softened, then remove from the oil with a slotted spoon.
❈ Add the fish to the wok and stir-fry for about 2 minutes or until white and cooked through. Return the pepper and onion, mix well, then pile into the center of a serving plate, arranging the fried pine nuts in a circle around the fish.

Guangzhou 广州

STEAMED TENCH FISH

Only the very best and freshest fish should be steamed, and only the merest hint of seasoning or other added ingredients is needed to highlight its freshness and flavor. At the peak of summer, when the thought of oily food dulls the tastebuds, steamed tench is very popular, both in restaurants and at home.

1 12-oz (375-g) fresh tench fish, catfish or bream
2 dried black mushrooms, soaked for 25 minutes
6 slices young fresh ginger
2 oz (60 g) lean pork fillet
2 green onions
2 tablespoons Superior Stock (*see page 124*)

SEASONING

2 tablespoons light soy sauce
½ teaspoon sesame oil
pinch of white pepper

STEAMED TENCH FISH

Clean and scale the fish and slash along the top of the backbone on either side. Place in the center of an oval heatproof dish that will fit inside a wok or steamer.
❈ Drain the mushrooms, squeeze out excess water and shred finely. Shred the ginger, pork fillet and the white parts only of the green onions. Arrange these ingredients along the top of the fish, set the dish on a rack in a wok or steamer, cover and cook the fish over gently simmering water for about 15 minutes or until very tender.
❈ Bring the stock and the seasoning ingredients to boil separately, pour over the fish and serve at once.

Sichuan 四川

CARP WITH BEAN JELLY

Jelly is a popular snack in Sichuan Province and is sold throughout the year in cities and in the country at hawkers' stands or in restaurants. The jelly can be made from powdered rice, beans or buckwheat, and is usually eaten cold.

This particular combination of carp with cubes of mung bean jelly is unique to Sichuan cooking.

2 10-oz (315-g) carp or other meaty white fish
1 tablespoon rice wine or dry sherry
1 teaspoon salt
1 piece pork caul fat
3 green onions, finely chopped
1 teaspoon grated fresh ginger
¾ teaspoon ground Sichuan peppercorns (Fagara or Sansho)
6 oz (185 g) green mung bean jelly

SEASONING

1½ tablespoons fermented black beans, chopped
1 teaspoon chopped garlic
2 tablespoons finely chopped bean sprouts or celery
2 tablespoons light soy sauce
1 teaspoon chili oil or chili sauce
¾ teaspoon sesame oil

Clean the carp and score diagonally across each side. Place in a heatproof dish and sprinkle with the wine and salt. Let stand for 5 minutes, then wrap each fish in a piece of the caul fat and return to the dish. Cover with the green onions, ginger and Sichuan pepper. Place on a rack in a wok or steamer, cover and steam for about 20 minutes or until cooked.
❈ Dice the jelly and simmer in boiling water for 2-3 minutes, then drain. Mix with the seasoning ingredients in the wok and heat through. Remove the fish from the steamer and remove the caul fat. Slide the fish into the wok and simmer gently for 2-3 minutes with the jelly and seasonings.
❈ Lift onto a serving plate and serve.

CARP WITH BEAN JELLY

SILVER CARP AND TURNIP IN BROTH

Sichuan 四川

SILVER CARP AND TURNIP IN BROTH

Fish simmered in broth is a great favorite throughout China. As far back as the Tang Dynasty (618-907AD) chefs cooked fish supplemented with mutton, rabbit and venison to make delicious pot meals. This dish was devised fifty years ago by the well-known chef Liao Chin-tin, who adapted the following recipe from an ancient one.

1 lb (500 g) silver carp or other meaty white fish steaks
4 tablespoons lard
1 fresh turnip
4 cups (1 l) Superior Stock (*see page 124*)

SEASONING

4 green onions
3 slices fresh ginger
2 pickled red chilies
½ cup (4 oz) rice wine or dry sherry
1 teaspoon salt

DIPPING SAUCE

3 tablespoons light soy sauce
1 tablespoon red or brown vinegar
1 teaspoon grated fresh ginger
1 teaspoon sesame oil

Wipe the fish steaks dry with paper towels. Heat the lard in a wok and fry the steaks on both sides until lightly browned. Drain and transfer to a casserole with a tight-fitting lid.
❀ Peel and shred the turnip. Stir-fry it in the remaining lard for 2 minutes, then add the stock and bring to boil. Pour into the casserole.
❀ Shred or dice the green onions, ginger and chilies and add all the seasoning ingredients to the casserole.
❀ Cover and simmer for 20 minutes or until the fish is tender. Do not overcook or the fish will begin to dry out.
❀ Mix the dipping sauce ingredients together and serve in several small dishes with the fish and broth.

Sichuan 四川

SPECIAL BRAISED ROCK CARP

Sichuan is a vast territory laced with rivers. The warm climate and fine water favor the reproduction of many different varieties of fish; rock or black carp in particular grow abundantly. Rock carp is characterized by its small head, thick body, small bones and rich meat. It is regarded as one of the most delicious freshwater fish in China.

1 1-lb (500-g) rock carp or other meaty white freshwater fish
6 oz (185 g) yam
3 green onions
3 slices fresh ginger
3 cloves garlic
2 tablespoons lard

SPECIAL BRAISED ROCK CARP

SAUCE

2 cups (16 oz) water
1 tablespoon rice wine or dry sherry
1 tablespoon hot bean paste
1 tablespoon sugar
1 tablespoon brown vinegar
1 tablespoon red fermented rice (wine lees)
1 tablespoon light soy sauce
pinch of salt

Clean the fish and make several diagonal slashes across each side. Peel and finely dice the yam. Chop the green onions, ginger and garlic finely.

❀ In a wok, sauté the yam in the lard for about 2 minutes until lightly colored, then place in the bottom of a casserole. Add the fish to the wok, sauté on both sides until lightly colored and place on top of the yam. Lightly fry the green onions, ginger and garlic in the lard and add to the casserole with the pre-mixed sauce ingredients.

❀ Bring to the boil, skim any froth and residue from the surface and reduce the heat. Simmer very gently, partially covered, until the fish is tender and the stock reduced to a thick clear layer over the fish.

❀ Chinese chefs call this cooking technique "gaining wonder from fire."

Sichuan 四川

CARP WITH SICHUAN HOT BEAN SAUCE

4-6 carp or other meaty white fish,
　5-7 oz (150-200 g) each
¾ cup (6 oz) oil for frying
3 cloves garlic, chopped
1½ tablespoons hot bean paste
1 green onion, chopped (garnish)

SEASONING/SAUCE

¾ cup (6 oz) water or fish stock
1 tablespoon brown vinegar
1 tablespoon rice wine or dry sherry
1 tablespoon dark soy sauce
1 tablespoon sugar
1 pickled red chili, chopped
2-3 slices fresh ginger, chopped
1½ teaspoons cornstarch
½ teaspoon salt

Clean the fish and rinse in cold water, then drain and dry thoroughly. Heat a wok with half the oil to the smoking point and fry half of the fish until lightly browned on both sides. Remove to a plate and keep warm.

※ Add the remaining oil and fry the remaining fish until browned, then place with the first batch. Cover and keep warm.

※ Pour the oil out; rinse the wok and return about 2 tablespoons of the oil. Stir-fry the garlic briefly, then add the bean paste and stir-fry for about 40 seconds. Add the pre-mixed sauce ingredients and bring to boil, stirring constantly. Slide the fish into the sauce, reduce heat, cover and simmer gently for about 20 minutes. Splash in a little more water from time to time if the mixture begins to dry up during cooking.

※ Use a wide spatula to transfer the fish onto a serving plate, stacking them together in the same direction. Scatter the green onion over the fish and pour on the sauce.

WHOLE GRASS CARP BARBECUED IN A BAMBOO TUBE

The fish cooked in the following typical country fashion is insulated by green bamboo and a net of pork caul fat to keep it tender and moist with no risk of burning. During cooking the marinade ingredients slowly permeate the fish, which takes on some of the unusual fragrance of the fresh bamboo.

1 1½-lb (750-g) whole grass carp or other meaty white fish
1 piece pork caul fat
a thick tube of green bamboo, or several layers of bamboo
    leaves and aluminum foil
thin wire to fasten

SEASONING

1 tablespoon ginger juice
1 tablespoon rice wine or dry sherry
1 teaspoon salt
pinch of white pepper

SAUCE

juice of 2 oranges
½ cup (4 oz) water
1 tablespoon sugar
1½ teaspoons cornstarch
½ teaspoon sesame oil

Scale, gut and thoroughly wash the fish. Place the caul fat on a board and lay the fish in the center. Rub the seasonings over the fish, inside and out, and wrap it in the caul fat.
❊ Split the bamboo in half lengthwise and place the wrapped carp in the hollow. Cover with the other piece of bamboo and tie the bundle securely with wire. Have ready a quantity of glowing charcoal. Place the bamboo in the charcoal to roast slowly until the fish is cooked, 30-40 minutes. If using bamboo leaves and aluminum foil the dried leaves must be soaked first to soften. Wrap the fish in at least 8 leaves and a double layer of aluminum foil. Roast for approximately 30 minutes.
❊ Mix the sauce ingredients and stir in a wok or saucepan over gentle heat until thickened. Pour into a gravy boat or small bowl. Unwrap the fish and serve with the sauce.

WHOLE GRASS CARP BARBECUED IN A BAMBOO TUBE

Sichuan 四川

CARP WITH LOTUS EGG

In Sichuan Province, the word lotus has several meanings and chefs have gotten into the habit of calling steamed egg white "lotus egg." This very popular steamed dish uses carp and lotus egg as its main ingredients. The result is very light and delicious.

3 6½-oz (200-g) small carp or other meaty white fish
4 egg whites
⅓ cup (2½ oz) fish stock
1 tablespoon cornstarch
½ teaspoon salt
¼ red bell pepper (garnish)
lemon rind or grated hard-cooked egg yolk (garnish)
cilantro (garnish)

SEASONING

1 tablespoon rice wine or dry sherry
1 tablespoon finely chopped green onion
½ teaspoon grated fresh ginger
pinch of white pepper
dash of chili oil or chili sauce

SAUCE

½ cup (4 oz) fish or chicken stock
salt and pepper
1 teaspoon rice wine or dry sherry
1 teaspoon cornstarch

DIP

1 tablespoon finely minced young fresh ginger
2 teaspoons sesame oil

Clean the carp and cook briefly in a saucepan of boiling water. Lift out, drain well and scrape off the skin. Arrange the fish side by side in a heatproof dish and add the pre-mixed seasoning ingredients. Place on a rack in a wok or steamer, cover and steam for about 15 minutes or until tender.

※ Beat the egg whites, fish stock, cornstarch and salt together and pour into a flat heatproof dish. Steam for about 6 minutes or until set, then cut into lotus petal shapes.

※ Finely shred the bell pepper and blanch in boiling water.

※ Mix the sauce ingredients except the cornstarch, pour into a wok and bring to boil. Mix the cornstarch with a little cold water, stir in and simmer until thickened. Add any liquid from the dish in which the fish were steamed and simmer again briefly.

※ Arrange the lotus egg around the fish and pour on the sauce. Add the garnish of bell pepper, lemon rind or grated egg and cilantro. Serve at once with the minced ginger and sesame oil in a separate dish to use as a dip.

CARP WITH LOTUS EGG

CARP WITH TRI-HOT FLAVORS

Sichuan 四川

CARP WITH TRI-HOT FLAVORS

1 14-oz (440-g) carp or other meaty white fish
oil for deep-frying
2-3 dried red chilies
1 teaspoon Sichuan peppercorns (Fagara or Sansho)

SEASONING

2 teaspoons fermented black beans
1 cup (8 oz) water
1¼ teaspoons sugar
1 teaspoon rice wine or dry sherry
1 teaspoon vinegar
pinch of salt

Clean and scale the carp, rinse under running cold water, then dry well inside and out. Make several diagonal slashes across each side.

❀ Heat the oil in a wok to the smoking point, lower the heat and deep-fry the fish on both sides until golden. Lift out and drain well.

❀ Pour off all but 2 tablespoons of the oil and stir-fry the whole chilies and peppercorns for about 1 minute or until crisp and dry. Remove from the oil, drain well and chop or grind coarsely.

❀ Chop the fermented beans finely, place in the oil and stir-fry for 30-40 seconds. Add the remaining seasoning ingredients and bring to boil. Skim off any froth, then place the fish in the wok, cover and simmer gently for about 3 minutes on each side. If the wok is tightly covered the liquid will not evaporate; if it does, add a little more water during cooking.

❀ Lift the fish onto a serving plate, pour on the sauce, sprinkle with the ground pepper and chili and serve.

Shanghai 上海

CARP STEAMED WITH EGG

1 12-oz (375-g) carp or other meaty white fish
3 large eggs
¾ cup (6 oz) chicken stock
½ teaspoon salt
1 slice cooked salted ham

Clean and scale the carp and make several deep diagonal slashes across each side.

❀ Lightly beat the eggs, add the chicken stock and salt and pour into an oval heatproof dish. Place the fish on top, then set the dish on a rack in a wok or steamer, cover and steam for about 12 minutes over simmering water until the fish is cooked through and the egg firm. When the dish is removed from the steamer the fish will have sunk halfway into the egg.

❀ Finely chop the ham and sprinkle over the fish. Serve at once.

❀ For extra flavor, add the ham halfway through cooking, when the egg has firmed up enough to prevent it from sinking through to the bottom.

CARP STEAMED WITH EGG

FRIED BLACK CARP IN A GRAPE-BUNCH SHAPE

Shanghai 上海

FRIED BLACK CARP IN A GRAPE-BUNCH SHAPE

This unusual traditional dish from Anhui Province is made from a big fillet cut from a large black carp, scored and coated so that when crisply fried it takes on the appearance of a bunch of grapes. Grape juice in the sauce adds to the flavor.

12-14 oz (375-440 g) thick central piece of white fish fillet
1 teaspoon grated fresh ginger
1 tablespoon finely chopped green onion
1 teaspoon salt
1½ cups (6 oz) cornstarch
oil for deep-frying
grapevine leaves and stem (garnish)

SAUCE

1 cup (8 oz) dark grape juice
3 tablespoons chicken stock
2 tablespoons light soy sauce
1½ tablespoons red vinegar
1 tablespoon cornstarch
1 teaspoon sugar
1 teaspoon lard
½ teaspoon salt

Place the piece of fish skin side down on a cutting board and cut a criss-cross pattern diagonally across it, cutting down to the skin but not through it. Place in a dish and scatter on the ginger, onion and salt. Let stand for 15 minutes, then coat thickly with cornstarch.

In a small wok or saucepan boil the pre-mixed sauce ingredients for about 3 minutes, stirring constantly. Check the seasoning and keep warm.

Heat the oil in a large wok to the smoking point, then reduce the heat slightly. Slide in the fish, skin side upwards, and deep-fry for about 5 minutes or until golden and cooked through. As it cooks, the skin will curl up, giving the fish the appearance of a bunch of grapes.

Drain, place on a dish and arrange the vine leaves and stem at the top of the "bunch." Pour on the sauce and serve.

GOLDEN CRISP FISH WITH SWEET AND SOUR SAUCE

Sichuan 四川

GOLDEN CRISP FISH WITH SWEET AND SOUR SAUCE

In a small town near a river, many many years ago, there was a popular snack called "Aromatic Fried Fish." The fish, probably a carp from the river, was cleaned and marinated, then coated thickly with a paste of soy flour and water before frying. This dish has been developed from the original by skillful Sichuan chefs.

1 2-lb (1-kg) carp or other meaty white fish
¾ cup (3 oz) soy flour or cornstarch
oil for deep-frying
3 green onions, shredded
2-3 fresh red chilies, shredded
cilantro leaves

MARINADE

2 tablespoons light soy sauce
1 tablespoon rice wine or dry sherry
2 teaspoons ginger juice (optional)
½ teaspoon salt

SAUCE

2 tablespoons vegetable oil
2 cloves garlic, crushed
1 teaspoon grated fresh ginger
1-2 fresh red chilies, chopped
2 tablespoons vinegar
1½ tablespoons sugar
¾ teaspoon sesame oil
1½ teaspoons cornstarch
¾ cup (6 oz) fish or chicken stock
pinch each of salt and white pepper

Clean and scale the carp, rinse well, then dry thoroughly inside and out. Place in a dish, rub on the pre-mixed marinade ingredients and let stand for 15 minutes. Mix the soy flour or cornstarch with enough water to make a batter of coating consistency.

Use a sharp knife or cleaver to cut deep scores across each side of the fish, cutting at an angle so that each segment of fish stands out like a large fish scale. Coat the fish lightly with additional soy flour or cornstarch, then dip into the batter, holding the fish by the tail so that the "scales" open and all the meat is covered evenly with the batter.

In a large wok heat the oil to the smoking point, add the fish, then lower the heat slightly and deep-fry for about 10 minutes, turning once. Lift out and drain well.

In another wok heat the oil for the sauce and fry the garlic, ginger and chilies over moderate heat for about 1½ minutes. Add the vinegar, sugar and sesame oil and increase the heat slightly, then stir the cornstarch into the stock and add to the wok. Boil briefly, adding salt and pepper.

Reheat the deep-frying oil and fry the fish again for about 2 minutes to make the surface very crisp. Drain and place on a serving plate.

Scatter the green onions, chilies and cilantro leaves over the fish and pour the sauce on immediately before serving.

Shanghai 上海

SMOKED POMFRET

1 1½-lb (750-g) pomfret or John Dory
½ cup (2 oz) black Chinese tea leaves
1½ tablespoons sugar
cucumber fans (garnish)
pickles or tomato slices (garnish)
mayonnaise or salad dressing

SEASONING/MARINADE

1½ tablespoons finely chopped green onion
1 tablespoon rice wine or dry sherry
1 tablespoon sugar
1 tablespoon grated fresh ginger
1 teaspoon salt

Clean the fish and cut through the body diagonally in three places. Place in a dish. Mix the seasoning/marinade ingredients together and rub thoroughly over the fish, then let stand for at least 1 hour to absorb the flavors.

Line the bottom of a heavy-duty wok, preferably an old iron one, with aluminum foil and put the tea leaves and sugar on this. Place over high heat until they begin to smoke. Set the fish on a metal rack over it, cover and smoke the fish over slightly reduced heat for about 25 minutes. The fish will take on a rich deep color, and the heat within the wok should be sufficient to cook the fish through.

Transfer to a serving plate, garnish attractively with fans of cucumber, a little brightly colored pickled vegetable or tomato slices and serve with the mayonnaise.

SMOKED POMFRET

MANDARIN FISH COOKED IN CHILI BEAN SAUCE

Shanghai 上海

MANDARIN FISH COOKED IN CHILI BEAN SAUCE

1 1-lb (500-g) mandarin fish (perch or sea bass)
4 oz (125 g) lard
2 green onions
6 slices young fresh ginger
¾ cup (6 oz) water

SEASONING

1-2 pickled red chilies
1 tablespoon chili bean paste
1 tablespoon rice wine or dry sherry
1 tablespoon sugar
½ teaspoon red vinegar

Select a live fish if possible; kill and clean it. Heat the lard in a wok and fry the fish on both sides until golden. Lift out and set aside.

✻ Cut the green onions into 1-in (2.5-cm) lengths and fry with the ginger in the wok for about 30 seconds. Add the seasoning ingredients (except the vinegar) and simmer for 1 minute, stirring constantly. Add about ¾ cup (6 oz) water and bring to boil. Return the fish and simmer, covered, for about 3 minutes, then remove the lid and continue simmering until the fish tender and the sauce is well reduced. A little cornstarch can be used to thicken the sauce if necessary.

✻ Transfer to a serving plate and sprinkle on the vinegar before serving.

BRAISED CHUB'S HEAD IN AN EARTHENWARE POT

Shanghai 上海

BRAISED CHUB'S HEAD IN AN EARTHENWARE POT

Chub is variegated carp, a delicious freshwater fish. All four kinds of carp – rock, silver, grass and variegated – are eaten and cooked in many different ways throughout China.

Chub's head is especially large, accounting for about one-third of the body size. The flesh near the gills and jaw, especially the walnut-shaped flesh inside the mouth, is fatty, tender and full of flavor.

The clay pot used to cook the fish heads allows them to simmer slowly, thus retaining their shape and producing a richly flavored clear sauce. This famous dish is served in the autumn and winter.

1 2½-lb (1¼-kg) variegated carp (chub) head or several large
   meaty fish heads, supplemented with extra fish meat,
   if necessary
4 oz (125 g) lard
2 bean sheets, soaked to soften*

SEASONING

3 tablespoons light soy sauce
1½ tablespoons soybean oil (optional)
1 tablespoon rice wine or dry sherry
1½-2 teaspoons salt
1 teaspoon sugar
½ teaspoon white pepper

Rinse the fish head and wipe dry. Heat the lard in a large wok and stir-fry the fish head until it takes on a light color, then transfer to an earthenware pot or casserole.

※ Cut the bean sheets into squares and place in the pot, adding the seasoning ingredients. Add enough water to just cover the fish, cover the pot and bring almost to boil. Simmer gently for about 1½ hours or until the fish is completely tender and the stock has become rich, whitish in color and well reduced. Serve in the pot.

Transparent edible sheets made from a paste of ground mung beans and water. If unavailable, substitute mung bean vermicelli, or use strips of bean curd skin, cubes of fried bean curd or soaked dried "wood ear" fungus.

Beijing 北京

PAN'S FISH

This dish was created by the chef of a high-ranking official in the Qing Dynasty (1644-1911 AD). This official, whose name was Pan, loved fish but abhorred the grease that normally results from frying. So Pan's chef steamed the fish and named the dish after him.

1 13-oz (410-g) fresh carp or other meaty white fish
4 dried black mushrooms, soaked for 25 minutes
6-8 dried shrimp, soaked for 25 minutes
1 green onion, chopped
3 slices fresh ginger

SEASONING

¾ cup (6 oz) chicken or fish stock
2 tablespoons rice wine or dry sherry
2 tablespoons light soy sauce
⅓ teaspoon salt

Scale and clean the fish, wash in cold water, then dip into a pot of boiling water for a few seconds and drain well. Make several slashes diagonally across each side and place in a heatproof bowl.

※ Drain the mushrooms and remove the stems; drain the shrimp. Arrange both over the fish, adding the green onion and ginger. Pour on the pre-mixed seasoning ingredients, place on a rack in a wok or steamer, cover and steam for about 20 minutes. The fish is ready when the thick flesh adjoining the head is tender and flakes easily.

※ Serve at once in the same bowl.

PAN'S FISH

STEAMED TRI-SHREDS ROLLED IN FISH

Shanghai 上海

STEAMED TRI-SHREDS ROLLED IN FISH

A variety of foods can be used as filling for these slender fish rolls. Although this dish is called tri-shreds, the number of ingredients can vary and include ham, winter bamboo shoots, black mushrooms, chicken meat, green onions and ginger.

By cooking them in a steamer, the original textures of the different ingredients are preserved, while the various flavors are able to permeate each other. In one tiny roll, you can experience the tender smoothness of fish, the salty flavor of ham, the crispness of bamboo shoots and the tasty, somewhat chewy consistency of mushroom, complemented by the pungency of onion and ginger.

1¼ lb (625 g) thick central piece of fresh rock carp or other
    white fish fillet
2-3 dried black mushrooms, soaked for 25 minutes
2 oz (60 g) salted ham
2 oz (60 g) fresh or canned winter bamboo shoots
2-3 green onions
12 slices fresh ginger

SAUCE

1 tablespoon rice wine or dry sherry
2 teaspoons light soy sauce
1 teaspoon rendered chicken fat, melted
1 teaspoon cornstarch
½ teaspoon salt

Holding the knife at a sharp angle, slice the fillet into very thin slices.

❖ Drain the mushrooms, remove the stems and finely shred the caps, together with the ham, bamboo shoots, green onions and ginger, keeping the slices about 2 in (5 cm) long.

❖ Place a few pieces of each ingredient in the center of each slice of fish and roll it around the filling, squeezing firmly into a smooth roll – the ingredients may be allowed to protrude slightly past the ends of the roll. Arrange on an oiled heatproof plate, place on a rack in a wok or steamer, cover and steam over gently simmering water for about 20 minutes or until cooked and tender. Remove, reserving the cooking liquid; keep warm.

❖ Mix the sauce ingredients together, adding the liquid from the steamed fish, and simmer, stirring, until thickened. Check the seasoning, then pour over the fish rolls and serve at once.

ZHUA CHAO YU FRIED FISH SLICES

Beijing 北京

ZHUA CHAO YU FRIED FISH SLICES

The story is told of the time the Empress Dowager Cixi picked out one dish of smooth, shining, tender fish slices from the many dishes on the table. When asked for the name of the dish, the cook, caught unawares, called it "Zhua Chao Yu," which means "grasping and frying."

Its distinctive feature is that it is first deep-fried and then stir-fried. It has a slight hint of sweet and sour flavors together with a touch of saltiness.

10 oz (315 g) fresh white fish fillets
1 cup (4 oz) cornstarch
oil, preferably peanut oil, for deep-frying

SAUCE

2 green onions, white parts only
2 slices fresh ginger
2 tablespoons lard
1 tablespoon light soy sauce
1 tablespoon brown vinegar
2 teaspoons sugar
1 teaspoon rice wine or dry sherry
½ teaspoon cornstarch
pinch each of salt and pepper

Cut the fish into long, thin slices. Mix the cornstarch with enough cold water to make a thin paste.

❖ Heat the oil in a wok to the smoking point, then reduce the heat. Dip the fish slices into the cornstarch paste and deep-fry 8 pieces at a time for about 1½ minutes or until golden and crisp on the surface and cooked through. Lift out, drain well and keep warm while the sauce is prepared.

❖ Very finely chop the green onions and ginger. Heat a wok with the lard and stir-fry the green onion and ginger for about 45 seconds, add the remaining pre-mixed sauce ingredients and heat through. When the sauce begins to thicken, slide in the fried fish and stir-fry, turning the fish carefully until coated with all the sauce. Serve at once.

STEAMED THREE-LAYER FISH

Beijing 北京

STEAMED THREE-LAYER FISH

1 1¼-lb (625-g) meaty white fish such as coral cod or grouper
9 dried black mushrooms, soaked for 25 minutes
6 oz (185 g) fresh or canned winter bamboo shoots
6 slices Yunnan or other salted ham
3 tablespoons fish or chicken stock
1 tablespoon rice wine or dry sherry
1 teaspoon melted lard
pinch each of salt and pepper
4 slices fresh ginger
3 green onions
8 oz (250 g) choy sum or other Chinese green vegetable
1 tablespoon vegetable oil
6-8 slices young fresh ginger (garnish)

SAUCE

½ cup (4 oz) fish or chicken stock
1 teaspoon melted lard
½ teaspoon cornstarch
½ teaspoon salt
pinch of white pepper

Clean and wash the fish, then scald with boiling water and drain. Cut off the head and tail and set aside. Use a sharp knife to remove the fillets from each side, then place skin side down on a board and carefully detach the skin from the fillet by holding firmly at the tail end and running the knife between skin and meat. Hold the knife at a sharp angle to the fillet and cut across it into slices. There should be 18 slices of fish, 9 from each fillet.

※ Drain the mushrooms, remove the stems and cut each cap in half. Cut the bamboo shoots and ham into pieces the approximate size of the fish slices.

※ Arrange the fish, mushrooms, bamboo shoots and ham alternately in two rows along an oval heatproof plate, then position the head and tail at either end. The head can be halved so that it will remain flat on the plate.

※ Mix the stock, wine, melted lard, salt and pepper together and pour over the fish, then place the ginger and green onion on top. Place on a rack in a wok or steamer, cover and steam over simmering water for about 20 minutes, or until done. Discard the onions, ginger and liquid.

※ Trim the choy sum and drop into a saucepan of boiling water with a tablespoon of oil. Simmer until tender, then drain well and arrange around the edge of the plate and along the center between the two rows of ingredients.

※ Cut the ginger for the garnish into butterfly or other decorative shapes and use to decorate the dish.

※ Boil the sauce ingredients in a small pan until thickened and pour over the fish immediately before serving.

BRAISED FISH WITH MINCED MEAT

Sichuan 四川

BRAISED FISH WITH MINCED MEAT

Braised Fish with Minced Meat is one of the many famous fish dishes of the Sichuan cuisine, and is very popular at banquets. The fish is supplemented by special Shiu Fu pickled potherb mustard and pickled red chilies, and is cooked using a special braising technique. The dish is known for its bright red color, fragrant aroma and slightly spicy, delicate taste with a strong local character.

2 8-oz (250-g) carp or other meaty white fish
2 cups (16 oz) lard or oil for frying
3 oz (90 g) *unsmoked* bacon
1 oz (30 g) pickled mustard greens
2 green onions
1½ pickled red chilies
2 slices fresh ginger

SAUCE

2 cups (16 oz) fish stock
1 tablespoon rice wine or dry sherry
1 tablespoon dark soy sauce
1 teaspoon light soy sauce
1 teaspoon salt
1 teaspoon sesame oil
1 teaspoon sugar

Clean and scale the fish, make several deep scores diagonally across each side and dry well with paper towels. Heat the lard or oil in a wok and slide in the fish. Fry gently on both sides until crisp and partially cooked, then lift out carefully and drain well.

※ Finely chop or grind the bacon, mustard, green onions, chilies and ginger.

※ Drain the wok, wipe out and return about 2 tablespoons of the oil. Sauté the bacon until lightly colored, then add the mustard, green onions, chilies and ginger and stir-fry briefly. Pour in the pre-mixed sauce ingredients and bring to boil.

※ Place the fish in the sauce, cover and simmer over gentle heat for about 45 minutes or until the fish is completely tender and the sauce is well flavored.

※ Serve the fish with the sauce in a deep serving dish.

SANDWICHED PERCH

Guangzhou 广州

SANDWICHED PERCH

5 oz (155 g) perch fillets, skinned
4 oz (125 g) chicken livers
3 oz (90 g) fatty pork
2 teaspoons rice wine or dry sherry
½ teaspoon sesame oil
⅓ teaspoon salt
½ cup (2 oz) cornstarch
2 eggs
oil for deep-frying
12 stalks young choy sum or other Chinese green vegetable

Cut the perch and pork into pieces 1½ x 1¼ in (4 x 3 cm); slice the livers thinly. Place the fish in a dish and add the rice wine, sesame oil and salt. Let stand for 20 minutes.
❊ Sandwich the ingredients together, layering fish, chicken liver and pork, and coat each sandwich thickly with cornstarch. Beat the eggs thoroughly.
❊ Heat 4-5 cups of oil in a wok to moderately hot. Dip the fish into the egg, coating evenly, then deep-fry, preferably in two batches, until cooked through and golden, about 6 minutes. Drain well and arrange on a serving plate.
❊ Drop the vegetables into a pan of boiling water and simmer briefly. They should remain crisp and brightly colored. Drain and arrange around the fish. Serve immediately.

Beijing 北京

LIGHT-FRIED AND SIMMERED MANDARIN FISH

The rivers and lakes to the south of the Yangtze River are teeming with fish for this dish. The preparation method, called "ta" in Chinese, allows time for the seasoning to penetrate the meat and means that the sauce will be well reduced and concentrated.

1 8-oz (250-g) piece of mandarin fish (perch or sea bass) fillet
1 tablespoon light soy sauce
½ cup (2 oz) all purpose flour
6 oz (185 g) lard
2 eggs, well beaten
2 tablespoons onion oil*

SAUCE

1½ cups (12 oz) chicken stock
1½ tablespoons rice wine or dry sherry
1 tablespoon light soy sauce
2 teaspoons ginger juice
½ teaspoon salt

Made by heating peanut or vegetable oil with sliced green or red onions until the onions are well colored. Strain and store the oil in a jar.

LIGHT-FRIED AND SIMMERED MANDARIN FISH

Cut the fish into a fish shape and pound with the side of a cleaver to tenderize. Sprinkle on the soy sauce and then coat with the flour. Heat the lard in a wok. Dip the fish into the beaten egg, coating it thickly, and fry on both sides until golden. Lift out and place in a casserole.
❊ Add the pre-mixed sauce ingredients and bring just to boil. Cover and simmer very gently for about 20 minutes. Pour on the onion oil and serve in the casserole.

Sichuan 四川

STIR-FRIED SQUID SHREDS

Squid can be dry and tough, unless it is gently cooked or soup is added. However, the chefs in Sichuan do not follow these common rules but cook squid using the stir-fry method. By cleverly handling the duration and degree of heat, they turn the dryness into crispness and toughness into puffiness, the result being tasty and aromatic.

1 2-oz (60-g) piece dried squid
4 oz (125 g) *unsmoked* bacon
8 oz (250 g) lard
2 teaspoons rice wine or dry sherry
3 oz (90 g) fresh silver sprouts*
1 tablespoon light soy sauce
1 teaspoon sesame oil
salt

Use a sharp cleaver to cut the dried squid and the bacon into very fine shreds; set aside.
❊ Heat the wok and add the lard. Stir-fry the squid shreds for about 2 minutes or until they are crisp and red-brown. Drain off the excess lard and add the bacon and the rice wine. Stir-fry together until the bacon is done, then add the bean sprouts and the remaining ingredients. Stir-fry together over high heat for 45 seconds, then serve.

Fresh mung bean sprouts from which the yellow seed pods and long tapering roots have been removed, leaving a slender, silver-colored sprout.

STIR-FRIED SQUID SHREDS

114

FRIED WHOLE FISH WITH DUMPLINGS

Sichuan 四川

FRIED WHOLE FISH WITH DUMPLINGS

1 1-lb (500-g) carp or other meaty white fish
6 oz (185 g) semi-fat pork
1 egg white
1 cup (4 oz) cornstarch
oil for deep-frying
five-spice salt*

SEASONING

2 tablespoons finely chopped green onions
1 tablespoon rice wine or dry sherry
1 teaspoon grated fresh ginger
½ teaspoon salt
pinch of white pepper

STUFFING

1 oz (30 g) pickled mustard greens
2 green onions
2 slices fresh ginger
1 teaspoon rice wine or dry sherry
2 teaspoons light soy sauce
1 teaspoon sugar
¼ teaspoon sesame oil
lard or oil for frying

DUMPLINGS

2 oz (60 g) flour
8 oz (250 g) spinach
2 cabbage leaves
⅓ teaspoon sesame oil

Clean the carp and make several slashes diagonally across each side. Place in a dish and add the pre-mixed seasoning ingredients, rub in well and set aside for 1 hour.

Very finely mince or grind a third of the pork and cut the remainder into fine shreds.

To prepare the stuffing, finely shred the mustard greens, green onions and ginger and mix with the remaining stuffing ingredients. Heat a little lard or frying oil in a wok and sauté the stuffing mixture and the shredded pork briefly until the pork turns white, then set aside to cool.

For the dumplings, sift the flour into a mixing bowl. Very finely chop the spinach and cook without water for about 7 minutes, then transfer to a colander and squeeze the liquid onto the flour. Knead into the flour to make a soft dough.

Finely chop the cabbage leaves, mix with the minced pork and season with the sesame oil.

Roll the dough out into a long sausage shape and divide into 18 pieces. Roll or pull each piece into a thin round dumpling wrapper and fill with a portion of the pork and cabbage filling. Fold over and pinch the edges together to enclose the filling. Arrange the dumplings on an oiled heatproof plate and set on a rack in a wok or steamer. Cover and steam for about 14 minutes or until tender.

Stuff the prepared stuffing into the cavity of the fish. Make a paste with the egg white and a little cornstarch to seal the opening, then brush the remaining paste over the fish and coat thickly with cornstarch.

Heat the oil in a wok to the smoking point. Add the fish, then lower the heat. Deep-fry for about 5 minutes, turning once, until cooked through and golden brown on the surface.

Lift out and drain well. Place in the center of a large serving plate and surround with the steamed dumplings. Pour the five-spice salt into a small dish and serve separately as a dip for both the dumplings and the fish.

*To make the five-spice salt, heat 1½ tablespoons fine table salt in a wok until it begins to crackle, add 1 teaspoon Chinese five-spice powder, remove from the heat, stir and cool.

CRISP FISH WITH GREEN ONION SAUCE

Guangzhou 广州

CRISP FISH WITH GREEN ONION SAUCE

1 2½-lb (1¼-kg) whole fresh fish
1 teaspoon salt
2 egg whites
1 cup (4 oz) cornstarch
oil for deep-frying

SAUCE

3 tablespoons peanut oil
¼ red bell pepper, finely diced
¼ green bell pepper, finely diced
3 green onions, finely chopped
1 clove garlic, crushed
1 teaspoon grated fresh ginger
2 dried black mushrooms, soaked and diced
2 oz (60 g) cha siew (Chinese roast pork), diced
2 tablespoons light soy sauce
½ teaspoon sesame oil
½ teaspoon salt
1 cup (8 oz) fish or chicken stock
1 tablespoon cornstarch

Clean, scale and wash the fish, then drain and dry thoroughly inside and out. Make several deep diagonal slashes across each side, then cut in the other direction to create a diamond-shaped pattern. Sprinkle with the salt.

※ Beat the egg whites until frothy and brush all over the fish. Coat thickly with the cornstarch and set aside.

※ To prepare the sauce, heat the peanut oil in a wok and stir-fry the peppers, onion, garlic and ginger for 2 minutes. Add the mushrooms and pork and stir-fry for another minute, then add the soy sauce, sesame oil and salt and toss together. Mix the stock with the cornstarch and pour into the pan. Simmer gently, stirring until thickened; set aside.

※ Heat the deep-frying oil in a very large wok to the smoking point. Slide in the fish and deep-fry for about 7 minutes, turning once or twice, until the fish is cooked through and crisp and golden on the surface.

※ Reheat the sauce to the boiling point and pour into a pitcher.

※ Carefully lift the fish onto a wide serving plate and take to the table with the hot sauce, which should be poured over the fish in front of the diners.

Guangzhou 广州

BRAISED FISH HEAD, COUNTRY-STYLE

Dishes offered by the teahouses in the Guangdong countryside generally use local ingredients, skillfully prepared in ways unfamiliar to town dwellers. Some even have their own small vegetable plots and fish ponds from which customers can select the ingredients for their meals.

Carp can grow to a massive size, and the heads, although bony, have deliciously sweet pockets of meat and give a unique gelatinous texture to a dish.

2 lb (1 kg) variegated carp (chub) head or several other meaty fish heads, supplemented with extra fish meat, if necessary
oil for deep-frying
12 cloves garlic
3 oz (90 g) lean pork
8 small cubes dried bean curd, soaked for 10 minutes
4-6 slices fresh ginger
6 dried black mushrooms, soaked for 25 minutes
12 small fresh or canned straw mushrooms, trimmed
12 stalks choy sum or other Chinese green vegetable

SEASONING/STOCK

3 cups (24 oz) Superior Stock (*see page 124*)
3 tablespoons light soy sauce
1 teaspoon sugar
1 teaspoon sesame oil
½ teaspoon salt
¼ teaspoon white pepper

Rinse the fish head, drain and wipe dry. Heat the oil and fry the head for several minutes or until it takes on a good color. Drain and transfer to a casserole.

※ Peel the garlic, shred the pork, drain the bean curd and squeeze out all the water. Place in a frying basket or large perforated ladle and deep-fry in hot oil for about 2 minutes; drain and arrange over the fish. Add the ginger, mushrooms and the seasoning/stock ingredients. Bring just to boil, then braise gently, half covered, until the fish is completely tender and the sauce is well reduced.

※ Boil or stir-fry the green vegetable separately, then arrange around the dish to serve.

BRAISED FISH HEAD, COUNTRY-STYLE

SHREDS OF FISH, GINGER AND PICKLED CUCUMBER

FISH SLIVERS WITH LOTUS FLOWER

Shanghai 上海

SHREDS OF FISH, GINGER AND PICKLED CUCUMBER

The following recipe describes a seasonal dish prepared at the end of summer and the beginning of autumn. Each ingredient complements the others to make this a sweet, tasty, tender, yet crisp and delightfully light dish.

12 oz (375 g) fillets of meaty fish
1 egg white
pinch of salt
8 slices young fresh ginger
2 tablespoons lard
1/2 teaspoon sesame oil

SEASONING

1/3 cup (2 1/2 oz) chicken or fish stock
1 teaspoon rice wine or dry sherry
1/2 teaspoon sugar
1/2 teaspoon salt
1/2 teaspoon cornstarch

PICKLED CUCUMBER

2 small cucumbers
1 cup (8 oz) boiling water
2 tablespoons white vinegar
1 tablespoon sugar
2 teaspoons salt

Make the pickled cucumber first, as it should be allowed to marinate for several hours before use. Peel the cucumbers thinly and cut into matchstick strips, discarding the ends and seed cores. Place in a bowl. Mix the remaining ingredients together, pour over the cucumber and let stand. Drain very thoroughly before use.
※ Cut the fish into shreds, place in a dish with the lightly beaten egg white and the salt and set aside.
※ Shred the ginger slices.
※ Heat a wok and add the lard. Stir-fry the fish shreds until white and firm, then remove to a strainer to drain.
※ Stir-fry the drained cucumber and the ginger together, adding the wine after about 30 seconds. Pour the remaining pre-mixed seasoning ingredients into the wok, and when the sauce begins to thicken, return the fish and stir-fry all together over high heat for a few moments.
※ Transfer to a serving plate and sprinkle on the sesame oil before serving.

Beijing 北京

FISH SLIVERS WITH LOTUS FLOWER

The lotus flower, with its light and pure fragrance and exquisitely shaped petals, found its way into the hearts of the Chinese people long ago as a symbol of beauty and perfection. The eating of lotus seeds is recorded in ancient Chinese writings, but the flower is bitter and is only used for its color and fragrance.

4 oz (125 g) white fish fillets
3 oz (90 g) canned bamboo shoots, drained
1 lotus flower
1 egg white, lightly beaten
1 tablespoon cornstarch
1 teaspoon rice wine or dry sherry
1 1/2 cups oil for frying

SEASONING

2 slices fresh ginger, shredded
1 teaspoon rice wine or dry sherry
1/2 teaspoon salt
1/3 teaspoon sesame oil

Hold the knife at a 45° angle to cut each fish fillet into thin slices and then into shreds. Shred the bamboo shoots and rinse the petals of the lotus flower.
※ Arrange the lotus petals on a serving plate, preferably jade green, in a lotus leaf shape.
※ Place the sliced fish in a dish. Add the egg white, cornstarch and rice wine and stir together lightly.
※ Heat the oil in a wok and deep-fry the fish in several batches over moderate heat until cooked through but not colored on the surface. Lift out and drain well.
※ Pour off all but 2 tablespoons of the oil. Stir-fry the bamboo shoots for 1 minute, then add the seasoning ingredients and stir-fry together briefly. Add the fish and cook slowly, mixing lightly so as not to break it up.
※ Transfer to the serving platter, placing the fish in the center of the "flower" and serve.

SAUTÉED FISH SLICES

Beijing 北京

SAUTÉED FISH SLICES

This dish is said to have appeared at every birthday banquet held for the Empress Dowager Cixi. It is especially suitable for the elderly because the fish is boned and the meat is extremely tender.

12 oz (375 g) white fish fillets
5-6 slices carrot, parboiled
2 tablespoons oil for frying
3 tablespoons fish or chicken stock
cucumber slices (garnish)
cilantro or watercress (garnish)

SEASONING

1 tablespoon rice wine or dry sherry
1 tablespoon cornstarch
1 teaspoon melted lard
1 egg white, well beaten
½ teaspoon sugar
½ teaspoon salt

Skin the fish and pat dry with a paper towel. Holding the knife at a sharp angle to the cutting board, cut each fillet into thin slices. Place in a dish with the pre-mixed seasoning ingredients and let stand for 20 minutes.
※ Cut the carrots into decorative shapes.
※ Heat the oil in a wok and quickly stir-fry the fish for about 2 minutes over high heat. Add the carrot slices and stir-fry for another minute, then pour in the stock and simmer briefly. Check the seasoning, transfer to a serving plate and garnish with cucumber slices and a sprig of watercress or cilantro. Serve immediately.

Beijing 北京

FIVE WILLOW FISH

Mandarin fish is a freshwater fish found in China's large rivers and lakes. They live in the Yihou Imperial Garden Lake in Beijing, where legend has it that every spring they feast on the peach blossoms that fall into the lake. As a result the meat of the mandarin fish is supposed to be especially fragrant. In reality, however, these fish are quite aggressive and their diet consists of prawns and smaller fish.

This recipe, with the fish garnished with five different ingredients, was inspired by the "Five Willow Hermit," so called because he dwelt near a lake surrounded by five willow trees. He loved to sit under one of these trees to write and recite poetry and essays. At times he would just scoop up a big fat fish, cook it on the spot and eat it all by himself.

1 14-oz (440-g) mandarin fish (perch or sea bass)
1 small carrot
2 slices pickled cabbage, soaked for 10 minutes
2 dried black mushrooms, soaked for 25 minutes
½ green bell pepper
5 slices young fresh ginger
2 tablespoons oil for frying

SEASONING/SAUCE

½ cup (4 oz) chicken or fish stock
1 tablespoon rendered chicken fat, melted
2 teaspoons rice wine or dry sherry
½ teaspoon salt
½ teaspoon sugar
small pinch of ground star anise
1 teaspoon cornstarch

Clean and scale the fish and make several diagonal cuts across each side. Set the fish in a heatproof dish and place on a rack in a wok or steamer. Cover and steam over simmering water until almost cooked through, then remove and place on a rack to drain.
※ Shred the carrot, drained cabbage and mushrooms, the bell pepper and ginger.
※ Heat the oil in a wok and slide in the fish. Carefully fry over moderate heat until cooked and lightly crisp on both sides, then lift onto a serving plate and keep warm.
※ Add the shredded vegetables in separate piles to the wok and pour in the pre-mixed seasoning/sauce ingredients except the cornstarch. Simmer gently, occasionally stirring carefully so as not to disorganize the groups of ingredients. Lift out separately and arrange across the top of the fish. Mix the cornstarch with a little cold water and stir into the sauce, boiling until the sauce thickens and clears. Pour over the fish and serve at once.

FIVE WILLOW FISH

STEAMED PORGY

Beijing 北京

STEAMED PORGY

This fish is commonly found in the East China Sea. Its texture is very fine; it is also snow white, full of nutritional value, and said to have properties that keep it fresh longer than other fish.

There is a legendary figure in Japan that carries such a fish under his arm. It is said to bring blessings of peace and prosperity to the country and its people.

1 1-lb (500-g) porgy, sea bass or bream
3 slices Yunnan or other salted ham
1 fresh bamboo shoot, parboiled or canned
3 dried black mushrooms, soaked for 25 minutes
2 tablespoons melted lard
2 green onions
3-4 slices fresh ginger
2 teaspoons cornstarch

SEASONING

2 teaspoons rice wine or dry sherry
1/2 teaspoon salt
1/4 teaspoon white pepper

Clean and scale the fish. Make diagonal slashes across each side, then hold it by the tail and dip briefly into a pot of boiling water. Lift out and dry thoroughly.

※Rub with the seasoning ingredients and place in a heatproof shallow dish. Cut the ham into decorative oval shapes and insert a piece into each of the cuts on the top side of the fish. Thinly slice the bamboo shoot, cut it decoratively and arrange along the fish. Drain the mushrooms well, remove the stems and halve the caps. Use the point of a sharp knife to shred the caps, leaving them connected in the center to give a chrysanthemum-like appearance. Place along the fish. Sprinkle on the lard, arrange the green onions and ginger along the fish and pour the seasoning ingredients over it. Leave for about 10 minutes to absorb the flavors, then place on a rack in a wok or steamer, cover and steam for 20 minutes or until tender.

※Discard the green onion and ginger, remove the fish to a serving plate and pour the liquid from the steaming dish into a wok. Bring to the boil and add the cornstarch mixed with a little cold water, stirring until the sauce is clear and thick. Pour over the fish before serving.

FRIED PERCH AND PORK WITH CRAB SAUCE

FISH BALLS WITH STRAW MUSHROOMS

Guangzhou 广州

FRIED PERCH AND PORK WITH CRAB SAUCE

6 oz (185 g) perch fillets, skinned
4 oz (125 g) pork fat*
1 tablespoon rice wine or dry sherry
1 cup (4 oz) cornstarch
3 egg whites
pinch each of salt and white pepper
oil for deep-frying

CRAB SAUCE

3 oz (90 g) fresh crabmeat
2-3 oz (60-90 g) fresh crab roe
2/3 cup (5 oz) fish stock
2 egg whites
1/2 teaspoon salt
pinch of white pepper
1 1/2 teaspoons cornstarch
3/4 teaspoon sesame oil

Cut the fish and the pork fat into pieces about 1 1/4 x 3/4 in (3 x 2 cm). Place in a dish and sprinkle with the wine. Let stand for 20 minutes, then sandwich pieces of pork and fish together. Coat each parcel thickly with cornstarch.

Lightly beat 3 egg whites, adding a pinch of salt and pepper.

Heat the oil to the smoking point, then reduce heat to moderate. Dip the meat parcels into the egg and fry gently in two or three batches, turning once or twice, until golden and cooked through, about 6 minutes. Lift out and drain well.

Pour the oil from the wok, rinse out and return about 1 tablespoon of oil. Add the crabmeat and roe and stir-fry briefly. Pour in the stock and bring just to boil. Lightly beat 2 egg whites and pour into the hot stock in a slow stream. Do not stir for about 40 seconds while the egg cooks. Add salt and pepper. Mix the cornstarch with a little cold water and stir into the sauce.

Arrange the perch and pork sandwiches on a serving platter. Cover with the crab sauce and sprinkle with sesame oil.

The fat just beneath the skin of a pork leg roast (fresh ham) is ideal.

Guangzhou 广州

FISH BALLS WITH STRAW MUSHROOMS

In many Guangdong dishes a starch dressing (sauce thickened with cornstarch or pea starch) is used to enhance the appearance of the food. This also increases the density of the dish, so it lingers on the taste buds, and keeps it moist.

8 oz (250 g) white fish fillets
1 egg white
2 tablespoons all purpose flour
3/4 teaspoon salt
12 fresh or canned straw mushrooms
1 green onion
3 slices fresh ginger
2 teaspoons rice wine or dry sherry
oil for deep-frying
2 teaspoons cornstarch
1 teaspoon sesame oil
cilantro and carrot slices (garnish)

SIMMERING SAUCE

1/2 cup (4 oz) fish stock
1/2 teaspoon sugar
pinch each of salt and white pepper

STARCH DRESSING

1/3 cup (2 1/2 oz) water
1 teaspoon mushroom soy sauce
1 teaspoon cornstarch

Check the fish for bones; cut the fish into small pieces and pound to a paste using the flat side of a cleaver or a food processor. Add the egg white, flour and salt and mix with your fingers to a smooth and sticky paste. Form into about 12 balls.

Trim the straw mushrooms, removing the straw and dirt fragments from the bases. Place in a wok with the green onion, ginger and wine and add 1 cup (8 oz) water. Cover and bring to boil, remove the lid and simmer for about 10 minutes.

Meanwhile, heat the oil in another wok and deep-fry the fish balls until golden, stirring with chopsticks to turn and color evenly. Remove and drain. Drain the oil from the wok and add the simmering sauce ingredients. Simmer for 5-6 minutes, turning from time to time.

Add 2 teaspoons cornstarch mixed with a little cold water to the simmering mushrooms and stir until thickened, then transfer the mushrooms and sauce to a serving plate. Place the fish balls on top of the mushrooms.

Boil the starch dressing separately, stirring until thickened. Pour over the dish and sprinkle the sesame oil on top. Garnish with cilantro and carrot slices.

FISH CAKES AS MANDARIN DUCKS

FRIED FLAT FISH

Beijing 北京

FISH CAKES AS MANDARIN DUCKS

Mandarin ducks live in lifelong couples, and the Chinese often compare them to husbands and wives. Guangdong people like to refer to things that are matching yet not completely alike as "mandarin ducks." A pair of chopsticks of different colors, for example, is called "yuan yang kuai zi" (mandarin duck chopsticks).

This dish is called "Fish Cakes as Mandarin Ducks" because the fish balls have been colored and flavored in two different ways. One batch is simmered in a milky soup and the other in a clear soup colored with molasses.

8 oz (250 g) pike or whiting
1/2 cup (4 oz) water
pinch of salt
3 egg whites
1/2 teaspoon salt
2 tablespoons rendered chicken fat, melted
1 green onion, shredded
2 slices fresh ginger, shredded
1 1/2 teaspoons rice wine or dry sherry
1 cup (8 oz) chicken stock
1 teaspoon molasses
1/2 cup (4 oz) milk
1/2 cup (4 oz) water

Finely chop the fish, then beat to a smooth paste with the side of a cleaver or in a food processor. Mix in 1/2 cup (4 oz) cold water, stirring in one direction only, and add a large pinch of salt. Beat the egg whites until stiff, then fold in the fish mixture and add half of the chicken fat.

Heat a large pan of water and add 1/2 teaspoon salt. When simmering, form the fish batter into ovals by molding between two wet tablespoons. Slide them into the water and simmer for about 5 minutes in gently bubbling water until they are cooked through but retain their shape. Lift out with a slotted spoon and drain.

Heat the remaining chicken fat in a wok and gently stir-fry the green onion and ginger for 40 seconds. Add the rice wine and boil briefly, then add the chicken stock and molasses and stir until dissolved. Add half the fish cakes and simmer gently, turning carefully when the underside is well colored. Continue to cook until there is little sauce left.

In another pan bring the milk and 1/2 cup (4 oz) water to a slow boil and add the remaining fish cakes. Simmer uncovered until the liquid is well reduced, then thicken with a little cornstarch mixed with cold water. Turn the fish cakes in the thickened sauce until well coated.

Arrange the fish cakes on a platter in pairs of gold and white.

Beijing 北京

FRIED FLAT FISH

1 12-oz (375-g) flat fish (sole, flounder or turbot)
2 teaspoons rice wine or dry sherry
1 teaspoon sesame oil
1/2 teaspoon salt
2 tablespoons cornstarch
1 egg white, well beaten
oil for frying
carrot slices (garnish)
sprigs of cilantro (garnish)

SAUCE

2 slices fresh ginger
2 green onions, roughly chopped
2 tablespoons rice wine or dry sherry
1 teaspoon sugar
pinch of salt

With slightly diagonal cuts, separate the head and tail of the fish and discard. Use a flexible-bladed knife to carefully trim off the skin of the remaining central section, scrape out the gut, then rinse the fish and dry well. Place in a dish, add the wine, sesame oil and salt and leave for 1 hour, turning once.

Coat the fish with cornstarch, then dip into the beaten egg white and coat with cornstarch again.

Heat the oil in a wok and fry the fish on both sides until golden and cooked through. Transfer to a serving plate.

Pour off the oil, rinse out the wok, then return to the heat and add about 2 tablespoons of the oil. Stir-fry the ginger slices and green onions until lightly browned, then discard. Add the rice wine, sugar and salt and bring to boil.

Spoon the sauce over the fish, then garnish with attractively cut carrot slices and sprigs of cilantro and serve.

SQUID SLICES WITH JASMINE TEA

Shanghai 上海

SQUID SLICES WITH JASMINE TEA

Artistically cut, curled slivers of pearly white squid, presented in a sauce flavored with fragrant jasmine tea and strewn with jasmine flowers, is an unforgettable dish.

1 lb (500 g) fresh squid
2 teaspoons jasmine tea leaves
2 teaspoons rice wine or dry sherry
⅔ teaspoon salt
2½ teaspoons cornstarch
1 tablespoon vegetable oil
3 cloves garlic, finely chopped
4 slices fresh ginger
1 green onion, roughly chopped
jasmine flowers (garnish)

Pull away the head, tentacles and stomach of the squid and dislodge the transparent skeleton. Cut the squid open and pull off the fins and skin. Rinse well under cold water and drain.

❈ Place outside downwards on a cutting board and score the inside very lightly lengthwise, then turn over. Holding the knife at a 45° angle to the board, make deep diagonal scores across the surface, then score from the other direction so that the surface has been dissected into points giving the appearance of the spines of a pine cone.

❈ Drop the squid into a bowl of boiling water, leave for about 20 seconds, then drain. The squid should curl attractively and the points rise up.

❈ Place the tea leaves in a pot or jug and add 1 cup (8 oz) of water, leave for 2-3 minutes, then pour the water off. Add another cup (8 oz) of boiling water, cover and leave for 2 minutes.

❈ Pour the tea into a wok, add the rice wine and salt and bring to boil. Drop in the squid and poach for 1 minute. Mix the cornstarch with a little cold water and stir into the sauce, simmering briefly.

❈ In another wok heat the vegetable oil and add garlic, ginger and green onion. Stir-fry for 1 minute until the garlic is lightly colored, then pour in the squid with its tea sauce and simmer briefly. Pick out the ginger and green onion and transfer the dish to a serving plate.

❈ Strew with fresh jasmine flowers and serve at once.

COUNTRY-STYLE FRIED STUFFED DACE

FRIED MELON DATES

Guangzhou 广州

COUNTRY-STYLE FRIED STUFFED DACE

The people of Guangdong are particularly fond of the smooth flesh, delicate flavor and rich protein of the dace. Its fine bones do, however, make it less enjoyable, but prepared the following way, the fish is boneless and tender. The meat is minced and mixed with diced sausage, dried mushrooms and shrimp to make a stuffing which is replaced in the skin and served in the original shape of the fish. Although it is difficult to skin fish, nearly every housewife in Shundeh County is an expert in preparing dace in this way. Whiting will give equally good results.

2 12-oz (375-g) dace or whiting
2 dried Chinese sausages or 1 oz (30 g) salted ham
2 tablespoons dried shrimp, soaked for 25 minutes
3 dried black mushrooms, soaked for 25 minutes
1-2 cloves garlic, crushed
½ cup (2 oz) cornstarch
2 cups (16 oz) oil for frying
1 tablespoon light soy sauce
2 teaspoons rice wine or dry sherry
⅔ cup (5 oz) fish or chicken stock
cilantro (garnish)

SEASONING

½ teaspoon sugar
⅓ teaspoon sesame oil
⅓ teaspoon salt
pinch of white pepper
2 teaspoons cornstarch

Clean and rinse the fish. Use a sharp knife to slit each fish along the backbone. Lift out the backbone and discard. Place the fish skin side down and carefully cut the meat from the skin, then do the same with the other side so that the skin remains attached to the head and tail while the meat has been completely detached. Pick or cut away the line of fine bones that runs down the center of each fillet. Chop the fish meat coarsely, then beat vigorously with the side of a cleaver until reduced to a smooth paste.

🐟 Steam the sausages on a rack in a wok or steamer for 5-6 minutes or until softened. Drain the shrimp and mushrooms. Finely dice all three ingredients and mix with the fish, adding the seasoning ingredients and the garlic.

🐟 Dust the inside of each fish skin lightly with cornstarch. Divide the mixture into two parts and spread half along the center of each fish skin, molding the stuffed fish into their original shape.

🐟 Coat the fish evenly with more cornstarch, brushing off the excess. Heat the oil in a wok and when quite hot fry the two stuffed fish until well colored on both sides. Carefully lift onto a serving plate.

🐟 Drain the wok, return about 1 tablespoon of the oil and add the soy sauce, wine and stock. Boil briskly, then thicken with about 1½ teaspoons cornstarch mixed with a little cold water. Pour over the fish and garnish with cilantro.

Guangzhou 广州

FRIED MELON DATES

This is a well-known Fujian dish, but the ingredients include neither melon nor dates. Its name comes from the yellow melon fish, which is plentiful along the coast of Fujian Province. This is sliced and rolled into date shapes, which are coated and fried and served on a bed of crisply fried salted vegetable leaves.

10 oz (315 g) melon fish or other white fish fillets
2 teaspoons rice wine or dry sherry
1 teaspoon ginger juice
½ teaspoon salt
lard or oil for frying
oil for deep-frying
6-8 leaves dried salted cabbage or bok choy, shredded
five-spice salt*

BATTER

3 egg whites, well beaten
3 tablespoons cornstarch
3 tablespoons all purpose flour

Cut the fish into strips and place in a dish, adding the wine, ginger juice and salt. Mix well and let stand for 1 hour.

🐟 Mix the batter ingredients, adding just enough cold water to make a thick batter.

🐟 Heat the lard or oil in a wok to the smoking point, then lower the heat slightly. Dip the fish into the batter and slide into the oil to fry for about 1¼ minutes or until golden, then drain and keep warm.

🐟 In another wok heat the oil for deep-frying to the smoking point. Place the shredded vegetable leaves in a frying basket, deep-fry for a few seconds until bright green and crisp, remove and arrange on a serving platter. Place the fish on top of the vegetables and serve with the five-spice salt as a dip.

*To make the five-spice salt, heat 1½ tablespoons fine table salt in a wok until it begins to crackle, add 1 teaspoon Chinese five-spice powder, remove from the heat, stir and cool.

JADE WHITE SLICED FISH

Sichuan 四川

JADE WHITE SLICED FISH

7 oz (220 g) white fish fillets
1 egg white, well beaten
3 tablespoons soy flour or cornstarch
2 cups (16 oz) oil for frying

SAUCE

6 thin slices fresh young ginger
1 pickled red chili
2 green onions, white parts only
1 clove garlic
12 sprigs fresh pea leaves or 2-3 lettuce leaves
½ cup (4 oz) fish stock
2 teaspoons cornstarch
1 teaspoon rice wine or dry sherry
1 teaspoon sugar
pinch each of salt and white pepper

Cut the fish into thin slices and place in a dish with the egg white. Mix well, then coat each slice of fish lightly on both sides with the soy flour or cornstarch.

🔅Heat the oil in a wok to the smoking point, then reduce the heat and fry the fish, about 8 pieces at a time, over moderate heat until just cooked through and still white. Lift out and drain well.

🔅To prepare the sauce, cut the ginger into decorative shapes, slice the chili and onions diagonally and chop the garlic. Chop the lettuce leaves into squares, if used.

🔅Drain off the oil and wipe out the wok. Return about 2 tablespoons of the oil and stir-fry the ginger, chili, onions and garlic for 1 minute over moderate heat. Add the remaining premixed sauce ingredients and bring to boil. Add the pea leaves or lettuce squares and the fish and simmer very gently, stirring to mix evenly. Transfer to a serving dish and serve at once.

Guangzhou 广州

SHARKS' FINS BRAISED IN BROWN SAUCE

Shark's fin is a delicacy which featured at most imperial banquets of the Qing Dynasty (1644-1911 AD). Its esteem in the Chinese cuisine comes from the culinary skills required to prepare it, as well as its high nutritional value. Shark's fin cooked in the method described here is golden and translucent, with a smooth texture and luscious aroma. A dish of this caliber is rarely made at home, but can be enjoyed in most fine restaurants.

9 oz (280 g) prepared dried sharks' fins
4 slices fresh ginger
2 green onions
2 tablespoons rice wine or dry sherry
1 tablespoon cornstarch
4 oz (125 g) silver sprouts*
2 red chilies
2-3 slices cooked ham
black or red vinegar

SUPERIOR STOCK

½ chicken
6 chicken feet
½ pig's trotter or knuckle
5 oz (155 g) lean pork
1 tablespoon dark soy sauce
½ teaspoon salt
pinch of white pepper
4 cups (1 l) water

Soak the sharks' fins in cold water for 2 hours, bring to boil and simmer gently for 30 minutes. Drain and cover with more cold water, soak for a further 2 hours, bring to boil and simmer 30 minutes again. Repeat this twice more, then rinse the fins well in cold water and drain.

🔅In the meantime, place the stock ingredients in a separate saucepan, bring to boil and skim. Continue boiling gently, covered, for 3 hours, until the liquid has been well reduced.

🔅Place the sharks' fins on a tightly woven bamboo rack and arrange the ginger and green onions on top, then sprinkle with the wine. Place the rack in a casserole and strain the stock over. Set the pot on a rack in a wok or steamer, cover and steam over simmering water for about 1½ hours. Replenish the water in the steamer from time to time. Remove the sharks' fins from the rack and place on a serving plate.

🔅Bring the stock to boil, thicken with the cornstarch mixed with a little cold water and simmer until the sauce becomes transparent. Adjust seasoning to taste and pour the sauce over the fins.

🔅Blanch the sprouts, finely shred the chilies and ham and arrange the three ingredients on several small dishes. Serve with the sharks' fins, together with dishes of black or red vinegar.

Fresh mung bean sprouts from which the yellow seed pods and tapered roots have been removed, leaving the silver-colored sprouts.

SHARKS' FINS BRAISED IN BROWN SAUCE

BRAISED SHARKS' FINS, TAN FAMILY STYLE

Beijing 北京

BRAISED SHARKS' FINS, TAN FAMILY STYLE

The famous Tan family, who started their first restaurant during the Qing Dynasty (1644-1911 AD), apparently had twenty ways of cooking sharks' fins. This one has been handed down for generations and is considered one of their best.

2½ oz (75 g) dried sharks' fins
1 2½-lb (1¼-kg) chicken
½ 3½-lb (1¾-kg) duck
5 dried scallops, soaked for 1 hour
4 oz (125 g) Yunnan or other salted ham, chopped
8 cups (2 l) water
1 tablespoon rice wine or dry sherry
1 teaspoon sugar
2 tablespoons light soy sauce
salt and pepper
2-3 teaspoons dried shrimp roe (optional)
red vinegar (dip)

Place the sharks' fins in a saucepan, cover with water and bring to boil. Simmer for 20 minutes, then drain and cover with cold water again. Bring to boil and simmer gently for about 2 hours. Leave to cool in the water, then pour the water off. Scrape away any tough pieces of skin, then rinse the fins, cover with cold water and bring to boil. Reduce the heat and simmer gently for another hour. Let the fins cool in the water.

❈ Drain the sharks' fins and place on a tightly woven bamboo rack in a wok; cover with another bamboo rack. Chop the chicken and duck into pieces and arrange on the top rack. Add the scallops, ham and the water. Cover, bring to boil and simmer gently for 3 hours, or until the sharks' fins are soft and tender and the stock is richly flavored.

❈ Remove the chicken, duck, scallops and ham to use in another dish.

❈ Bring the sharks' fins and their stock to boil, season with the wine, sugar and soy sauce, and add salt and pepper to taste. Sprinkle with the shrimp roe, if used, and simmer, uncovered, for about 15 minutes or until the liquid has reduced to just cover the fins.

❈ If shrimp roe has not been used, very finely dice a little of the ham and use this to garnish the dish.

❈ Serve with small dishes of red vinegar dip.

125

Shanghai 上海

EEL SHREDS WITH SESAME OIL

Eel is delicious and highly nourishing. Traditional Chinese folk medicine holds that eel gives one energy and helps in the treatment of rheumatism.

Eel has different distinctive features during each of the four seasons. It is tender and delicately flavored in spring, most delicious during the rice transplanting time from the end of spring to early summer, tough in autumn and fat in winter.

Eels should be killed just before cooking, as the meat deteriorates quickly and acquires a muddy and strong fishy flavor.

2 lb (1 kg) freshwater eels
3 tablespoons lard
6 slices young fresh ginger
1 tablespoon sesame oil
½ teaspoon white pepper

SEASONING/SAUCE

¾ cup (6 oz) chicken or fish stock
2½ tablespoons light soy sauce
1 tablespoon rice wine or dry sherry
1½ teaspoons sugar
⅓ teaspoon powdered ginger
1 teaspoon cornstarch

EEL SHREDS WITH SESAME OIL

Drop the eels into boiling water to kill, then remove. Cut off the heads and use a sharp knife to remove the meat in long fillets from the backbone; cut into shreds. (Eels do not need to be skinned if they are young and small.)

Rub out a wok with an oiled cloth, add the lard and heat to the smoking point. Drop in the eel meat and stir-fry over very high heat until it changes color and is cooked through. Remove to a plate. Add the pre-mixed seasoning ingredients, except the cornstarch, to the wok and stir until boiling. Return the eel, cover and simmer gently for 2-3 minutes.

Mix the cornstarch with a little cold water and pour into the sauce, stirring until thickened. Transfer the eel and sauce to a serving dish.

In another pan heat the sesame oil until very hot. Make a small well in the center of the eel meat and pour in the oil, then sprinkle on the pepper. The hot oil will sizzle and make the dish very fragrant. Serve at once.

Guangzhou 广州

EEL STEWED IN A CLAY POT

"When the north wind blows, the wind eel is plump" is an old Chinese saying. The wind eel is a highly nutritious seafood delicacy. Every winter the eels swim out from the Zhu Jiang River into the ocean, where spawning takes place on the sea bed some 1,300 feet (400 meters) deep. The young fry later swim back to the mouth of the river, where they continue to grow buried in the silt, emerging between the end of autumn and early winter when the north winds blow and the temperature falls. Thus they have become known as "feng shan," or wind eel.

Apart from pot roasting and stewing, wind eels are also eaten sliced and poached, or made into a porridge with glutinous rice — a milk-colored, rich, warming dish.

1 1½-lb (750-g) feng shan eel or other meaty eel
1 tablespoon mushroom soy sauce
5 oz (155 g) roasted or boiled *unsmoked* bacon
10 cloves garlic
6-8 dried black mushrooms, soaked for 25 minutes
oil for deep-frying
6 slices fresh ginger
2 pieces dried orange peel, soaked for 10 minutes
1 tablespoon cornstarch
1 tablespoon vegetable oil (optional)
cilantro (garnish)

SEASONING/STOCK

2 cups (16 oz) hot fish stock, or Superior Stock (*see page 124*)
2 tablespoons light soy sauce
1 tablespoon rice wine or dry sherry
¼ teaspoon salt
¼ teaspoon white pepper

Kill the eel by severing the head. Place in a strainer and pour over boiling water, then rinse thoroughly. Cut into 2-in (5-cm) pieces, rub with the mushroom soy sauce and let stand for 10 minutes.

Slice the bacon. Peel the garlic and leave whole; drain and shred the mushrooms.

Heat the oil in a wok and fry the eel until well colored. Using a slotted spoon, transfer the eel to a clay pot or casserole. Fry the bacon and garlic in the oil until lightly colored.

Arrange the bacon, garlic, mushrooms, ginger and orange peel over the eel. Add the seasoning/stock ingredients, cover tightly and simmer for about 20 minutes until the eel is tender. Thicken with the cornstarch mixed with a little cold water and add the vegetable oil, if used. Garnish with cilantro.

EEL STEWED IN A CLAY POT

广州
Guangzhou

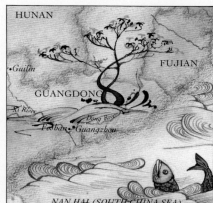

HUNAN

FUJIAN

•Guilin

GUANGDONG

Xi River

Dong River

Foshan •Guangzhou

NAN HAI (SOUTH CHINA SEA)

广州

Guangzhou
THE JAGGED COAST

ETWEEN China's two major islands, Taiwan and Hainan, 1,000 miles (1,600 kilometers) of jagged coastline curves in a gigantic arc. Taiwan, with its snowy peaks, rich rain forests and sandy beaches, straddles the straits off the province of Fujian. The island of Hainan, a tropical paradise where coconut palms wave above plantations of exotic fruit, guards the Gulf of Tonkin from the full fury of the Dai Fung, the typhoons that sweep in over the South China Sea. These two islands, and thousands of other less significant outcrops that speckle the coast, rim the southern flank of China. This indented coastline provides the rich bounty that forms the basis of China's best-known cuisine: Cantonese food, in all its diverse and splendid variety.

The coastline between the islands has everything that generous nature can bestow. Narrow river valleys broaden into fertile plains, and the sprawling estuary of the Pearl River delta provides a wonderland of twisting waterways where fish and fowl luxuriate. Countless coves and bays glow at night with the flaring twinkle of sampan lamps guiding juicy tiger prawns into the nets. On steep cliffs above azure waters fishermen tend long snap nets drooping from bamboo poles, ready to hoist ashore any school of fish unwary enough to venture past.

Out from land, on the expanse of the South China Sea, the sails of junks flap in the monsoon breeze as their nets haul taut behind. Most junks today have engines, but the romance of the sailing junk is inseparable from the legends of the China coast. Closer inshore, under the craggy rocks, tiny sampans bob in the surf as their occupants dangerously pluck shellfish from cliffs pounded by the waves. Seaweed, disdained and discarded in the West, is a profitable crop on the China coast. Jellyfish also grace the table along with sea urchins and slugs that crawl along the ocean bed.

More than half the area of the beautiful island of Hainan is an autonomous prefecture for the Li and Miao peoples. The market in their mountain capital of Tongshi offers a rewarding glimpse of their varied

A FISHING FLEET OFF HAINAN ISLAND   PAUL LAU

131

(previous page) SUNRISE OVER HAINAN ISLAND   PAUL LAU

THE YUSHAN MOUNTAINS, A MISTY BACKDROP TO THE MEI JIANG RIVER, JIANGXI PROVINCE   LEO MEIER

WORKING IN THE FIELDS, JIANGXI PROVINCE

cuisine. Rice is the staple in this fertile paradise, but it is often accompanied by jungle delicacies such as stewed freshwater turtle or baked civet cat. Almost every Li household has a shotgun, and hunting is a passion. Even today, when much of the farmland grows rubber, sisal, peppers, cocoa, coffee and other tropical cash crops, the traditional hunting parties go out into the hills after game. The catch is still distributed in the ancient manner: the man who fired the successful shot gets a quarter and the rest of the quarry is divided among members of the hunting party, and any strangers they meet on the way home.

The southern coast, and more specifically the vast steamy delta of the Pearl River, has given the Western world the flavor of Chinese food. This is not surprising, as most of the original American–Chinese came from this region: three hundred and fifty thousand Californians can trace their roots back to the county of Toishan, a former pirate haven and bandit den. The men from the delta left in a wave of despair to dig the gold mines of the sierras and hack the railroads across the Rocky Mountains. Foshan men went to the gold diggings in Australia, Hakka hill villagers left to grow pineapples in Hawaii and pan gold in New Zealand, and the Guangzhou city dwellers went to every port in the world. With them they took not only commercial cunning and a staggering ability to work, but also a gastronomic legacy that has enriched every land they reached.

The Cantonese cuisine found outside China is, however, unlike that of Guangdong Province. The dishes have been adapted to local tastes: steamed chicken with bamboo shoots, for example, has a flavor in Sydney different from the dish of the same name served in San Francisco or Liverpool. It is no coincidence that all three of these great cities with their big Chinatowns are major ports, because it was by ship that the Guangdong exodus

LEO MEIER

132

reached the Western world, and it was by ship, when they had enough money to buy a tiny plot of the good earth of China, that they planned to come home. Very few left the delta with the intention of settling overseas. Their aim was to work to buy a wife and a plot of land back in their native village. But as the presence of thirty million overseas Chinese vividly testifies today, the dream of returning to the Middle Kingdom was for many of them a forlorn hope.

The land they left behind is very different these days from the piratical coast of the mid-nineteenth century. Nowhere in the entire country do climate and geography play a more vital role in shaping cuisine than along the jagged southern coastal rim. Food is fresh and bursting with vigor, juice and goodness. The astonishing bounty of the seas is rushed alive to market. In even the most humble of restaurants, live fish, crabs, prawns, lobsters and eels swim in large tanks before the eyes of appreciative diners. Seafood in the Cantonese kitchen has been elevated to an art. It is the supreme food of the southern school of cooking, the preparation of which calls for great skill. The love of fish is coupled with a compulsion for fresh food, so the main item on a menu is likely to be swimming in a fish tank one minute and the next served steaming on a platter with a whisper of green onions and a hint of ginger.

To the adoration of seafood add a great desire for vegetables. Once again the gentle southern climate, hot and steamy for most of the year like some gigantic glass-

VIBRANT COSTUMES AT FOSHAN FESTIVAL, GUANGDONG PROVINCE   JACKY YIP

BOAT RACES AT FOSHAN FESTIVAL, GUANGDONG PROVINCE   JACKY YIP

HAINAN ISLAND

PAUL LAU

house given by the gods, provides the best that nature can offer. From lowland fields, which produce six crops of prime vegetables every year, farmers come to market bringing the splendid results of their labor. It is said that the Chinese agriculturalist is more a gardener than a farmer – perhaps, but the men and women who stoop endlessly over their patches of fertile earth are more lovers of the soil than simple gardeners. The earth is their passion as well as their pride. The summer rains soak deeply into the fertilized soil, the sun blazes, the tiller of the soil walks between the rows of glowing vegetables giving each plant its own private dousing from a bamboo watering can. The steam rises, the fruit hangs heavy in the summer noon, the very air reeks of fertility. The coastal rim and its inland valleys produce a range of vegetables probably unequaled on earth, and they are picked every day to be carried or trucked to markets in Fujian, Guangdong, Taiwan and Guangxi, where the housewives are unbending in their insistence on the freshest of foods, and refuse to contemplate cooking something not picked that very day.

The pride and the passion of the farmers is matched by the fanaticism to be found among the chefs in any southern kitchen. Cantonese cooks are the best in the world. Chefs in other provinces agree with this, and there is no higher praise than that. Cooking and eating the best that nature has to offer is a vital part of southern life. Much of that life is spent in the pursuit of excellent

A COLORFUL DISH FROM GUANGXI PROVINCE   PAUL LAU

A FINE EXAMPLE OF CHINESE INTERIOR ART IN A GUANGZHOU DINING ROOM

MICHAEL COOK

food. Day begins in many a city of the south with old men walking with their caged birds to special restaurants where their pets can twitter at each other as their owners eat. At the most famous teahouse on earth, the Panxi in Guangzhou, every morning long before public transport starts, regular breakfast customers walk great distances to stand in line to be first at the tables when the doors open at 6a.m. The Panxi is noted for its invention of thousands of new varieties of dim sum and, of course, everyone wants to be first to try the newest version of the ancient tidbits.

Devotees of the southern kitchen like to announce to visitors that they will eat anything. The newcomer to their ways should not doubt it, or he might find himself feasting on owl, anteater or cobra, all firmly favored by Cantonese gourmets. Wild cats and plump, black-tongued Chow dogs are also bred for the pot. "We eat anything whose backbone does not point to heaven" goes one old saying. True, but that was before men of the delta emigrated to South America and found the sloth that hangs upside down in trees, and discovered that this also provided the basis of a dainty treat.

"Be born in Suzhou" urges a traditional poem much quoted in the Pearl River delta. Suzhou, near Shanghai, is said to produce the most beautiful women in China. Be born in Suzhou; live in Hangzhou where the nation's finest silk comes from; die in Luzhou where the wood best suited for noble coffins grows; and eat where the best food in the world can be found – in the kitchens of Guangzhou, naturally.

The people of Guangzhou like to point out the predominant position they have held in the kitchens of China and the world over the centuries. Cantonese cuisine is, however, a varied mixture. Within the province of Guangdong alone there are major variations. The Hakka people, the gypsies of China who settled on the southern rim after fleeing from barbarian invaders in the north, have their own style of cooking. The gastronomic delights of Chiu Chow cuisine are in a class of their very own. Fujian Province rivals even Guangdong in its pursuit of treasures from the sea, and the aboriginal tribes on the east coast of Taiwan make a seafood soup that is more ambitious than the heartiest bouillabaisse to be found on the waterfront of Marseille.

The strength that underlies the region is provided by nature. From the sea, the land and the ponds that harbor fat carp and contented duck, the stress is on natural, fresh goodness. It is on this basis of fresh food that Cantonese cuisine is built. Along the entire coast nature's abundance has provided raw materials that make life easy for master chef and imaginative housewife alike. Few additional flavorings are needed: a hint of ginger, a small dash of salt, a gentle sprinkling of green onions. The natural goodness and sweet taste of food straight from the garden or the water is the trademark of the famous Cantonese kitchen.

SUNSET OVER HAINAN ISLAND   PAUL LAU

(following page) TERRACED HILLSIDES IN GUANGXI PROVINCE

PAUL LAU

NOMADS TEND THEIR SHEEP ON THE GRASSLANDS OF NORTHERN SICHUAN

LEONG KA TAI

肉類
Meat

肉類

Meat 肉類

WHEN a Chinese chef talks of meat, it is almost certain that the animal to which he refers is the pig. In every corner of the land pork is the most common and preferred meat. The only exceptions are the Muslim areas of the northwest, and even there the increasing settlement of Han Chinese has led to pork becoming commonly available. It is no coincidence that in Chinese script the character for "home" consists of the ideogram for a "pig" under a "roof." For centuries the home was where the pig lived, often sharing a modest hut in a tiny village with its owner. Pigs are still common throughout China, although they are now raised by agronomists using more scientific methods as well as by farmers' wives in the barnyard.

Chefs use pork in at least seven out of every ten meat dishes. The reasons are historic, culinary and economic. Pigs are easy to raise and can live virtually anywhere there are people. They are cheap to feed, simple to care for and adaptable. They grow quickly and produce meat of high quality that can be sliced, shredded or cubed for any style of cooking. Pork has no strong flavor of its own, making it ideal to use as a base on which to build a combination dish with virtually any vegetable. It can be covered with honey and roasted whole, or ground to make the ideal raw ingredient for the beloved meatball. Indeed, if the pig did not exist a Chinese cook would have to invent it.

Pork in one guise or another appears prominently in every regional cuisine. A thousand years ago recipe books contained instructions for the dutiful housewife on how to prepare pork for sacrifices to ancestors and family deities. Today there is keen provincial rivalry about which area produces the best ham in China; but the most famous, with much justification, comes from Yunnan. The bacons of Hunan, laid out to dry in the winter sun, are renowned. Winter sausages, strongly akin to the spicy sausages of Hungary, are a specialty of Shanxi. Shanghai chefs use ground pork in soup and inside pastries; and heavy hearty dumplings – each large enough to feed three hungry people in the northern winter – are famous in Liaoning. Guangdong prides itself on whole suckling pigs suspended from a chain in a special kiln, which bakes them crisply to produce the incomparable roast pork of Guangzhou. As the pig cooks,

A PIG SELLER, SICHUAN PROVINCE

PAUL LAU

the fat drains off to sizzle in a pan of water at the bottom of the huge upright oven, which then fills with steam so the meat stays sweetly succulent as it roasts.

Pork may be predominant, but every other sort of meat has at one time or another, somewhere in the country, been enjoyed. Historically, beef has been rare in China. For the past two thousand years there simply has not been sufficient land to raise grazing herds. The only cattle generally seen by the average Chinese is the dignified old water buffalo, more a friend and a tool to the peasant farmer with whom the creature grows up and works the fields for most of its life. Only when old and useless, after years of toil which have developed muscles instead of meat, does the buffalo ever find its way into the cooking pot, by which time it is disdainfully rejected by the gourmet.

A strongly held article of faith of many southerners is that they simply cannot abide the strong smell of sheep or goat. No such prejudices prevent the northerner from enjoying lamb, kid or mutton. A dish that is a delight to a Beijing gourmet, like lamb fried with cilantro, will be eaten swiftly and without pleasure by someone from Guangzhou who is taking it as a medicine instead of a meal. But although repelled by the thought of eating sheep, the southerner will go to considerable trouble and spend as much as necessary to enjoy a bowl of dog stew. This delicacy is not only believed to warm the blood and help the circulation during the chilly winter months, but is also a gastronome's joy.

Although they are the proud inheritors of the oldest agrarian tradition on earth, the Chinese have always been keen hunters. The hunt, strictly for the pot, is an interest that continues today all over the country except in the most densely populated areas. Even in provinces with huge populations there still remain large areas of mountain and forest where game is abundant. There is now no necessity for peasants to hunt to eat; starvation is no longer the spur, but the sport is enjoyed and rare creatures that are not grown domestically sometimes add spice to the family table. Venison, rabbit, bear, tiger, snake, boar, pangolin, mountain goat, hare and other game are prized species which feature prominently in ancient recipe books. Alas, for the modern gourmet they are now more difficult to find.

YAKS, A SOURCE OF MILK AND MEAT FOR NOMADIC TIBETAN TRIBES · LEO MEIER

GOATS AND OXEN GRAZE IN MOUNTAINOUS NORTHERN YUNNAN

GREGORY HEISLER

Sichuan 四川

APPETIZERS IN A LACQUER BOX

A banquet in Sichuan will often begin with an assortment of cold appetizers served in a multi-sectioned box made of lacquered wood. This classical and elegant presentation displays the efforts of the chef and the host, together with the traditional craft of lacquer work.

The contents of these boxes vary according to season, but each item must have a different taste and cooking method. Some may be salted, others quick-fried, others mixed. The cutting methods too must differ – slices, chunks, dice, strips, curls, rolls.

The colors must present attractive patterns and contrast. Flavors must complement – some mild, others strong.

THIS SELECTION COMPRISES

Steamed, thinly sliced Yunnan ham
Salt-simmered duck with broad beans
"Thousand-year" eggs
Cabbage rolls with dried chilies
Thinly sliced Chinese sausage
Sliced poached winter bamboo shoots
Dry-fried beef with Sichuan pepper and chilies
Diamonds of boiled winter melon interlaced with
  dried shrimp
Curls of green onion centered with slivers of red chili,
  served on a bed of edible black moss and dried shrimp

Guangzhou 广州

SKEWERED PORK DIPPED IN MALT SUGAR

Slightly fatty pork should be used in this dish; otherwise it will burn and dry out during the cooking process. The malt sugar, brushed over the pork during roasting, gives a rich, red-brown glaze and adds a crisp texture and salty sweet taste.

1 lb (500 g) pork leg with a little fat
3 tablespoons malt sugar (maltose)
½ cup (4 oz) boiling water

SEASONING

2 tablespoons soybean oil
1½ tablespoons light soy sauce
1 tablespoon dark or mushroom soy sauce
1 tablespoon Fen liquor, rice wine or dry sherry
1 tablespoon sugar
1 teaspoon sesame oil
¼ teaspoon salt

Cut the meat into strips and place in a dish with the pre-mixed seasoning ingredients. Mix well and marinate for 2-3 hours, turning frequently.

❁Thread the strips of pork on a thick metal skewer and suspend them in a preheated hot oven (400°F/200°C) over a drip tray to roast for 10 minutes.

❁Mix the malt sugar and boiling water together, stirring until the sugar has melted. Remove the pork from the oven and brush liberally with the syrup, then return to the oven to roast for a further 5 minutes. Brush again with syrup, roast again very briefly, then remove from the oven and brush with a final coating of syrup.

❁Cut into slices and arrange on a serving plate. Can be served warm or cold.

(inset) APPETIZERS IN A LACQUER BOX

SKEWERED PORK DIPPED IN MALT SUGAR

LOTUS EGGS WITH BARBECUED PORK

DEEP-FRIED SHREDDED PORK

Guangzhou 广州

LOTUS EGGS WITH BARBECUED PORK

The lotus, it is said, "grows out of the mud but is not stained. It stands firmly against the wind, elegantly beautiful and mildly scented." Many noted historical personalities praised it and even compared the lotus to the beauty of women. In Guangdong cuisine, when egg is an important ingredient in a dish, the name of the dish often incorporates the word lotus (fuyong). This alludes to the resemblance of the egg's delicate texture and pale color to the beauty of the lotus.

2 eggs
4 egg whites
4 oz (125 g) barbecued pork
1½ oz (45 g) fresh or canned bamboo shoots
2 green onions, white parts only
2-3 tablespoons lard or oil for frying
¾ teaspoon salt
pinch of pepper

Beat the eggs and egg whites together thoroughly and set aside.

Cut the barbecued pork, bamboo shoots and green onions into fine shreds. Heat the lard or oil in a wok and sauté the shredded ingredients briefly.

Season the egg with salt and pepper, pour over the shredded ingredients and cook over moderate heat, stirring only occasionally, until golden brown underneath. Turn the whole omelet without cutting and gently cook the other side until the egg is just firm, then slide onto a serving plate.

Beijing 北京

DEEP-FRIED SHREDDED PORK

10 oz (315 g) pork fillet (tenderloin)
½ cup (2 oz) cornstarch
2½ cups (20 oz) peanut oil
¼ small red bell pepper, shredded
¼ small green bell pepper, shredded
2 green onions, white parts only, shredded
1 teaspoon chili oil or chili sauce

SEASONING

1 tablespoon light soy sauce
2 teaspoons ginger juice
2 teaspoons rice wine or dry sherry
2 teaspoons brown vinegar
½ teaspoon salt

Cut the pork fillet into paper thin slices, then into shreds finer than matchsticks. Mix the cornstarch with enough cold water to make a thin paste. Add the pork and mix well until each shred is thinly coated with the paste.

Heat the peanut oil in a wok to the smoking point and deep-fry the pork shreds until crisp, using wooden chopsticks to separate the shreds. The pork will turn a light golden brown and rustle slightly when drained, as soon as it is done. Remove and set aside.

Drain the oil, leaving about 1 tablespoon. Add the pre-mixed seasoning ingredients and bring to boil. Return the fried pork and stir-fry in the sauce until evenly coated, add the peppers and onions and toss all together, then sprinkle on the chili oil, toss well and transfer to a serving plate.

Sichuan 四川

PORK WITH SICHUAN PRESERVED CABBAGE

Chinese preserved cabbage, and especially that from Fulin in Sichuan, is famous for its unique flavor and has been exported all over the world. In the preparation it is seasoned with a great variety of condiments, in particular fennel, pepper, licorice root, Chinese cassia, chili, salt and spirits.

6 oz (185 g) Sichuan preserved cabbage
12 oz (375 g) pork fillet (tenderloin)
1 leek or 2-3 green onions
3 slices fresh ginger
1-2 fresh red chilies
3 tablespoons lard or vegetable oil

SEASONING

2 tablespoons rice wine or dry sherry
1 tablespoon light soy sauce
1 tablespoon cornstarch
½ teaspoon sugar

Soak the salted cabbage in cold water for 1 hour. Drain and squeeze out as much water as possible, then cut into strips of about 2 x ½ in (5 x 1 cm) and set aside.

Very thinly slice the pork, cutting across the grain, then stack the slices and cut them into fine shreds. Place in a dish with the pre-mixed seasoning ingredients, mix well and let stand for 20 minutes.

Cut the leek, ginger and chilies into fine shreds.

Heat the lard in a wok to smoking point. Stir-fry the pork and cabbage together until the pork changes color. Push to one side of the wok and add the remaining ingredients, stir-frying for 1 minute. Mix with the pork and cabbage, add 1 tablespoon water, check the seasoning and serve.

PORK WITH SICHUAN PRESERVED CABBAGE

STIR-FRIED DICED PORK WITH CASHEW NUTS

Guangzhou 广州

STIR-FRIED DICED PORK WITH CASHEW NUTS

The cashew nut grows abundantly in subtropical climates. Its strange-looking fruit consists of two parts: the upper part, called the "pear" or "false fruit," is soft and juicy with the flavor of musk, and is eaten as a fruit; the lower part comprises the shell and crescent-shaped kernel of the cashew.

Deep-fried cashew nuts are extremely crisp, with a flavor surpassing that of the peanuts which are often used in Chinese cooking.

10 oz (315 g) lean pork
2 green onions
1/3 red bell pepper
1/3 green bell pepper
2 cloves garlic
2 dried black mushrooms, soaked for 25 minutes
oil for deep-frying
3-4 oz (90-125 g) raw cashew nuts

SEASONING

2 teaspoons cornstarch
1 teaspoon rice wine or dry sherry
3/4 teaspoon sugar
1/2 teaspoon salt

SAUCE

1/3 cup (2½ oz) chicken stock or water
1 teaspoon dark soy sauce
1 teaspoon cornstarch
1/2 teaspoon salt
1/2 teaspoon sugar
pinch of white pepper

Dice the pork finely, add the seasoning ingredients, mix well and leave for 20 minutes.

Cut the green onions into short lengths, dice the peppers, finely chop the garlic and squeeze the water from the mushrooms before cutting into small dice.

Heat the oil in a large wok and deep-fry the pork in a frying basket or large perforated ladle for about 3 minutes or until cooked through. Remove and drain well. Deep-fry the cashew nuts until they begin to color and remove quickly. Do not overcook or they will be bitter. Set aside.

Drain the wok, reserving about 1 tablespoon of the oil, and stir-fry the vegetables and garlic for 2-3 minutes. Mix the sauce ingredients together and pour into the wok, stirring to thicken. Add the pork and toss together until well coated with the sauce and mixed with the vegetables.

Transfer to a serving plate and arrange the cashews on top. Serve at once.

SWEET AND SOUR PORK

Guangzhou 广州

SWEET AND SOUR PORK

9 oz (280 g) *unsmoked* bacon
1/2 teaspoon salt
2 teaspoons rice wine or dry sherry
1 egg, well beaten
1 medium size green bell pepper
2 oz (60 g) fresh or canned bamboo shoots
2-3 green onions
3 cloves garlic
1 cup (4 oz) cornstarch
oil for deep-frying
1/2 teaspoon sesame oil (optional)

SWEET AND SOUR SAUCE

2 tablespoons sugar
1 tablespoon oil for frying
3 tablespoons brown vinegar
1/2 cup (4 oz) stock
1 teaspoon cornstarch
salt and pepper

Use a sharp knife to closely crosshatch the bacon skin, then cut the meat into cubes, each with a piece of skin attached. Place in a dish with the salt, rice wine and egg, mix well and set aside.

Cut the pepper in half, remove the seeds, stem and inner ribs and cut into squares. Thinly slice the bamboo shoots and the green onions and finely chop the garlic.

Place the cornstarch in a plastic bag, add the bacon and shake vigorously to coat thickly and evenly. Transfer to a colander and shake off the excess.

Heat the oil in a wok to the smoking point and deep-fry the meat for 1 minute, then lower the heat slightly and continue to fry for about 3 minutes or until well cooked and crisp on the surface. Remove and drain well.

Drain off the oil and wipe out the wok. Return 2 tablespoons of the oil and stir-fry the pepper, bamboo shoots, green onions and garlic for about 1½ minutes. Add the bacon and mix well, then remove to a plate.

Pour the sugar and oil of the sauce ingredients into the wok and cook until it turns a light caramel color, stirring occasionally. Add the vinegar and remaining sauce ingredients and bring to boil, stirring.

Return the meat and vegetables, stir in the sauce until evenly coated, sprinkle on the sesame oil and serve.

FRIED PORK FLAVORED WITH LAUREL

PORK "COINS" WITH HONEY

Shanghai 上海

FRIED PORK FLAVORED WITH LAUREL

Flowering laurel is a treasured aromatic plant in China, being used for ornamental and medicinal purposes. Chefs often use the flowers in cooking to enhance the color, taste and aroma of the food. The pork in this dish is golden, light and tender, with the added fragrance of laurel flowers. Served with a sweet and sour sauce and peppercorn salt it is especially delicious, and is a traditional specialty of the Shanghai area.

9 oz (280 g) lean pork
2 eggs
¾ cup (3 oz) cornstarch
oil or lard for deep-frying
2 green onions, white parts only
1 teaspoon sesame oil
silver laurel flowers
peppercorn salt*

SEASONING

1 tablespoon light soy sauce
1 tablespoon rice wine or dry sherry
1 tablespoon finely chopped green onion
¼ teaspoon salt

SAUCE

1 tablespoon light soy sauce
2 teaspoons rice wine or dry sherry
1 teaspoon sugar

Cut the pork into thin slices and pound with the side of a cleaver or a rolling pin to flatten and tenderize, then cut into strips. Place in a dish and add the pre-mixed seasoning ingredients, mix well and let stand for 20 minutes.
❋ Beat the eggs and mix into a batter with the cornstarch.
❋ Heat the oil in a wok over moderate heat. Dip the pork into the batter, then deep-fry in the oil for about 1 minute. Remove and drain well. Increase the heat and fry the pork again for about 20 seconds. Remove, drain and fry again, cooking until the surface is crisp and the pork cooked through. Remove and drain well.
❋ Finely chop the green onions.
❋ Heat a clean wok and add a little oil. Stir-fry the green onions with the pork, adding the sesame oil. Add the pre-mixed sauce ingredients and toss the pork over high heat until the sauce is absorbed. Sprinkle on the laurel flowers, stir in and serve with the peppercorn salt as a dip.

To make peppercorn salt, dry-fry 1 teaspoon Sichuan peppercorns (Fagara or Sansho) in a wok until fragrant, then grind finely. Heat 1 tablespoon fine table salt in the wok, add the pepper, mix together and cool before using.

Beijing 北京

PORK "COINS" WITH HONEY

The name of this dish derives from the way the meat is skewered for cooking. When removed from the skewer each piece of meat has a hole in the center similar to an old Chinese coin.

Although the meat is barbecued over an open fire, the interlayered pork fat prevents the normally dry fillet from becoming parched and tough.

1 lb (500 g) pork fillet (tenderloin)
8 oz (250 g) duck livers or fresh ham
1½ lb (750 g) pork fat
½ cup (5 oz) clear honey
½ cup (4 oz) peanut oil

PORK MARINADE

1 egg white, lightly beaten
1½ tablespoons sugar
1 tablespoon dark soy sauce
1 tablespoon rice wine or dry sherry
1 teaspoon five-spice powder
pinch of salt

PORK FAT MARINADE

2 teaspoons rice wine or dry sherry
2 teaspoons sugar
1 teaspoon salt

Cut the pork, livers and fat into thin slices, then shape into rounds of approximately 1¾-in (4-cm) diameter. Place the pork fillet and the pork fat in separate dishes and add their respective pre-mixed marinade ingredients, mix well and let stand for 20 minutes.
❋ Use thick metal or wooden skewers; soak wooden ones in water for 1 hour to prevent burning, and rub them with oil. Thread the pork, liver and fat in alternate layers along the skewers.
❋ Cook over a moderately hot charcoal fire, brushing alternately with honey and oil to keep the meat moist. Or roast in a preheated oven at 350°F (180°C) for about 30 minutes, turning several times during cooking. Serve at once.

Guangzhou 广州

BARBECUED PORK

Skewered and barbecued meat, usually lamb, is a specialty of the wandering tribes of the northwestern regions of China. The southern Chinese have devised a similar recipe using pork, which they prefer to lamb. The ingredients used to flavor the meat impart a sweetish taste, a bright red-brown color and a crispness to the surface. Cooked over charcoal, the meat gets a mouthwateringly delicious smoky taste. It can be served as a main course or as a starter with drinks.

2 lb (1 kg) lean pork (loin or picnic shoulder)
fresh pineapple (garnish)
cucumber (garnish)

SEASONING/GLAZE

⅔ cup (4 oz) malt sugar (maltose)
3 tablespoons boiling water
2 tablespoons rice wine or dry sherry
1 tablespoon light soy sauce
1 tablespoon oyster sauce
1 teaspoon sesame oil
½ teaspoon salt
½ teaspoon orange or red food coloring (optional)

Cut the pork into long strips about 2 in (5 cm) wide, and place in a dish. Mix the seasoning/glaze ingredients together, first mixing the malt sugar and boiling water until dissolved. Pour over the pork and let stand for at least 5 hours, turning from time to time.

※ Prepare a charcoal fire or preheat oven to 450°F (240°C). Hang the strips of meat on metal butchers' hooks and suspend over the fire, or hang from a rack in the oven, placing a drip tray underneath.

※ Roast for about 15 minutes, then remove and brush thickly with the remaining marinade. Return to the oven to complete roasting until just cooked through and very crisp on the surface.

※ Cut into thick slices and pile onto a serving plate. Surround with pineapple and cucumber. Serve warm or cold.

BARBECUED PORK

PORK IN WINE LEES

KIDNEY SLICES WITH SESAME PASTE DRESSING

Guangzhou 广州

PORK IN WINE LEES

In Chinese cooking, the chef pays careful attention to the choice and use of seasoning ingredients, the red fermented rice used in this recipe being one such specialty. This is polished glutinous rice prepared through a process of steaming, fermenting and filtration; it is a local product of Fujian Province. Because it is bright red and has the fragrant smell of wine, it is often known as wine lees. Fujian dishes are characterized by their frequent use of this ingredient.

10 oz (315 g) pork fillet (tenderloin)
1 medium cucumber
2 egg whites, lightly beaten
3 tablespoons cornstarch
3 tablespoons red fermented rice (wine lees)
8 oz (250 g) lard

SEASONING/SAUCE

¾ cup (6 oz) chicken stock
2 tablespoons rice wine or dry sherry
2 teaspoons cornstarch
1½ teaspoons sugar
¾ teaspoon salt

Cut the pork fillet and unpeeled cucumber into small cubes, discarding any tendons and sinews from the meat and the seeds from the cucumber.

※ Mix the pork with the egg whites, then place in a plastic bag and add the cornstarch. Shake briskly until the meat is well coated, then transfer to a plate and add the red fermented rice, mixing in well.

※ Heat the lard in a wok and stir-fry the pork over high heat until bright red, separating pieces that stick together. Add the cucumber and stir-fry briefly, then remove the pork and cucumber and drain off the fat.

※ Return the pork and cucumber and add the pre-mixed seasoning/sauce ingredients, stirring over high heat for about 45 seconds before serving.

Beijing 北京

KIDNEY SLICES WITH SESAME PASTE DRESSING

The cooking method described in the following recipe is unusual. The thin slices of kidney are scalded several times in boiling water, dipped in the sesame paste dressing and then served. The scalding removes the strong taste and aroma of the kidney while cooking it just enough to preserve its delicate texture.

2 pork kidneys
salt
1 teaspoon rice wine or dry sherry
cucumber slices

DRESSING

2 tablespoons sesame paste (tahini)
1 tablespoon sugar
2 teaspoons dark soy sauce
½ teaspoon sesame oil
pinch of salt

Cut the kidneys in half horizontally to expose the inner core of white fat. Remove this and the connected veins, and place the kidneys in a dish of cold water to soak for several hours. Change the water 3-4 times. Drain well, then slice the kidneys very thinly.

※ Bring a saucepan of water to boil. Scald the kidneys for just a few seconds, then remove and drain. Boil a second pot of water and scald again, just long enough for them to lose their pink color. Drain well and sprinkle with a little salt and rice wine.

※ Mix the dressing ingredients together, adding cold water if the paste is very thick – depending on the brand of sesame paste used.

※ Arrange slices of cucumber on a serving plate and pile the kidney slices on top. Pour on the sesame paste and serve.

PORK SHREDS AND BELL PEPPER

BALSAM PEAR WITH PORK AND PRAWN FILLING

Sichuan 四川

PORK SHREDS AND BELL PEPPER

Pickled red bell pepper is served with many Sichuan meals as a side dish, as it is said to stimulate the appetite. Being a good source of vitamin C, and growing and bearing fruit readily, bell peppers have been an essential part of the Sichuan cuisine for many centuries.

8 oz (250 g) pork fillet (tenderloin)
1 large or 2 small red bell peppers
3 oz (90 g) canned or cooked fresh bamboo shoots
6 garlic chives
4 slices young fresh ginger
2 tablespoons cornstarch
pinch of salt
3 tablespoons lard or vegetable oil

SEASONING/SAUCE

2/3 cup (5 oz) chicken or veal stock
1 tablespoon light soy sauce
2 teaspoons rice wine or dry sherry
1 teaspoon cornstarch
1/2 teaspoon salt
pinch of white pepper

Slice the pork into paper-thin slices, cutting across the grain, then stack the slices into piles of five or six, cut into matchstick shreds and set aside.

Cut the peppers in half, trim and cut lengthwise into narrow shreds. Cut the bamboo shoots, garlic chives and ginger into similar-sized pieces.

Stir the cornstarch into the pork shreds, coating them evenly.

Heat the wok over moderate heat and stir-fry the pepper shreds without oil until browned on the edges and half tender. Add a large pinch of salt, stir, then remove.

Add the lard and stir-fry the pork over high heat until white. Add the bamboo, garlic chives and ginger and stir-fry for another minute, then add the pre-mixed seasoning/sauce ingredients and return the pepper to the wok. Simmer, stirring, until the sauce thickens and clears, then serve.

Guangzhou 广州

BALSAM PEAR WITH PORK AND PRAWN FILLING

Balsam pears are said to be able to lighten the heart and brighten eyesight, promote respiration and reduce fever. There is a folk song in Guangdong which goes: "They say the balsam pear is bitter/But I take it to be sweet/Sweet or bitter to your choice/How can there be sweetness without bitterness?" This implies that the bitter balsam pear (commonly referred to as Chinese bitter melon) can be made sweet. The bitter taste of the balsam pear is not, however, passed on to other ingredients cooked with it. Hence it is said to possess a "gentleman's behavior."

3-4 balsam pears (Chinese bitter melons)
pinch of baking soda
6 oz (185 g) fatty pork
3 oz (90 g) fresh prawn or shrimp meat
1/2 teaspoon salt
cornstarch
oil for frying

SAUCE

1 tablespoon fermented black beans
3 cloves garlic
1 teaspoon finely chopped fresh ginger
2 teaspoons rice wine or dry sherry
2 teaspoons mushroom soy sauce
1 teaspoon sugar
pinch of white pepper
1/2 cup (4 oz) chicken stock
1 teaspoon cornstarch

Cut the balsam pears into 1/2-in (1.5-cm) slices, scoop out the seeds and fibrous centers, then place in a saucepan with cold water to cover. Add the baking soda and bring to boil. Simmer until the pears are beginning to soften, then drain.

Very finely mince or grind the pork and prawn meat to a smooth paste, using two cleavers simultaneously or a food processor. Add the salt and mix well. Dust the inside of the pear rings with cornstarch and fill with the pork and prawn paste, smoothing the tops. Coat lightly with cornstarch.

Heat about 1/2 in (1.5 cm) of oil in a skillet and fry the pears gently on both sides, until the filling is crisp on the surface and the pear rings are bright green and tender. Remove from the skillet, drain and arrange on a serving plate.

Drain the skillet, reserving about 2 tablespoons of the oil. Finely chop the black beans and garlic and fry briefly in the hot oil, add the ginger and fry briefly again. Add the wine and soy sauce, then after a few seconds add the sugar, pepper and the stock mixed with the cornstarch. Bring to boil, stirring, then pour over the prepared dish and serve at once.

Guangzhou 广州

ROAST SUCKLING PIG

Roast suckling pig is a renowned traditional Chinese delicacy. During the fifth century, it was considered by the common people to be "Yao Shu" (important art). In the Qing Dynasty (1644-1911 AD) it was one of the dishes featured in banquets held at the Qing Palace, and even today, roast suckling pig appears only at grand banquets and is always considered one of the highlights of the meal.

The pig has a characteristic bright red coloring, a sweetish flavor and skin that is smooth as glass, yet crisp and feather light. Special large iron forks are used to hold the prepared pig over glowing charcoal, and it is slowly rotated – usually by hand – until cooked to perfection. In a quality restaurant one of the master chefs will often tend the roasting over a tub of charcoal on the veranda or footpath outside the restaurant.

1 12-16-lb (6-8-kg) suckling pig (to serve about 24)
1 cup (6 oz) malt sugar (maltose)
½ cup (4 oz) red vinegar
boiling water

SEASONING

½ cup (4 oz) sugar
½ cup (4 oz) soy milk
½ cup (5 oz) bean paste
½ cup (5 oz) sesame paste (tahini)
½ cup (4 oz) vinegar
3 tablespoons Fen liquor, rice wine or sherry
3 tablespoons peanut oil
1 tablespoon mushroom soy sauce
1 tablespoon crushed garlic

Have the butcher slit the pig down the center underneath, cutting through the head as well so that the whole pig can be pressed out as flat as possible. Pierce with a large iron fork which will hold the pig open, or devise a cooking method which suits your equipment or circumstances. Have ready a large quantity of charcoal for roasting.

Hold the pig over the sink and pour over plenty of boiling water. This will contract the skin and help make it crisp. Mix the malt sugar and red vinegar with enough boiling water to make a thick syrup and paint this over the skin of the pig. Hang in an airy place for several hours or until the skin feels dryish to the touch.

Mix the seasoning ingredients together, stirring until the sugar has dissolved and all ingredients are well blended. Coat the pig thickly on the underside with the seasoning preparation and rub the remainder over the skin.

Roast slowly over glowing charcoal until no pink liquid runs off when the pig is pierced through the thickest part of the thigh. This will take several hours. During cooking, pierce any bubbles which appear on the skin with a large needle or skewer to ensure that the skin remains flat and smooth.

There is a traditional way to serve this delicious dish. First, slice the crisp red skin from the back of the pig, place the whole pig on a large platter and put the skin back in place. At the first serving, only the skin will be eaten. Return the pig to the kitchen, where the choicest pieces of meat will be cut into serving portions and reassembled on the carcass. This is presented as the second course.

The first and second courses are usually accompanied by multi-layered white buns or thin pancakes and dips of sweetened soy sauce or sweet bean paste. Green onion bulbs or curls and crisp sweet-sour pickled vegetables, such as beet, cucumber, turnip or radish, are also served. The meat is dipped into the sauce, then eaten with the bread or pancake and a piece each of vegetable and onion. This combination of ingredients counteracts the richness of the pork and provides an interesting contrast of tastes and textures.

Finally, the bones may be simmered and made into a rich broth, or the remaining pieces of meat stir-fried – usually with ginger and onions – to make a third course.

ROAST SUCKLING PIG

BRAISED RUMP OF PORK

Guangzhou 广州

BRAISED RUMP OF PORK

2 lb (1 kg) pork rump (upper leg/fresh ham)
8 cups (2 l) oil for deep-frying
8 slices fresh ginger
4-5 green onions
12 dried black mushrooms, soaked for 25 minutes
8 oz (250 g) choy sum or other Chinese green vegetable
vegetable oil

SEASONING/SAUCE

3 tablespoons light soy sauce
1 tablespoon dark soy sauce
1 tablespoon rice wine or dry sherry
1 tablespoon sugar
1½ teaspoons salt
1 teaspoon sesame oil

Wipe the skin of the pork with paper towels. Heat the oil in a large wok and when quite hot, deep-fry the pork, skin side down, until it turns a light golden color and bubbles appear on the skin. Take care at this stage, as the frying pork is inclined to spatter. Lift out and place immediately in a casserole half filled with cold water. This causes the skin to ripple and it will be very tender when braised.

Add the ginger, whole green onions, drained mushrooms and the seasoning ingredients. Cover and bring to boil, then simmer gently for about 2 hours or until the meat is very tender.

Trim the choy sum or other vegetable and stir-fry in a hot wok with a little vegetable oil. Add 2-3 tablespoons water, cover and cook until almost tender.

Arrange around the edge of a serving dish. Place the pork in the center, and slice. Arrange the mushrooms over the meat and pour over a generous serving of sauce.

152

Shanghai 上海

MEATBALLS IN MYRICA BERRY SHAPES

Including the juice of the myrica berry in the preparation of meatballs is a specialty of Anhui Province. They are both sweet and sour, invigorating and useful for treating hangovers.

The Chinese have an expression, "Looking at the berry quenches one's thirst," which derives from the late Han Dynasty, around the year 200 AD, when General Cao Cao was leading his exhausted soldiers on a long march. To revitalize them he told them of a forest of berry trees ahead. Their spirits picked up and they marched swiftly towards their imaginary goal.

13 oz (410 g) *unsmoked* bacon
3 tablespoons myrica berry juice, tamarind water or a tart
  mixture of fruit and lemon juice
1 cup (4 oz) dry breadcrumbs
4 cups (1 l) oil for deep-frying

SAUCE

¾ cup (6 oz) water
2 tablespoons sugar
2 tablespoons vinegar
1 tablespoon lard
2 teaspoons light soy sauce
2 teaspoons cornstarch
pinch of salt

Finely mince or grind the pork and mix with the fruit juice. Form into small balls and coat with the breadcrumbs.

🦋 Heat the oil in a wok to the smoking point and add one-third of the meatballs. Deep-fry until cooked through and golden brown, about 3 minutes, then cook the remainder in two batches.

🦋 Insert a small twig or pick into the top of each meatball so that they resemble berries; pile on a serving plate.

🦋 Boil the sauce ingredients in another wok, stirring until thickened. Pour over the meatballs and serve.

MEATBALLS IN MYRICA BERRY SHAPES

PORK TWICE-COOKED

Sichuan 四川

PORK TWICE-COOKED

Sichuan cooking makes much use of pork. Records show that even six thousand years ago the inhabitants of Ba and Shu (the ancient names of the east and west parts of Sichuan) kept domesticated pigs.

The following recipe, incorporating two separate cooking processes, is especially good with pork. It eliminates some of the fat, making it easier to digest and very tender.

12 oz (375 g) *unsmoked* bacon
1 medium size red bell pepper
2 oz (60 g) canned or cooked fresh bamboo shoots
2 green onions or garlic chives
4 slices fresh ginger
2 tablespoons lard

SEASONING

2 tablespoons water
1 tablespoon light soy sauce
1 tablespoon sweet bean paste
2 teaspoons hot bean paste
2 teaspoons rice wine or dry sherry
1½ teaspoons sugar
1 teaspoon mushroom soy sauce

Place the pork skin side up on a rack in a wok or steamer over simmering water. Cover and steam gently for about 25 minutes or until the pork is soft, but not completely cooked through.

🦋 Cut the pepper and bamboo shoots into squares and the green onions or garlic chives into 1-in (2.5-cm) lengths; shred the ginger.

🦋 Remove the pork from the steamer and let stand for about 20 minutes to cool and firm up.

🦋 Use a very sharp knife to cut the pork into thin slices, then into pieces about 2 in (5 cm) long. The slices should curl up like rose petals during frying.

🦋 Heat the lard in a wok and stir-fry the pepper and bamboo shoots until softened, then add the green onions or garlic chives and ginger and stir-fry briefly. Push to one side of the wok or remove, and stir-fry the pork slices until cooked through and crisp on the edges; the fat should turn translucent. Mix in the pre-mixed seasoning ingredients and stir-fry with the pepper and other vegetables over high heat for about 1½ minutes, then serve.

CANDIED FRIED PORK

PORK WITH FRUIT SAUCE

Beijing 北京
CANDIED FRIED PORK

12 oz (375 g) *unsmoked* bacon
6 cups (1½ l) chicken stock
4 oz (125 g) Chinese rock candy or caramelized white sugar
1 teaspoon finely chopped fresh red chili
1 tablespoon finely chopped green onion
oil for deep-frying

BATTER

2 egg whites, well beaten
½ cup (2 oz) all purpose flour
½ cup (2 oz) cornstarch

Cover the meat with stock and simmer gently for about 1 hour or until very tender. Cool in the stock, drain and remove the fat. Cut the meat into slices approximately 2 x 1 in (5 x 2 cm).

Crush the rock candy finely and set aside.

Mix the egg whites, flour and cornstarch to make a batter of coating consistency, adding a little cold water if needed. Dip the pork into the batter and deep-fry several pieces at a time until golden and crisp on the surface. Drain and keep warm.

Heat the rock sugar in a heavy wok or saucepan until it caramelizes. Add the chili and green onion, turn off the heat and turn each piece of meat in the caramel until coated.

Arrange on a lightly oiled plate and serve at once.

Guangzhou 广州
PORK WITH FRUIT SAUCE

9 oz (280 g) boneless lean pork
1 egg, well beaten
1 cup cornstarch
oil for deep-frying
12 shrimp chips
1 cup (8 oz) pineapple or apricot juice
½ teaspoon sesame oil

SEASONING

1 tablespoon finely chopped green onion
2 teaspoons rice wine or dry sherry
1 teaspoon grated fresh ginger
½ teaspoon salt

Cut the pork into slices and place on a board. Pound with the side of a cleaver or a rolling pin to tenderize. Place in a dish, add the pre-mixed seasoning ingredients, mix well and let stand for 20 minutes.

Add the egg to the above ingredients, mix well and then coat each slice thickly with cornstarch.

Heat the oil in a large wok to the smoking point. Deep-fry the pork slices for about 3 minutes or until crisp and well colored on the surface, stirring constantly to prevent them from sticking together. Lift out and drain well.

Fry the shrimp chips in the oil until puffed up and lightly colored; lift out and drain. Arrange in the center of a serving plate.

Pour off the oil and return the meat, adding the fruit juice. Simmer until the juice has been absorbed, then spoon onto the plate. Sprinkle with the sesame oil and serve at once.

Beijing 北京
PLAIN BOILED PORK SLICES

This dish was introduced with the Manchurians who conquered and ruled the country as the Qing Dynasty (1644-1911 AD). It was a custom during that era for the king to bestow his favor on the subjects who came to wish him happiness during the New Year by treating them to this simple but delicious dish. Similarly Manchurian nobility offered this specialty at weddings and other festive occasions. Each person would cut meat for himself from a large piece of pork and guests were invited to eat as much as they could. The more one ate of this dish, the more delighted the host would be.

2 lb (1 kg) meatier portion of pork picnic shoulder
1 teaspoon salt

BROWN BEAN SAUCE DIP

1 tablespoon brown bean sauce
1 teaspoon sugar
1 teaspoon sesame oil

GARLIC SAUCE DIP

3 cloves garlic, crushed
1 tablespoon vegetable oil
1 teaspoon salt

CHILI SAUCE DIP

1 fresh red chili, finely chopped
2 tablespoons light soy sauce

Place the pork in a wok skin side down, add the salt and cover with water. Bring to boil, cover and simmer for at least 2 hours or until the pork is very tender. A chopstick will easily penetrate the skin when the pork is cooked through. Remove from the heat and leave in the stock to cool.

Cut off the skin and part of the fat before cutting the pork into paper-thin slices. Arrange in overlapping rows on a serving plate.

Mix the three sauce ingredients and serve as cold dips in small dishes.

DICED PORK STIR-FRIED WITH PEPPER AND SOYBEAN PASTE

DRAGON AND PHOENIX HAM

Shanghai 上海

DICED PORK STIR-FRIED WITH PEPPER AND SOYBEAN PASTE

12 oz (375 g) *unsmoked* bacon
2 tablespoons dried shrimp, soaked for 25 minutes
½ green bell pepper
½ red bell pepper
1-2 dried red chilies
3 tablespoons vegetable oil
2 tablespoons soybean paste

SEASONING/SAUCE

1 tablespoon rice wine or dry sherry
1½ tablespoons light soy sauce
1 teaspoon sugar
¼ teaspoon salt
⅓ cup (2½ oz) chicken stock
1 teaspoon cornstarch

Cut the pork into very small dice, discarding any skin and fragments of bone. Drain the shrimp. Cut the peppers into small squares, removing the stems, seeds and inner ribs. Finely chop the chilies.

※ Heat the vegetable oil in a wok to the smoking point. Stir-fry the peppers for about 1½ minutes, then remove and set aside. Stir-fry the pork until it changes color. Add the chili and soybean paste and continue to cook over high heat for 3-4 minutes or until the meat is cooked through, stirring constantly.

※ Add the peppers and the seasoning ingredients, except the chicken stock and cornstarch, and stir-fry briefly. Mix the stock and cornstarch together and stir into the dish. Simmer until thickened, then serve.

Sichuan 四川

DRAGON AND PHOENIX HAM

There are many legends about the dragon and the phoenix in China. In ancient times, people thought of the dragon as the embodiment of a king and the phoenix as that of a queen. Sometimes the dragon and phoenix are combined into one symbol of glory, honor, riches and good luck. At wedding or birthday celebration banquets people always like to have dishes using dragon and phoenix names.

12 oz (375 g) boneless duck meat
8 oz (250 g) pork
3 oz (90 g) water chestnuts
10 chicken wing bones
2 pieces pork caul fat
5 slices salted ham
5 slices white bread
oil for deep-frying

SEASONING

3 tablespoons cornstarch
2 tablespoons light soy sauce
2 tablespoons water
1 egg yolk
2 teaspoons rice wine or dry sherry
¾ teaspoon salt
¼ teaspoon white pepper

Very finely grind the duck meat and pork together with the water chestnuts until reduced to a smooth, sticky paste. Add the pre-mixed seasoning ingredients and stir briskly with a wooden spoon until completely amalgamated, then form into 10 oblong shapes resembling drumsticks. Cut each piece of caul fat into 5, giving 10 similar-sized pieces. Insert one chicken bone into the narrow end of each "drumstick," wrap them in pieces of the caul fat and set aside.

※ Cut the ham and bread slices in half and trim them into rectangular shapes of equal size. Place the ham on a rack in a wok or steamer, cover and steam until tender. In the meantime lightly toast the bread.

※ Heat the oil in a wok to the smoking point and slide in the "drumsticks," several at a time. Deep-fry for about 3 minutes or until cooked through, then drain well.

※ Place a piece of ham on top of each slice of toast, arrange the "drumsticks" and ham sandwiches alternately around a large platter and serve.

YUNNAN HAM SHAPED AS PLUM FLOWERS

Sichuan 四川

YUNNAN HAM SHAPED AS PLUM FLOWERS

The Chinese love plum flowers as much as the Japanese revere the cherry blossom. For three thousand years they have cultivated plum trees and praised the characteristics of the plum. It can bloom in snow, is very resistant to bitter cold and hardship, and is the first to greet the spring. The poet Chen Liang of the Song Dynasty (960-1279 AD) said: "One plum flower blooms first, hundreds of flowers follow; they spread the news of spring, even while it is behind the snow."

5 slices Yunnan or other well-salted ham
lemon rind, optional
6 oz (185 g) white fish fillets
1 green onion, minced
⅓ teaspoon grated fresh ginger
⅓ teaspoon salt
pinch of white pepper
1 egg white
4 oz (125 g) pork fat
lard

Use a sharp knife or vegetable cutter to cut or stamp out plum flower designs from the ham. Make a hole in the center of each, then cut small pieces of the lemon rind, if used, to fill these holes, to create the center of the blossoms.
❀ Cut the fish into small pieces and pound with the flat side of a cleaver, or use a food processor, to make a smooth paste. Add the green onion, ginger, salt, pepper and egg white and mix with your fingers until smooth.
❀ Spread the fish over a large sheet of very thinly sliced pork fat, then cut into diamond shapes large enough for the ham blossoms to fit in the center (*see photograph above*). Place the ham in position.
❀ Heat a wide skillet and wipe out with a little melted lard. Gently fry the fish cakes until the pork fat is crisp and melting. Cover halfway through cooking so that the top is cooked by steam.
❀ Lift onto a serving plate, arrange attractively and garnish with a carved vegetable rose.

BRAISED PORK WITH DRIED VEGETABLE

BOILED AND FRIED PORK LEG IN BROWN SAUCE

Guangzhou 广州

BRAISED PORK WITH DRIED VEGETABLE

The meat used for this dish is pork belly (unsmoked bacon), which consists of alternating layers of fat and meat with a thin skin. The dried vegetable is a salted and sun-dried leaf mustard, the best of which is the "Huizhou" dried vegetable that is exported around the world. This has a thick heart and well-flavored leaves and is frequently used in vegetarian cooking.

1½ lb (750 g) *unsmoked* bacon
1 heart of Huizhou dried vegetable (mui-choy)
2 tablespoons peanut oil
2 tablespoons mushroom soy sauce
2 tablespoons sugar
½ teaspoon sesame oil

Scald the pork in boiling water, then leave to drain. Soak the vegetable in cold water for 30 minutes, rinse well and squeeze dry; repeat several times.

❋ Heat a wok or large saucepan and add the peanut oil. Fry the pork over high heat until brown on both sides. Add the mushroom soy sauce and sugar, then reduce the heat. Turn the pork several times until it is coated with the sauce. Add the whole piece of vegetable, cover the meat with boiling water and bring back to boil.

❋ Reduce heat to very low and simmer for at least 2 hours or until the pork is very tender and has a smooth, almost gelatinous texture. Add the sesame oil.

❋ Lift out the vegetable, cut into pieces and arrange on a serving plate.

❋ Carefully lift out the pork and cut into slices. Arrange in its original shape on top of the vegetable.

❋ Reduce the sauce further, if it is not yet thick and syrupy, or add a little extra water if it has become too concentrated. Spoon over the pork and serve.

Shanghai 上海

BOILED AND FRIED PORK LEG IN BROWN SAUCE

Boil-and-fry is a technique particularly suitable for the cooking of large joints of meat such as pork leg. It reduces the fat content while tenderizing the meat and enhancing the flavor.

In ancient times, the village people in the Shanghai area often cooked large fish or massive joints of meat for wedding banquets, funeral gatherings, and other celebrations.

1½ lb (750 g) boneless pork leg or butt
1½ teaspoons salt
1 tablespoon dark soy sauce
3 cups (24 oz) lard or vegetable oil
12 stalks Chinese kale (gai larn) or spinach
2 tablespoons light soy sauce
1½ tablespoons rice wine or dry sherry
1 teaspoon sugar
salt and pepper

Place the pork in a saucepan, cover with water and add the salt. Bring to boil, then reduce heat and simmer for about 30 minutes. Drain, then wipe the skin and meat as dry as possible with kitchen towels, piercing any bubbles in the skin, as these can expand and splatter during frying.

❋ Rub the pork with the dark soy sauce and let stand to dry for 1 hour.

❋ Heat the lard or vegetable oil in a wok, add the pork skin side down and deep-fry over moderate heat for about 3 minutes. Turn and cook the other side for 1-3 minutes, then lift out, drain and place in a clean casserole.

❋ Cover with cold water and set aside for 10 minutes, then add the remaining ingredients and simmer gently until the meat is very tender with a texture similar to bean curd.

Shanghai 上海

FRIED AND BRAISED SPARERIBS

Spareribs are an inexpensive ingredient, being quite bony with little meat. However, when cooked as in this recipe the result is lustrous with finger-licking succulence.

1½ lb (750 g) pork spareribs
¾ cup (3 oz) water chestnut powder or cornstarch
shrimp chips
oil for deep-frying

SEASONING

¾ cup (6 oz) Superior Stock (*see page 124*)
2 tablespoons tomato ketchup
2 tablespoons tomato juice
2 tablespoons rice vinegar
2 tablespoons sugar

Cut the ribs into short lengths and toss in the water chestnut powder or cornstarch to coat thickly. Shake off the excess.

❋ Heat the oil in a wok to moderately hot and deep-fry the shrimp chips until well expanded and crisp. Do not allow to color. Remove, drain well, then place around the edge of a serving dish and set aside.

❋ Place the ribs in the oil and deep-fry for about 6 minutes or until well colored, crisp on the surface and almost cooked through. Remove with a slotted spoon and set aside.

FRIED AND BRAISED SPARERIBS

SHREDDED PORK WITH SPECIAL SAUCE

※ Drain off the oil and add the pre-mixed seasoning ingredients to the wok. Bring to boil and boil for 2-3 minutes, then add the ribs, cover and braise for about 10 minutes or until the ribs are very tender and the sauce has reduced to a thick glaze on the meat.

※ Spoon into the center of the dish and serve.

Beijing 北京

MEATBALLS WITH SESAME SEEDS

1 lb (500 g) *unsmoked* bacon
½ cup (4 oz) water
2 tablespoons cornstarch
3 cups (24 oz) peanut oil
¾ cup (3 oz) white sesame seeds
1 cup (7 oz) sugar

Mince or grind the pork finely, adding first the water, then the cornstarch. The mixture should be very smooth.

※ Heat the peanut oil in a wok to the smoking point, then reduce the heat slightly.

※ Form the meat into small balls about the size of a walnut and drop into the oil. Fry in several batches for about 3 minutes or until cooked through and well colored on the surface. Lift out and drain well.

※ Spread the sesame seeds on a plate.

※ Pour the sugar into a clean wok, adding 2 tablespoons of the hot oil. Cook gently without stirring until it turns to a pale caramel color, then turn off the heat and quickly roll each meatball through the caramel to coat evenly. Roll in the sesame seeds and place on a lightly oiled serving plate.

Sichuan 四川

SHREDDED PORK WITH SPECIAL SAUCE

7 oz (220 g) lean pork, preferably fillet (tenderloin)
½ teaspoon salt
pinch of white pepper
1½ tablespoons cornstarch
1-2 pickled red chilies
2 slices fresh ginger
2 cloves garlic
2 green onions
2 tablespoons lard or oil for frying

SAUCE

3 tablespoons stock
1 tablespoon light soy sauce
2 teaspoons sugar
1 teaspoon brown vinegar
¾ teaspoon sesame oil
½ teaspoon cornstarch

Very thinly slice the pork across the grain, then cut into fine shreds and place in a dish. Add the salt, pepper and cornstarch, mix well and set aside.

※ Finely chop the chilies, ginger, garlic and green onions. Mix the sauce ingredients.

※ Heat the wok and stir-fry the pork shreds in the lard or oil until white. Push to one side of the pan and add the chopped chilies, ginger, garlic and green onions and stir-fry quickly, then mix in with the pork.

※ Add the sauce ingredients. Heat quickly over high heat, stirring into the pork, and serve.

MEATBALLS WITH SESAME SEEDS

STIR-FRIED PORK TENDERLOIN

FRIED MEAT-FILLED EGG ROLLS

Beijing 北京

STIR-FRIED PORK TENDERLOIN

12 oz (375 g) pork fillet (tenderloin)
3 tablespoons peanut oil
1 tablespoon finely chopped green onion
½ teaspoon finely chopped fresh ginger
1 tablespoon brown vinegar
2 teaspoons sugar

SEASONING

1 tablespoon rice wine or dry sherry
1 tablespoon dark soy sauce
1 tablespoon cornstarch
½ teaspoon salt
pinch of pepper

Cut the pork into thin slices and place in a dish with the pre-mixed seasoning ingredients, mix well and let stand for 20 minutes.

Heat the wok and add the peanut oil. Stir-fry the pork for about 2 minutes over high heat or until lightly colored and cooked through. Remove and set aside.

Add the green onions and ginger and stir-fry briefly, then add the vinegar and sugar and toss together for a few seconds. Return the meat and stir-fry together until the meat is well coated with the ingredients. Serve immediately.

Beijing 北京

FRIED MEAT-FILLED EGG ROLLS

10 oz (315 g) fatty pork, finely minced or ground
½ cup (2 oz) all purpose flour
4 eggs
2 tablespoons peanut oil
oil for deep-frying

SEASONING

1 tablespoon finely chopped green onion
1 teaspoon cornstarch
1 teaspoon sesame oil
½ teaspoon grated fresh ginger
½ teaspoon salt
pinch of white pepper

Mix the pork with the seasoning ingredients, squeezing the mixture through your fingers until it is smooth and sticky; set aside.

Add enough water to the flour to make a sticky paste.

Beat the eggs with 2 teaspoons of the peanut oil. Heat a wok or omelet pan over moderate heat and wipe out with a cloth dipped in the peanut oil. Pour in half of the egg batter and tilt

the pan so that the egg spreads out as much as possible and is very thin. Cook evenly, moving the pan constantly until the egg is lightly colored underneath, then cook the other side briefly. Cook the other omelet and leave them both on a work surface to cool.

Spread the flour paste over the omelets, then spread on a layer of the pork filling, leaving a border all around. Roll up, tucking the sides in securely. Heat the deep-frying oil to the smoking point, then reduce heat slightly. Cut the rolls into 2½-in (4-cm) lengths and deep-fry in several batches until golden. Lift out and drain well, then serve at once.

Beijing 北京

STIR-FRIED KIDNEYS

4 pork or lamb kidneys
2 tablespoons lard
1 teaspoon finely chopped fresh ginger
1 tablespoon sugar

SAUCE

1 tablespoon water or chicken stock
1 tablespoon rice wine or dry sherry
1 tablespoon dark soy sauce
1 tablespoon finely chopped green onion
1 teaspoon cornstarch
½ teaspoon salt

Soak the kidneys in cold water for 1 hour, then drain. Cut in half and remove the fatty core, then turn the cut sides down and score deeply with diagonal cuts.

Soak in cold water for 20 minutes, then drain very thoroughly and cut each kidney into several pieces.

Heat a wok and add the lard. Stir-fry the ginger briefly, then add the kidneys and stir-fry over high heat until just cooked through. They should remain pink inside but no blood should run out when pierced; do not overcook or they will toughen. Stir the sugar in and place on a serving plate.

Add the pre-mixed sauce ingredients to the wok and bring to boil. Simmer, stirring, until slightly thickened. Return the kidneys and toss in the sauce until thoroughly coated and the sauce is reduced to a glaze, then serve immediately.

Shanghai 上海

STEWED LARGE MEATBALLS

The Chinese call these meatballs "lion heads." Stewed large meat-balls have long been a traditional specialty in the Yangzhou area and are prepared principally with ground pork, although they may consist of a combination of meats and sometimes contain a delicious filling, such as crabmeat. The delicate colors of the dish – the light pink of the meatballs and the bright green of the tender cabbage – plus the rich aroma and flavor create a meal to delight the senses.

1¼ lb (750 g) lean pork (preferably fillet/tenderloin)
2½ tablespoons finely chopped green onion
1 teaspoon grated fresh ginger
1½ teaspoons salt
1 tablespoon rice wine or dry sherry
1-1½ lb (500-750 g) Chinese cabbage
lard or vegetable oil for frying
chicken stock or Superior Stock (*see page 124*)

Cut the pork into small pieces, then mince or grind it finely using two cleavers simultaneously or a food processor.

Mix in the green onion, ginger, salt and wine and work the meat with your fingers until smooth and sticky. Form into 3-4 large meatballs.

Wash the cabbage and cut lengthwise into quarters. Stir-fry it briefly in a wok in lard or vegetable oil, adding a generous pinch of salt.

Spread half of the cabbage across the bottom of a casserole and place the meatballs on top, then cover with the remaining cabbage.

Add enough boiling stock to just cover the meatballs. Cover the casserole tightly and simmer over low heat for about 1½ hours or until the meatballs are melt-in-the-mouth tender.

Serve in the casserole, pushing the vegetables to one side to expose the meatballs.

161

MANDARIN DICED KIDNEY

FRIED BEEF AND WATER SPINACH WITH SHRIMP PASTE

Sichuan 四川

MANDARIN DICED KIDNEY

8 oz (250 g) pork kidneys
1½ tablespoons cornstarch
2 cloves garlic
3 slices fresh ginger
2 green onions
2 dried red chilies
3 tablespoons lard or oil for frying
1 teaspoon ground Sichuan peppercorns (Fagara or Sansho)
1 teaspoon rice wine or dry sherry
large pinch of red chili powder or chili oil (optional)

SEASONING/SAUCE

½ cup (4 oz) chicken stock
2 tablespoons light soy sauce
2 teaspoons red vinegar
2 teaspoons sugar
2 teaspoons cornstarch
pinch of salt

Cut the kidneys in half horizontally, remove the skin and cut away the fatty inner section. Use a sharp knife to deeply score each piece in crosshatch fashion. Place in a dish and sprinkle on the cornstarch, mixed to a thin paste with water. Stir until the kidney pieces are evenly coated, then set aside.

❊ Finely chop the garlic, ginger, green onions and chilies.

❊ Heat the lard or oil in a wok to the smoking point. Stir-fry the chopped chilies and Sichuan peppercorns for 20-30 seconds, then add the kidneys and the garlic, ginger and onions and stir-fry together over high heat until the kidneys are partially cooked. Add the wine and chili powder, if used, reduce heat and continue cooking until the kidneys are tender. Then add the pre-mixed seasoning/sauce ingredients and simmer, stirring, until the sauce thickens; serve at once.

Guangzhou 广州

FRIED BEEF AND WATER SPINACH WITH SHRIMP PASTE

Water spinach is one of the main green vegetables available in Guangdong during the hot summer. It is cultivated on floating rafts made of reeds, with small holes through which the water spinach grows. The jade-like vegetable must be cooked with care. If underdone, it will be astringent; if overdone, yellow, dull and with little flavor.

6 oz (185 g) beef fillet (tenderloin)
8 oz (250 g) water spinach or young leaf spinach
1 green onion
2 cloves garlic
½ cup (4 oz) vegetable oil
salt
½ teaspoon fresh ginger
2 teaspoons shrimp paste
1 teaspoon rice wine or dry sherry
½ teaspoon cornstarch
3 tablespoons chicken stock
⅓ teaspoon sesame oil

SEASONING

1 tablespoon vegetable oil
1 tablespoon water
1 teaspoon dark soy sauce
1 teaspoon fish sauce or anchovy paste
1 teaspoon cornstarch
½ teaspoon baking soda

Very thinly slice the beef, cutting across the grain, then cut into narrow, short strips. Place in a dish and add the pre-mixed seasoning ingredients. Mix well and let stand for 20 minutes.

❊ Thoroughly wash the spinach and drain well. Chop the green onion into 1-in (2.5-cm) lengths. Finely chop the garlic.

❊ Heat the vegetable oil in a wok and stir-fry the spinach over high heat for about 2 minutes or until the leaves wilt and the stems soften but retain crispness. Add a sprinkling of salt, then use chopsticks to lift onto a serving plate.

❊ Reheat the wok, add the beef and stir-fry over very high heat until it changes color. Remove from the wok. Stir-fry the ginger, garlic and green onion until tender, then return the beef. Add the shrimp paste and wine and toss all the ingredients together until well mixed. Stir the cornstarch into the stock and pour over the beef, stirring until the sauce thickens.

❊ Arrange the beef on or near the vegetables, sprinkle with the sesame oil and serve.

Sichuan 四川

BOILED BEEF WITH CHILI

This is a traditional dish famed for its characteristically heavy, hot and spicy, yet tender and delicious flavor. It originated in the salt mining area of Sichuan, where people usually cooked beef by boiling it in a soup heavily seasoned with chili, bean paste and pepper. This old recipe was very popular for its heavy flavor, which banishes cold and whets the appetite. Over the years many improvements have been made to the dish and it is now a local specialty.

10 oz (315 g) beef steak (rump/sirloin/loin)
6-8 lettuce leaves
1 tablespoon chili oil
½ teaspoon fried Sichuan peppercorns (Fagara or Sansho) ground
1 teaspoon finely chopped garlic (optional)

SAUCE

2 tablespoons lard or oil for frying
6 dried chilies
1 teaspoon Sichuan peppercorns (Fagara or Sansho),
1 tablespoon fermented black beans, finely chopped
3 cloves garlic, finely chopped
3-4 slices fresh ginger, finely chopped
6-8 garlic chives or 3 green onions, chopped
1 tablespoon hot bean paste
½ cup (4 oz) water

Cut the meat across the grain into paper-thin slices and set aside. Rinse the lettuce and tear into small pieces.

To make the sauce, heat the lard or oil in a wok and fry the dried chilies and Sichuan peppercorns for about 30 seconds, then remove and chop them finely. Add the black beans to the wok and fry for about 30 seconds, then add the garlic, ginger, garlic chives or green onions and the bean paste and fry together until aromatic. Return the chilies and pepper, add the water and bring to boil, then set aside.

Heat a large saucepan of water to the boiling point. Add the beef and cook just long enough for the meat to change color, then drain well.

Add the meat to the wok with the sauce, reheat and stir-fry together until all the sauce has adhered to the meat slices, then stir in the lettuce.

Transfer to a serving plate and splash on the chili oil. Sprinkle on the ground Sichuan pepper and the chopped garlic, if used, and serve at once.

STEWED BEEF WITH TENDER GARLIC CHIVES

Sichuan 四川

STEWED BEEF WITH TENDER GARLIC CHIVES

1 lb (500 g) stewing/braising beef
2 tablespoons lard or vegetable oil
1 tablespoon soybean paste or mashed fermented black beans
3 cups (24 oz) beef stock
10 slices fresh ginger
2 green onions, halved
1 tablespoon soy flour or cornstarch

SEASONING

1 tablespoon rice wine or dry sherry
2 teaspoons sugar
1 teaspoon salt
½ teaspoon Sichuan peppercorns (Fagara or Sansho)

GARNISH

2 fresh red chilies
20 garlic chives or green onions
1 tablespoon oil for frying

Cut the beef into slices about ½ in (1 cm) thick, then into sticks about 3 x 1 in (8 x 2 cm).

Heat a wok over moderate heat and add the lard. Stir-fry the bean paste or mashed black beans for about 40 seconds or until fragrant, then add the beef and stir-fry over high heat until lightly colored and well sealed on all surfaces.

Pour in the stock, heat through briefly over high heat, then reduce the heat and simmer for about 1 hour, covered, until the beef is tender and the liquid is reduced to about 1 cup (8 oz).

Halfway through cooking, add the ginger and green onions and the pre-mixed seasoning ingredients.

Meanwhile prepare the garnish. Cut the chilies into long thin shreds, discarding the seeds. Use only about 2 in (5 cm) of the white end of the chives or green onions. Use a toothpick or bamboo skewer to make a hole in one end of each piece of onion and insert a sliver of chili to resemble the wick of a candle or firecracker. Heat another wok or pan and add the oil. Stir-fry the onions quickly and carefully. Sprinkle with 1 tablespoon water to help them soften, simmer until evaporated, then set the garnish aside.

Mix the soy flour with a little cold water and stir into the sauce with the beef. Simmer, stirring, until it thickens and the oil floats on the surface.

Spoon into the center of a serving plate and arrange the onions around the edge of the plate.

Shanghai 上海

STEAMED THREE SHREDDED MEATS

This much revered dish, incorporating pork, ham and chicken meat with cooked bamboo shoots, is a traditional food in Shanghai homes. Locals often serve it during festival times and family get-togethers. The three kinds of shredded meats packed closely together imply a reunion.

8 oz (250 g) ham
8 oz (250 g) lean pork
8 oz (250 g) chicken breast
2 dried black mushrooms, soaked for 25 minutes
6 oz (185 g) canned or cooked fresh bamboo shoots, thinly sliced
1 cup (8 oz) clear chicken stock

Place the ham, pork and chicken in a saucepan, cover with water, bring to boil, then simmer gently for 1 hour. Remove, drain and cut the meat into fine shreds.

Select one or two heatproof bowls large enough to contain all of the ingredients. Place a black mushroom, cap downwards, in the bottom of the bowl. Arrange the shredded meats and the bamboo shoots in the bowl and set on a rack in a wok or steamer with simmering water. Cover and steam for about 10 minutes or until the meat is compact.

Turn the bowl upside down into a serving dish and remove the bowl so that the meat retains its shape. Boil the stock up, pour over the meat and serve.

This is delicious as a main course or is enough for 12 guests as an appetizer.

STEAMED THREE SHREDDED MEATS

DEEP-FRIED BEEF ROLLS FILLED WITH QUAIL EGGS

Guangzhou 广州

DEEP-FRIED BEEF ROLLS FILLED WITH QUAIL EGGS

8 oz (250 g) lean beef steak
1 small carrot
2 teaspoons cornstarch
½ teaspoon baking soda
10 quail eggs, fresh or canned
oil for frying
¼ teaspoon powdered cloves (optional)

SEASONING

2 teaspoons light soy sauce
1 teaspoon rice wine or dry sherry
1 teaspoon sugar
½ teaspoon sesame oil
½ teaspoon salt
pinch of ground star anise
pinch of white pepper

Using two cleavers, one in each hand, mince the meat very finely, or process to a smooth pulp in a food processor. Grate the carrot finely and add to the beef with the cornstarch, baking soda and the seasoning ingredients. Mix with your fingers to a smooth paste. On a piece of waxed paper or thick plastic wrap spread the meat in a rectangle about 12 in (30 cm) long and 5 in (12 cm) wide.

※ Boil the fresh quail eggs for 5 minutes, place under cold running water to cool and remove the shells. Dry the eggs and arrange end to end along the center of the meat. Use the paper or plastic to lift the meat up around the eggs so that they are completely encased within a long sausage of meat. Pinch the ends together. Coat the roll thickly with cornstarch, brushing off the excess.

※ Heat about 1 in (2.5 cm) of oil in a wide skillet or large wok and fry the beef roll over moderate heat until well and evenly colored all over. Roll it gently in the pan, using two wide spatulas, to ensure it does not break during cooking. Lift out, drain and sprinkle with powdered cloves, if used. Slice to serve.

TWICE-COOKED BEEF

Beijing 北京

TWICE-COOKED BEEF

2 lb (1 kg) beef bottom round
3 tablespoons peanut oil
3 pieces star anise
2 pieces dried tangerine peel
3 green onions
6 slices fresh ginger
4 cloves garlic
2 teaspoons Sichuan peppercorns (Fagara or Sansho)
3 tablespoons rice wine or dry sherry
½ cup (4 oz) light soy sauce
3 tablespoons dark soy sauce
2 tablespoons brown bean sauce
1 tablespoon sugar
salt and pepper
2 teaspoons cornstarch
1 teaspoon sesame oil

Cut the beef into thick slices, then into square pieces. In a wok, heat the oil to the smoking point and fry the beef in several batches until well colored. Lift out and set aside.

※ Drain off most of the oil. Stir-fry the star anise, peel, whole onions, ginger, garlic and peppercorns for 2 minutes or until fragrant. Add the wine and soy sauces and simmer for 4 minutes. Discard the star anise, green onion, ginger and garlic, then add the beef slices, bean sauce and sugar and cover with water.

※ Bring to boil, then reduce heat to very low and simmer, covered, for about 3 hours or until the beef is very tender.

※ Season the sauce with salt and pepper and thicken with cornstarch mixed with cold water. Sprinkle with the sesame oil and serve at once.

DEEP-FRIED BEEF CROQUETTES

Beijing 北京

DEEP-FRIED BEEF CROQUETTES

This dish is also called "Tien Dan Regains Chi," a name which can be traced back to 279 BC. Tien Dan, the great general of the Kingdom of Chi, was suffering from the onslaught of the warring Kingdom of Yen, which had captured some seventy Chi cities. In desperation he devised a remarkable plan.

His men gathered together a thousand cows, tied swords and knives to their horns and hay soaked with oil to their tails. In the dead of night they set fire to the hay and sent the cows charging into the enemy camp, followed by five thousand soldiers.

Victory was theirs, the cities were recovered and great honors were bestowed on Tien Dan.

The red beef fillet in this dish represents the fire-cows of Tien Dan, hence its name.

12 oz (375 g) beef fillet
4 water chestnuts, finely shredded
5 oz (155 g) ham, finely shredded
1 stem Chinese kale (gai larn) or spinach, shredded
1 tablespoon rice wine or dry sherry
1 teaspoon salt
12 oz (375 g) chicken meat
½ egg
1 tablespoon cornstarch
pinch of salt
deep-fried dried vegetable leaves or fresh sprigs
   of cilantro (garnish)

COATING

½ cup (2 oz) all purpose flour
1 egg, beaten
1 cup (4 oz) dry breadcrumbs
oil for deep-frying

Cut the beef into long, thin slices, then beat gently with the side of a cleaver to flatten.

⁂ Season the shredded ingredients with the rice wine and salt.

⁂ Mince or grind the chicken meat finely and mix with the egg and cornstarch, adding a pinch of salt.

⁂ Place a few strands of shredded ingredients in the center of each strip of beef and roll up into cylinders. Cover each roll with a thin coating of chicken paste, then dust with flour, dip into beaten egg and coat with breadcrumbs.

⁂ Heat the oil in a large wok and deep-fry the croquettes in batches until cooked through and golden brown. Lift out and drain well.

⁂ Arrange the croquettes on a bed of deep-fried vegetable leaves or surround them with sprigs of fresh cilantro and serve at once.

KASAYA BEEF

Beijing 北京

KASAYA BEEF

China raises a great number of cattle of many varieties, including Mongolian cattle and the pien niu – the offspring of a bull and a female yak. The pien niu can withstand hardship better than cattle; it produces more milk than a yak and is easy to tame.

Beef used in Beijing cooking usually comes from Inner Mongolia; it is rich and tender with a delicious aroma. It is said to strengthen bones and muscles and to reduce water retention.

In this recipe the fillet is pounded to a paste and spread between two layers of omelet before being crisp-fried.

8 oz (250 g) beef fillet (tenderloin)
2 egg whites, lightly beaten
2 tablespoons cornstarch
2 teaspoons rice wine or dry sherry
2 tablespoons finely chopped green onion
1 teaspoon finely grated fresh ginger
2 cloves garlic, finely chopped
¾ teaspoon salt
2 eggs
2½ cups (20 oz) peanut oil
½ teaspoon sesame oil
3 tablespoons cornstarch

Very finely mince or grind the beef, removing any sinews. Add the beaten egg white, cornstarch and rice wine and mix well, then add the green onion, ginger, garlic and salt and beat with a wooden spoon until the mixture is very smooth and slightly sticky.

⁂ Beat the eggs well. Heat a wok and rub with a piece of paper towel dipped in sesame and peanut oil. Pour in half of the egg mixture and tilt the pan until it spreads into a thin, wide sheet about 13 in (33 cm) in diameter. When firm and lightly colored on the underside, turn and lightly cook the other side. Repeat with the remaining egg.

⁂ Lay out one omelet and spread the beef paste over it. Cover with the other omelet, pressing it firmly into place. Cut into diamond shapes and dip the cut edges into the cornstarch. Heat the peanut oil and add the sesame oil. Fry the "sandwiches" in batches over moderate heat until crisp and golden. Make sure that the meat filling is cooked through before removing from the oil. Drain well and stack on a serving plate. Serve at once.

BEEF SLICES STIR-FRIED IN OYSTER SAUCE

STIR-FRIED FILLET OF LAMB

Guangzhou 广州

BEEF SLICES STIR-FRIED IN OYSTER SAUCE

8 oz (250 g) beef fillet (tenderloin)
1 egg white, well beaten
3 tablespoons oil for frying
1 green onion, chopped
2 slices fresh ginger, shredded
2 teaspoons cornstarch
2 tablespoons water

SEASONING

2 tablespoons oyster sauce
2 tablespoons beef stock
1 tablespoon rice wine or dry sherry
1 tablespoon light soy sauce
1 teaspoon mushroom soy sauce
1 teaspoon sugar
pinch each of salt and white pepper

Cut the beef across the grain into very thin slices, then cut into small squares. Place in a dish with the egg white and mix well. Add the pre-mixed seasoning ingredients and let marinate for 20 minutes.

⁂Drain the beef, reserving the marinade. Heat a wok with the oil and stir-fry the beef over high heat until it changes color. Remove immediately.

⁂Add the green onion and ginger to the wok and stir-fry for 45 seconds, then return the beef, the marinade ingredients and the cornstarch mixed with water. Stir over very high heat until thickened, then serve at once.

Beijing 北京

STIR-FRIED FILLET OF LAMB

6 oz (185 g) lamb fillet (tenderloin)
1 egg white
1½ tablespoons cornstarch
½ teaspoon salt
pinch of pepper
2 oz (60 g) canned bamboo shoots, drained
1 2-in (5-cm) piece cucumber
1 small red bell pepper
2 green onions
3 slices fresh ginger
2½ cups (20 oz) peanut oil
2 teaspoons rice wine or dry sherry

Use a sharp knife to cut across the fillet into thin slices. Stack the slices together and cut into narrow shreds. Place in a dish.

⁂Lightly beat the egg white, adding the cornstarch, salt and pepper, and pour over the lamb. Mix well and let stand for 20 minutes.

⁂Shred the bamboo shoots, the skin and flesh of the cucumber, the pepper, onions and ginger.

⁂Heat the oil in a wok and deep-fry the lamb strips for 1½ minutes over moderate heat, using chopsticks to separate the shreds. Lift out and drain well.

⁂Pour off all but 2 tablespoons of the oil and stir-fry the bamboo shoots, cucumber and pepper for 2 minutes, then add the onions and ginger and stir-fry together briefly.

⁂Return the lamb and toss the ingredients together over very high heat. Add the rice wine and toss again, then serve.

Beijing 北京

DEEP-FRIED LAMB SLICES

9 oz (280 g) lamb fillet (tenderloin)
¾ cup (3 oz) cornstarch
oil for deep-frying

SAUCE

½ cup (4 oz) water
2 tablespoons light soy sauce
2 teaspoons sugar
1½ teaspoons rice wine or dry sherry
1½ teaspoons vinegar
1 teaspoon ginger juice
1 teaspoon cornstarch

Slice the lamb very thinly across the grain; cut into thin strips.

⁂Mix the cornstarch with water to a very thin batter.

⁂Heat a wok with the oil to the smoking point. Coat the meat with the batter and deep-fry in several batches, stirring with chopsticks to separate the strips. The meat will take about 1 minute to be cooked through and well colored on the surface. Remove and drain well.

⁂In another wok bring the pre-mixed sauce ingredients to boil, add the meat slices and simmer, stirring carefully, until the sauce glazes the meat. Spoon onto a serving plate and serve at once.

DEEP-FRIED LAMB SLICES

Beijing 北京

IT'S LIKE HONEY!

A story is told about a special mutton dish cooked for the Empress Dowager Cixi. Being very pleased with it, she asked the chef for the name of the dish. He did not dare to venture an answer and instead asked her to name it. She said casually, "It's like honey!" and that has been the name of this dish ever since.

The lamb pieces in this recipe are brownish-red in color, and very tender. The dish really tastes like honey, with a slightly sour aftertaste.

7 oz (220 g) lamb fillet
1 tablespoon hoisin sauce
2 tablespoons cornstarch
3 tablespoons peanut or other oil for frying
⅓ teaspoon sesame oil

SEASONING
1 tablespoon light soy sauce
2 teaspoons sugar
1 teaspoon brown vinegar
1 teaspoon rice wine or dry sherry
1 teaspoon ginger juice
½ teaspoon cornstarch
¼ teaspoon molasses

Very thinly slice the lamb across the grain. Place in a dish and add the hoisin sauce, mixing well, then sprinkle with the cornstarch and mix until coated evenly.
Mix the seasoning ingredients together and set aside.
Heat the oil in a wok and stir-fry the lamb over moderate heat until reddish-brown and just cooked, stirring constantly with chopsticks to separate the slices. Remove and drain well.
Pour off most of the oil and add the seasoning ingredients. Bring to boil and add the sesame oil. Return the lamb and stir quickly over high heat until the seasoning ingredients coat the lamb. Serve at once.

MONGOLIAN FIRE POT

Beijing 北京

MONGOLIAN FIRE POT

The traditional Mongolian Fire Pot, or Hot Pot as it is also known, is positioned in the center of a large round table over a charcoal fire. The pot is filled with simmering stock and everybody cooks his own meal by using wooden chopsticks or small wire baskets to suspend pieces of meat and vegetables in the hot stock. Plates with paper-thin slices of lamb, bean thread vermicelli and different sorts of vegetables are arranged around the fire pot. The meat and other cooked ingredients are dipped into one or more of the seasonings, served separately in small bowls on the table. At the end of the meal all the remaining vegetables and side dishes are added to the stock and the banquet is finished off with bowls of the resulting rich soup.

10 cups (2½ l) chicken stock
2 tablespoons dried shrimp
6 dried black mushrooms, soaked for 25 minutes
2 lb (1 kg) lean lamb loin
1 lb (500 g) Chinese cabbage
3 oz (90 g) dry bean thread vermicelli
3 oz (90 g) canned pickled garlic
large bunch cilantro

SEASONINGS/DIPS

3 tablespoons sesame paste (tahini)
½ cup (4 oz) rice wine or dry sherry
⅓ cup (4 oz) preserved bean curd
2 tablespoons chili oil
½ cup (4 oz) dark soy sauce
2 tablespoons shrimp paste
½ cup (4 oz) light soy sauce

Fill the fire pot or other vessel suitable for tabletop cooking with the stock and add the dried shrimp. Drain the mushrooms, remove the stems, dice the caps and add to the stock.
❧ Slice the lamb very thinly (easier if meat is partially frozen) and arrange on plates. Rinse the cabbage, cut into squares and place in a dish. Pour boiling water over the vermicelli to soften, drain and arrange on a plate. Place the garlic and cilantro on plates. Arrange all the plates around the fire pot on the dining table. Serve at least 2 small bowls of each seasoning/dip and place these on the table with spoons.
❧ Give each guest one bowl to eat from, one or two small bowls for mixing the sauce, and a pair of wooden chopsticks.

LAMB TENDERLOIN WITH CILANTRO

Beijing 北京

LAMB TENDERLOIN WITH CILANTRO

12 oz (375 g) lamb fillet (tenderloin)
1 tablespoon rendered chicken fat
4 oz (125 g) broccoli or other green vegetable
2 dried black mushrooms, soaked for 25 minutes
4 stalks cilantro
1 green onion
2 teaspoons rice wine or dry sherry
1 tablespoon dark soy sauce
½ teaspoon salt

SEASONING

2 teaspoons sugar
2 teaspoons cornstarch
1 teaspoon sesame oil

Cut the lamb into thin slices, then into strips; rinse with cold water. Drain and dry thoroughly. Place in a dish and add the pre-mixed seasoning ingredients, mix well and leave for 15 minutes.

Heat the chicken fat in a wok and stir-fry the shredded lamb until just cooked, then remove and set aside.

Trim and slice the broccoli. Drain the mushrooms, remove the stems and shred the caps. Rinse the green onion, dry well and cut into 2-in (5-cm) lengths. Trim and chop the cilantro.

Add the vegetables to the wok and stir-fry together until the broccoli is tender, then add the wine, soy sauce and salt, return the meat and toss together over high heat for 1 minute. Add the cilantro and serve immediately.

Beijing 北京

ROAST LAMB ON SKEWERS

Muslims along the northwestern borders of China have a high regard for this delicious dish of cubed, seasoned lamb, tossed in sesame seed and roasted on skewers over charcoal.

The dish was introduced into Beijing some twenty years ago and now a number of restaurants include it in their menu.

2 lb (1 kg) lamb fillet (tenderloin)*
3 eggs
¾ cup (3 oz) all purpose flour
¾ cup (4 oz) finely minced green onions
1 tablespoon salt
1½ teaspoons pepper
1½ teaspoons ground Sichuan peppercorns (Fagara or Sansho)
2 large tomatoes, finely chopped, seeds discarded
3 tablespoons white sesame seeds

ROAST LAMB ON SKEWERS

Cut all the white sinews and membrane off the meat, then cut the meat into small, uniform cubes.

Beat the eggs lightly and mix with the remaining ingredients except the sesame seeds. Pour the marinade over the meat cubes and stir in evenly. Cover with plastic wrap and let stand for at least 3 hours.

Toss the meat cubes in sesame seed and thread onto lightly oiled metal skewers. Take six or seven pieces of meat for each skewer.

For best results roast over a charcoal burner with gently glowing coals. Turn skewers once to ensure even cooking. When the meat turns reddish-brown, after 3-4 minutes, it is done. Tender lamb should be crisp and browned on the surface but still pink inside, as it dries out with prolonged cooking.

Serve on the skewers.

Less expensive cuts, such as boneless leg meat, can be used, but the result will be a tougher-textured meat with a stronger flavor.

Beijing 北京

HAND-GRASPED LAMB

Hand-grasped lamb is a traditional dish of the nomadic desert dwellers of northwestern China. At the end of a journey they prepare a fire, slaughter a lamb, cook it simply and enjoy the hearty meal. The name of this dish comes from their practice of grasping the rib bones while eating the meat.

4 lb (2 kg) lamb ribs (approximately 20 ribs)
1 green onion, finely chopped
3 fresh red chilies, finely chopped
1 tablespoon grated fresh ginger
2 tablespoons finely chopped fresh cilantro

SEASONING

2 tablespoons rice wine or dry sherry
1 fresh red chili, sliced
2 green onions, roughly chopped
4 slices fresh ginger
2 star anise
2 cloves garlic, crushed
1 2-in (5-cm) stick cinnamon
1 teaspoon salt

Cut the meat into sections of two ribs each, then trim away the meat and fat at the end of the bones.

Place the ribs in a large saucepan and cover with water. Add the seasoning ingredients and bring to boil. Cover and simmer gently for about 1½ hours or until the meat is very tender. Let cool in the stock, then drain well.

Arrange on a serving plate. Serve with small dishes of raw green onion, chili, ginger and cilantro.

BARBECUED MUTTON

Beijing 北京

BARBECUED MUTTON

When night falls on the northern seafront of China, all is peaceful and quiet except for the brightly lit small restaurants along the shore, filled with the laughter of happy diners. The aroma of barbecued mutton fills the air.

The meat chosen for this traditional dish comes from the hind leg of a certain type of sheep. The crescent-shaped knife used to slice the meat and even the grid on which the mutton is cooked are especially made for this purpose. In the past even a special pose was adopted as one cooked and feasted on the barbecued meat. With one foot on the ground and the other on top of a stool, the cooking, chatting and feasting might have brought to mind stories handed down by nomadic ancestors.

The following recipe shows an improved version of the traditional dish, consisting of richly marinated shreds of mutton, quickly barbecued with shredded leeks. It is stuffed into sesame-covered pocket bread and eaten sandwich-style, often with pickled garlic.

1 lb (500 g) lean lamb
3 tablespoons light soy sauce
1½ tablespoons rice wine or dry sherry
2 teaspoons ginger juice
1½ tablespoons sugar
2 teaspoons sesame oil
pinch of salt
2 leeks
cilantro
pickled garlic

Cut the meat across the grain into very thin slices, then stack several slices together and cut into shreds. Place in a dish and add the soy sauce, wine, ginger juice, sugar, sesame oil and salt and mix well. Let stand for at least 30 minutes.

⚹ Rinse the leeks thoroughly, cut into 2-in (5-cm) lengths and shred lengthwise.

⚹ Heat a barbecue grill over a charcoal fire. Rub with oil and spread the leeks over it. Place the meat in a single layer on top of the leeks, then use a pair of long-handled chopsticks to turn the leeks and meat over and over until the leeks are soft and the meat is cooked through and tender.

⚹ Stuff the pocket bread with the meat and cilantro leaves; serve the pickled garlic separately.

SESAME POCKET BREAD

3 tablespoons vegetable oil
3½ cups (14 oz) all purpose flour
¾ cup (6 oz) boiling water
3 tablespoons cold water
2 teaspoons salt
2-3 tablespoons white sesame seeds
oil for frying

Heat the vegetable oil in a wok, add ½ cup (2 oz) flour and cook over low heat until the mixture is smooth and golden, stirring constantly. Set aside to cool.

⚹ Pour the remaining flour into a bowl, reserving 1 tablespoon. Pour in the boiling water and stir quickly, using the handle of a wooden spoon, to form a smooth dough, adding the cold water to make it soft and pliable. Knead for about 7 minutes on a lightly oiled board. Roll out into a long sausage shape and divide into 10-12 pieces. Cover with a damp cloth.

⚹ Roll each piece out separately into a square-shaped cake about 5 in (12 cm) wide. Spread with a coating of the flour and oil dough and sprinkle with salt and some of the reserved flour. Fold in two sides to overlap in the center, seal the edges by pinching the two ends, then fold the other two sides in to just overlap in the center. Roll in the direction of the folds into a rectangular shape. Dip the smooth side into sesame seeds, pressing lightly.

⚹ Bake on an oiled and floured baking sheet in a preheated 425°F (220°C) oven or fry on both sides until puffed and golden. Cut in half to fill.

SICHUAN RABBIT CAKE

Sichuan 四川

SICHUAN RABBIT CAKE

Confucius taught the Chinese to be meticulous about fine food and in particular ground meat. Food should be savored rather than devoured: it is the quality, not the quantity, of the food that counts. As for ground meat, the finer the grind the better, as it should be easily digested and easily absorbed.

In this dish the rabbit meat is ground, seasoned, steamed into cakes and then deep-fried until crisp. A rich Sichuan sauce containing minced ginger, green onion and garlic is poured over before serving. The meat is tender and salty, sweet, sour and peppery hot.

1 1¼-1½-lb (625-750-g) rabbit
2 egg whites, well beaten
½ cup (4 oz) water
1½ tablespoons cornstarch
¾ teaspoon salt
cornstarch
oil for deep-frying

SAUCE

2 pickled red chilies
3 cloves garlic
3 green onions
3 slices fresh ginger
½ cup (4 oz) chicken or rabbit stock
1½ tablespoons brown vinegar
1 tablespoon sugar
1 tablespoon light soy sauce
1½ teaspoons cornstarch
pinch each of salt and Sichuan pepper (Fagara or Sansho)

Remove the rabbit meat from the bones and mince or grind very finely. Add the egg whites, water, cornstarch and salt and mix thoroughly until the paste is smooth, picking out all the fine sinews. Spread the mixture in a lightly oiled heatproof dish and place on a rack in a wok or steamer, cover and steam for about 14 minutes or until the cake is firm. Remove and let cool. Cut into thick slices about 2 in (5 cm) long and coat thickly with cornstarch.

For the sauce, finely mince or grind the chilies, garlic, green onions and ginger. Mix the remaining sauce ingredients together and set aside.

Heat the oil in a wok to the smoking point and deep-fry the slices of rabbit cake, several at a time, until golden brown; drain well.

In a clean wok sauté the chilies, garlic, green onions and ginger in a little oil until fragrant. Add the rabbit cake, mix in evenly, then pour in the other pre-mixed sauce ingredients and bring to boil. Stir carefully and serve.

STUFFED OXTAIL

Beijing 北京

STUFFED OXTAIL

Oxtail meat is different from the meat of all other parts of the ox. It is bright red, finely textured and contains a sticky substance which is especially pleasing to some palates. In this recipe the star-shaped central bone is removed and the cavity is filled with a mixture of minced fish and chicken.

1 2-lb (1-kg) oxtail
5 cups (1¼ l) beef stock
2 green onions
2 slices fresh ginger
1 teaspoon salt
1 tablespoon rice wine or dry sherry

STUFFING

4 oz (125 g) white fish
4 oz (125 g) chicken meat
1 egg white
2 teaspoons rice wine or dry sherry
½ teaspoon salt

SAUCE

2 green onions, chopped
2 slices fresh ginger, chopped
2 tablespoons lard or oil for frying
¾ cup (6 oz) chicken or beef stock
2 teaspoons rice wine or dry sherry
1 tablespoon cornstarch

Have the butcher cut the oxtail through between the joints. Place the meat in a large saucepan and add the stock, onions, ginger, salt and rice wine. Cover and bring to boil. Skim off the froth, then reduce the heat and simmer gently for about 2 hours.

Allow to cool slightly, then remove the meat from the stock and drain well. Use a knife with a narrow sharp blade to remove the central bone from each piece of meat.

Finely mince or grind the fish and chicken together, adding the egg white, rice wine and salt. Knead to a smooth paste, then stuff into the holes in the pieces of oxtail. Arrange them on a lightly oiled heatproof plate and set on a rack in a wok or steamer. Cover and steam for about 15 minutes or until the filling is cooked through.

For the sauce, stir-fry the green onions and ginger in the lard or oil until softened, then add the remaining sauce ingredients and bring to boil, stirring constantly.

Stir the liquid from the dish in which the oxtail was steamed into the sauce. Pour sauce over the meat and serve.

Shanghai 上海

COLD DISHES

On the lower reaches of the Yangtze River there is a shop that specializes in selling cold dishes and game. It is said that when this shop was over a hundred years old, business was slack because of poor management.

One day a beggar came into the shop and asked to stay overnight. Seeing that he was tired and hungry, the owner gave him a meal. During the night the beggar spread out his mat to sleep, and before leaving the next morning the beggar left his mat in grateful repayment. The shop owner thought it useless and burnt it in his cooking fire. But the pork cooked over the fire that day was delicious, and business soon picked up. The beggar was said to have been an incarnation of the deity Lu Dongbing, and as the story spread, the owner changed the shop's name to Lu Gaojian to honor the god, selling pork stewed in soy sauce in the spring, goose pickled in grain in the summer, duck in autumn, and mutton, roast fish, roast eggs, duck stewed in soy sauce, prawns, pigs' trotters, game and more in the winter.

COLD DISHES ON A SINGLE PLATE

Cold, cooked food is often served as the first course at a dinner, and cold dishes in Shanghai have undergone several stages of development. A hundred years ago, each food was served on a separate plate. At a banquet, there would be dried and fresh fruit, cold and hot plates, beverages and so on. Even at the simplest dinner there were at least four cold dishes, and usually there were six or eight.

The food was finely cut and served neatly on plates. For instance, ham was cut into thin slices of equal size and thickness. Pai ham was cut into squares and Qiao ham was cut into thin pieces and placed on a plate in the shape of an arched bridge.

ASSORTED COLD DISHES OF TWO OR THREE INGREDIENTS

Forty or fifty years ago, cold dishes developed into assortments. Usually one assorted dish was made up of two or three ingredients, and four to six such dishes were served at dinner. There were also assorted cold dishes of five or six ingredients, but these were only served at informal dinners.

Assorted cold dishes vary according to their ingredients, shapes, colors and cuisines. Particular care is taken in selecting and arranging the ingredients so as to combine the colors well.

LARGE ASSORTED COLD PLATTERS

About thirty years ago large assorted cold dishes became popular. A large round or oval plate would contain ten or twelve ingredients. All were carefully prepared, boned and well presented. Preparation involved skill in slicing, matching colors and artful arrangement.

The photograph below shows a typical assorted cold platter of beautifully arranged cold cooked meat including ham, beef, chicken, luncheon meat, vegetarian "chicken" and bamboo shoots, with poached prawns and shredded marinated cabbage in the center.

Beijing 北京

Fried Red and White Meats

This is a traditional Shanxi specialty found on the menus of many of the restaurants in northern China. There are two kinds of meat in this dish: white chicken meat and red pork fillet. They complement each other and are both tender. Black wood ear fungus and green vegetable strips give additional color.

RED MEAT

8 oz (250 g) pork fillet
½ egg, well beaten
3 tablespoons cornstarch
½ cup (4 oz) peanut oil
1 tablespoon brown vinegar
1 green onion, sliced
2 cloves garlic, sliced
3 pieces dried wood ear fungus, soaked for 20 minutes
1 stalk Chinese kale (gai larn) or spinach, sliced diagonally

SAUCE

2 teaspoons rice wine or dry sherry
2 teaspoons dark soy sauce
½ cup (4 oz) chicken stock
large pinch of five-spice powder

WHITE MEAT

8 oz (250 g) chicken breast meat
1 egg white, well beaten
3 tablespoons cornstarch
2 tablespoons lard
½ cup (4 oz) chicken stock
¾ teaspoon salt
1 tablespoon rice wine or dry sherry
1 green onion, sliced
3-4 slices fresh ginger, shredded
3-4 slices cucumber, seeds removed
1 tablespoon rendered chicken fat, melted

Slice the pork fillet thinly, then cut into smaller pieces. Place in a dish and add the egg and cornstarch, coating the pork evenly.
🎇 Heat the peanut oil in a wok and fry the pork until cooked through, stirring constantly to separate the slices. Remove and set aside.
🎇 Add the vinegar, green onion, garlic, drained fungus and vegetable slices and stir-fry for 2 minutes, then return the pork and stir-fry briefly before adding the pre-mixed sauce ingredients. Cook, stirring, until the sauce coats the ingredients, then spoon onto one side of a serving dish and keep warm.
🎇 Slice the chicken and place in a dish with the egg white and cornstarch, mixing until each piece is well coated.
🎇 Heat a wok and add the lard. Stir-fry the chicken over high heat, adding the chicken stock, salt and rice wine. Then add the green onion, ginger and cucumber and simmer gently until the chicken is tender and the sauce is reduced to a glaze.
🎇 Arrange beside the pork on the plate and serve.

THE WILD RUSH OF THE DADU RIVER, WESTERN SICHUAN

LEO MEIER

四川
Sichuan

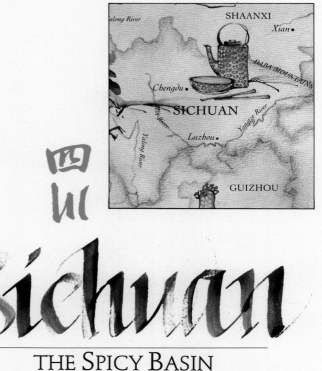

Sichuan

THE SPICY BASIN

IN THE geographical heartland of China is the huge natural bowl of Sichuan. Surrounded by range after range of mountains and slashed by the gathering flood of the Yangtze, the plains of the Red Basin are one of the most fertile areas in all China. Into these lowlands the Yangtze comes bursting with the ice-melt from the high ranges of remote Qinghai. When it leaves the red earth of Sichuan to carve its way through the Daba mountains to the east China plains, the Yangtze is mightier still — swollen by the waters of four substantial tributaries. These four rivers, the Min, Jialing, Yalong and To, give the province its name: Sichuan means Four Streams. They also give the area much of the agricultural muscle that has helped shape its gastronomic heritage and which today feeds a hundred million people with one of the best balanced and most spectacular cuisines on earth.

Three centuries before Christianity began, and sixteen centuries before Sichuan became a province of China, the flow of the mighty Min river was harnessed to water the thirsty land. A huge barrage built by human might diverted the river away from its natural channel into the surrounding plains. The flow was halved again and again, until countless irrigation streams trickled through the fields covering the plains on which the present provincial capital of Chengdu now stands. From these fields peasants harvested rich crops. They still do, and their produce gives the province its proud and spicy culinary legacy, which in recent years has swept the dinner tables of the world.

Sichuan cuisine today is a happy medley of many traditions and influences. The tangy tastes of India are blended into Sichuan cooking. Travelers brought Buddhism into the province more than two thousand years ago. The traders and missionaries carried Indian spices, herbs and cooking techniques with them as well as Buddhist teachings, and the strong vegetarian legacy is still very much alive in such family dishes as peppery hot bean curd and Sichuan pickled vegetables — items which sometimes take pride of place at a meatless table.

A WARM WELCOME FROM TIBETAN VILLAGERS IN WESTERN SICHUAN

LEO MEIER

AT SHIMIAN VILLAGE MARKET, SICHUAN PROVINCE

HARALD SUND

GREEN ONIONS, AN ESSENTIAL INGREDIENT OF CHINESE COOKING

The provincial cooking also has links with the cuisines of Indochina to the south. The Thai people trace their beginnings back through the mists of time to the shrouded mountains that surround the Sichuan basin, and many aspects of the cooking of Thailand bear a close similarity to Sichuan cooking. Thai-speaking tribes still live in the mountains, as do Miao, Li and other hill peoples whose racial relatives are scattered over the highlands of Vietnam, Laos and Kampuchea.

Vegetarian dishes flourish in Sichuan in staggering variety. For two thousand years Buddhist customs dictated a meatless diet for a large minority of the population, and imaginative chefs created an exhaustive repertoire of dishes from the abundant produce of the land. As the huge population grew, grazing space for animals dwindled as every available piece of land went under the plow. The animal that pulled the plow, the faithful, plodding water buffalo, the eternal tractor of China, was more often than not the only source of meat.

Many vegetarian dishes are garnished with the memorable and delicious, but wrongly named, Fish Flavored Sauce. This splendid example of culinary ingenuity tastes like fish, but its unforgettable flavor comes from a careful mixing of vinegar, garlic, ginger, green onions and hot bean paste. There is an old saying in Sichuan that a cook could pour the searingly spicy Fish Flavored Sauce over rocks washed up on the banks of the Min River and hungry diners would devour them with enthusiasm.

LEO MEIER

Another old saying concerns the seven flavors used in the cooking of provincial specialties. This is the first lesson given to a novice cook and it stays with him throughout his career: *sweet* (tien) comes from honey or sugar; *sour* (suan) from vinegar; *salty* (tien) from salt or soy; *fragrant* (xiang) from garlic and ginger; *bitter* (ku) from green onions or leeks; *nutty* (ma) from sesame seeds or oil; and, most importantly for Sichuan, *hot* (la) from the red chili.

Beans and bean curd, together with flavorful ingredients like green onions, garlic, peppercorns and ginger, combine with sesame oil, vinegar and the ubiquitous chili to form memorable dishes. To these are added carefully tended crops from the deep rich soil, the products of the wild mountains and steep valleys that make up ninety per cent of the 210,000 square miles (540,000 square kilometers) of the province.

In these mountains, covered in semitropical forests rising to cool growths of pine, are gathered some of the most highly praised mushrooms and fungi in China. Here, too, in magnificent towering stands, grow the imposing bamboos for which Sichuan is famous. The bamboo provides a delicacy not only for human gourmets but also for the nation's most famous animal, the giant panda. The bamboo forests are home and refuge for these bulky black and white animals, and the people of Sichuan are as proud of the pandas as they are of their distinctive cuisine. The animals are totally protected, and on cold winter nights often venture down from their mountain strongholds to seek shelter, which is given willingly in highland farmyards. Peasants in the mountains go to the aid of the pandas during periods of drought or flood when their delicate staple diet is threatened. Like the human inhabitants of Sichuan, the pandas are connoisseurs of the food of the province, and their

TASTY AND COLORFUL SPICES ADD FLAVOR TO REGIONAL DISHES   LEO MEIER

NOMADIC TIBETAN SHEPHERDS IN THE GRASSLANDS OF NORTHERN SICHUAN

LEO MEIER

preferred diet is fresh bamboo shoots which grow in plenty only in their remote and misty mountains. When the supply is threatened, local farmers carry loads of bamboo on their backs up steep tracks to feed the animals that are the symbol of Sichuan.

Although Chengdu is 1,800 miles (2,900 kilometers) up the Yangtze from the East China Sea, fish figures prominently in the diet. Until railways were forged through the mountains earlier this century, the great waterway provided the only reliable form of communication with the outside world. Today the waters of the Yangtze yield a good catch, but a good deal of the fish, freshwater crabs, eels and such consumed in the province are raised for the wok in fishponds, canals and irrigation ditches. A bonus of plump frogs, juicy turtles and tender snakes is also harvested by farmers going to their fields and children tending their ·flocks of wandering ducks. But despite its location, saltwater fish also appear on Sichuan menus, and for many hundreds of years junks loaded with dried or salted fish and seaweed have been towed by armies of toiling coolies through the narrow Yangtze gorges.

If the cuisine of Sichuan Province is built on a solid foundation of red-hot, mouth-pursing chilies, then that tradition is even more apparent over the border in neighboring Hunan. This landlocked province has a hot, humid summer and a winter that brings bracing chills. To open the pores and keep cool in the summer and to heat the blood in the cold months are two reasons that Hunan people give for flavoring so many dishes with chilies. As in Sichuan, there is an awesome variety of chilies and peppers. They range from the familiar, harmless large green bell pepper to the tiny red pepper known as the delayed action bomb. Why the name? Any innocent visitor will be able to tell you. Just ask the question five minutes after he has eaten one and, if he can splutter out an answer while trying to quaff bucket after bucket of cold water, he will explain that the peppers need a little while to take effect. When the fire is lit, however, it is hard to put out – perhaps one reason why the people of Sichuan and Hunan are also known for their ample consumption of prime beers to wash down the hearty, spiced meals.

Not all Sichuan food is hot, either in temperature or in flavor. Especially in summer, a meal will start with a selection of cold dishes or a platter holding a selection of cold meats. And the famed peppercorn of the province, used in moderation, tends to be tasty rather than hot. But let the visitor beware of the small scarlet peppers that are used as the raw ingredient of pungent red oil and to add the fire to fermented hot bean paste. When they grow, and they are harvested on every patch of earth in Sichuan, the chilies lift themselves upright on the branches. That is why they are called "reach for the sun" chilies – belief has it that they are striving to get closer to the warmth of the sun to take in more of its fire.

CARD PLAYERS IN A TRADITIONAL TEAHOUSE

HARALD SUND

THE TIBETAN VILLAGE OF ANLANG, SICHUAN PROVINCE

HARALD SUND

TIBETAN MOUNTAIN VILLAGERS

LEO MEIER

(following page) TIBETAN HOUSES CLIMB
THE QIONGLAISHAN MOUNTAINS, WESTERN SICHUAN

LEO MEIER

糧食豆品

Grains & Curd

糧食豆品

Grains & Curd

糧食豆品

NORTH of the Yangtze, wheat; south of the river, rice; all over China, beancurd. Like most schoolboy maxims, this one is too simplified to be completely true, but it is basically correct. While one of the seven thousand varieties of long-grained rice is the staple staff of life for people of the south and centre of China, northerners build their sturdy diet on a foundation of steamed buns or noodles. People don't say "Hullo" in Cantonese, the polite phrase is "Have you eaten rice yet?" In Shanghai, holding a secure job in the government is said to be like having an iron rice bowl – the bowl can't be broken and the public servant can't be sacked. While rice-eating has been ingrained for centuries in the south where benevolent nature provides ample rain and sunshine to harvest up to three bumper crops a year, the cold, dry plains of the north support mainly wheat, barley and millet. In Manchuria the farmers have to move quickly to harvest their crops before the freezing winter snaps down after the all too brief summer.

Throughout the southern provinces life revolves around the paddy field. Landscapes are painted in different shades of green, from the brilliant emerald of the newly transplanted rice to the deep luxuriant greens of the mature plants. Thousands of years of experience has laid down immutable laws for peasant farmers to follow as they bring in the white gold of the rice crop. The rice plant provides a greater yield in the flooded fields than any other crop, and it brings to the table a much-loved staple that plays a vital role in the daily diet of most Chinese. Eaten three times a day, it is an integral part of every meal – much more so than bread and potatoes in a Western kitchen. Rice to many Chinese is not just part of a meal, but the body on which the delicacies of meat, fish and vegetables are the gorgeous clothes: "A meal without rice is like a beautiful girl with one eye" says an old proverb.

The situation is quite different in the northern provinces, where the people feel deprived if they cannot enjoy the buns and noodles they were weaned on. The basic dough used reflects the no-nonsense approach to food of a busy farmwife who has crops, a home and children to attend to as well as a family to cook for. One part

of water and two parts of flour are the simple ingredients of the pancake of northern China. Add a thousand choices of different stuffings or accompaniments and you have the start of many northern meals. Plain steamed buns or thin fried pancakes can be eaten with the filling stews of Hebei and Shandong or to mop up the remains of a bubbling Mongolian Fire Pot.

Whether from rice flour or wheat, a staggering variety of pasta is made in China. Fat or thin, flat or round, pasta comes in sheets, strings, strands and nodules. Noodles can be cooked by themselves or as a steaming bed on which to serve a regional delicacy. They can be fried, stewed, boiled or baked, and eaten for breakfast, lunch, dinner, as an in-between meal or a midnight snack.

While rice and bread give Chinese cuisine much of its carbohydrates, a lot of the protein comes from the miraculous soy bean. Cultivated since the beginning of China's recorded history, over five thousand years ago, there are more than two thousand five hundred varieties of the soy bean. They grow easily in the harsh climate of the north, even in frigid Manchuria; they produce an immense yield, are easy to grow, simple to harvest and are processed into a vast range of healthy and edible products. Dieticians say the beans in one form or

GEORG GERSTER   TERRACES LINE THE LIPING VALLEY, GUIZHOU PROVINCE

another provide almost everything needed by the human body. Certainly, in the form of beancurd, the soy bean provides a high-protein meat substitute healthier than the original animal product it so flatteringly copies.

Beancurd has for a long time provided protein for those who could not afford meat, and today, in a more health-conscious world, beancurd is often used in place of meat by the more prosperous societies. Over the centuries chefs have invented tens of thousands of recipes using beancurd. The Buddhist influence which seeped gently through many eras of China and spread the gospel of a meatless diet did much to take the humble bean and elevate it to be a gourmet's delight. Stir-fried with vegetables, stewed with seafood, braised along with meat, boiled to add body and potency to soups, beancurd is a versatile addition to the diet.

Another well-known by-product of the bean is soy sauce; indispensable in Chinese cooking, it adds a unique flavour to any dish. With sugar added the soy bean becomes a health drink or a dessert sweet. The bland bean picks up the flavour of whatever it shares a pot with. In the hard years that have come so often to China, countless lives of poor peasants have been saved by this modest culinary chameleon.

MAKING DIM SUM, A FAMILY AFFAIR   WHEELER PICTURES

Sichuan 四川

PEPPERY HOT BEAN CURD

This deliciously hot and aromatic dish was created by pockmarked grandmother Ch'eng, who operated a small bean curd stall on a street corner in Chengdu centuries ago. Using a few cakes of bean curd, a little ground meat and local seasonings, she produced one of the tastiest and most nutritious of Chinese dishes, yet one of the least expensive. Today the dish is still called after her "Ma Po Dofu"(pockmarked mother's bean curd).

4 4½-oz (140-g) squares soft bean curd
6 oz (185 g) lean beef, preferably fillet (tenderloin)
3 green onions
2-3 tablespoons vegetable oil
3 cloves garlic, crushed

SEASONING/SAUCE

1 teaspoon grated fresh ginger
1 tablespoon fermented black beans, chopped
2 pickled red chilies, chopped
2 tablespoons light soy sauce
1-2 teaspoons hot bean paste
1½ teaspoons sugar
½ teaspoon salt
½ teaspoon Sichuan peppercorns (Fagara or Sansho), ground
1 cup (8 oz) chicken stock
1 tablespoon cornstarch

Cut the bean curd into small cubes and set aside. Very finely grind the beef and finely chop the green onion.

Heat the oil in a wok and stir-fry the beef, green onions and garlic until half cooked.

Add the ginger, black beans, chilies, soy sauce and hot bean paste and stir-fry together for about 1½ minutes, then add the remaining seasoning/sauce ingredients, except the cornstarch, and bring to boil. Slide in the bean curd and simmer for about 5 minutes over gentle heat. Carefully stir in the cornstarch mixed with a little cold water, simmering gently until thickened.

For extra flavor, sprinkle on some flaked red chili and a little crushed Sichuan pepper just before serving.

Sichuan 四川

BEAN CURD IN CONSOMMÉ

6 4½-oz (140-g) squares soft bean curd
3 egg whites
1 tablespoon softened lard
1½ tablespoons cornstarch
7 cups (1¾ l) clear chicken or vegetable stock
salt to taste
white pepper
1 lb (500 g) lettuce, Chinese cabbage or other leafy
    Chinese green vegetable

Place the bean curd in a dish and mash smoothly. Beat the egg whites well and stir into the bean curd. Add the lard and the cornstarch, mixed with a little cold water, and beat the whole mixture together until thoroughly amalgamated. Pour into a lightly oiled square pan and place on a rack in a wok or steamer. Cover and steam for about 14 minutes or until firm, then remove and let cool.

Cut the bean curd mixture into rectangular pieces.

Boil the stock and season with salt and pepper.

Rinse the vegetables thoroughly and separate the leaves. Place them in the bottom of a serving bowl and arrange the bean curd on top. Invert the sliced bean curd onto the vegetables, cover with the boiling stock and serve at once.

BEAN CURD IN CONSOMMÉ

PEPPERY HOT BEAN CURD

STUFFED BEAN CURD TRIANGLES

Sichuan 四川

STUFFED BEAN CURD TRIANGLES

4 4½-oz (140-g) squares bean curd
1 cup (8oz) vegetable or peanut oil
2 1½-oz (45-g) slices ham
8 water chestnuts
4oz (125g) fatty pork
2 tablespoons finely chopped bamboo shoots
1 egg white, lightly beaten
½ cup (2oz) cornstarch
4 slices fresh ginger
2 green onions, sliced
4 cloves garlic, chopped

SAUCE

¾ cup (6oz) chicken stock
1 tablespoon light soy sauce
2 teaspoons rice wine or dry sherry
2 teaspoons cornstarch
½ teaspoon salt
½ teaspoon sugar

Hold each square of bean curd in the palm of your hand and carefully cut into four triangular-shaped pieces. Heat the oil in a wok and fry the bean curd until the surface is crisp and slightly bubbly. Lift out and drain well. Make a slit in one side of each piece of bean curd.

✹ Finely mince the ham, water chestnuts, pork and bamboo shoots, mix together and stuff into the bean curd triangles. Dip the cut edges in the egg white, then into cornstarch, and fry gently in the oil for about 2½ minutes or until the bean curd has become very crisp and the stuffing has cooked through. Remove, drain well and arrange on a serving plate.

✹ Sauté the ginger, green onion and garlic in the oil for about 45 seconds, then add the pre-mixed sauce ingredients and simmer, stirring, until the sauce thickens. Pour over the bean curd and serve at once.

Sichuan 四川

BRAISED CARP WITH BEAN CURD

1 1¼-lb (625-g) carp or other meaty white fish
4 4½-oz (140-g) squares bean curd
1 cup (8oz) peanut oil
1½ tablespoons red fermented rice (wine lees)
1½ tablespoons sweet bean paste

SEASONING/SAUCE

3 tablespoons finely chopped green onions
2 tablespoons dark soy sauce
1½ tablespoons fermented black beans
1 tablespoon rice wine or dry sherry
1 teaspoon finely grated fresh ginger
1 teaspoon finely chopped garlic
½ teaspoon ground Sichuan peppercorns (Fagara or Sansho)
½ cup (4oz) chicken stock

Clean the fish, dip into boiling water, drain and dry well. Make several deep scores diagonally across each side. Cut the bean curd into cubes and slide into a pot of simmering water. Boil gently for 2 minutes, then drain well.

✹ Heat the oil in a wok and fry the fish on both sides until well colored. Pour off most of the oil, then add the pre-mixed seasoning/sauce ingredients, except the stock, and fry for 1 minute. Add the stock and bean curd, cover the dish and simmer gently until the flavors are well absorbed. Add the fermented rice and sweet bean paste, simmer briefly and transfer to a serving dish. Serve at once.

BRAISED CARP WITH BEAN CURD

Beijing 北京

BEAN CURD IN AN EARTHENWARE POT

3-4 dried black mushrooms, soaked for 25 minutes
1 dried scallop, soaked for 25 minutes
1 tablespoon dried shrimp, soaked for 20 minutes
2 oz (60 g) chicken breasts, finely ground
2 oz (60 g) lean pork, finely ground
1 oz (30 g) prawn or shrimp meat, ground
4 4½-oz (140-g) squares bean curd
4 green onions
3 slices fresh ginger
1 teaspoon salt
pinch of pepper
sesame oil
3 cups (24 oz) Superior Stock (*see page 124*) or chicken stock

Place the mushrooms, scallop and shrimp in separate heat-proof dishes on a rack in a wok or steamer. Cover and steam over high heat for about 15 minutes or until softened, then drain well.

Cut the stems from the mushrooms and finely dice half of the caps. Mix the ground chicken, pork and prawn meat together and season lightly with salt.

Cut each square of bean curd into four and make a slit through the center of each quarter. Fill one end of each slit with the ground filling and the other with the diced mushrooms, and place in an earthenware pot.

Slice the green onions diagonally and add to the pot with the ginger, remaining mushrooms, shredded scallop and the shrimp meat, then add the salt, dried pepper, sesame oil and stock.

Bring to boil and simmer gently for about 30 minutes. Serve in the pot.

SAN XIAN STUFFED BEAN CURD

"SILVER FISH" WRAPPED IN SNOW

Beijing 北京

SAN XIAN STUFFED BEAN CURD

Bean curd was first made some two thousand years ago by an emperor of the Han Dynasty (206 BC-220 AD). An accomplished scholar well versed in medicine and astrology, he assembled a group of researchers to look for new medicines, and in the course of their research they produced bean curd. They found it both cheap and very nutritious. Since that time bean curd has remained one of the most highly regarded Chinese foods, and many different ways of preparing and cooking it have been devised.

2 4½-oz (140-g) squares firm bean curd
3 oz (90 g) chicken breasts, finely ground
2 oz (60 g) fresh prawn or shrimp meat
2 tablespoons finely chopped, soaked and prepared sea cucumber (optional)
1½ tablespoons finely chopped green onion
¼ teaspoon grated fresh ginger
1 egg white, well beaten
1 tablespoon rice wine or dry sherry
½ teaspoon sesame oil
½ teaspoon salt
oil for frying

BATTER

1 cup (4 oz) all purpose flour
1 egg

SAUCE

1 cup (8 oz) chicken stock
1½ teaspoons rice wine or dry sherry
1 teaspoon cornstarch
½ teaspoon salt

ONION OIL

3 tablespoons peanut oil
1 small red onion, very thinly sliced

Cut the bean curd squares in halves and slice each piece thinly to give about 28 square slices.
❈ Make a reasonably smooth filling by mixing the chicken breasts, prawn meat, sea cucumber (if used), green onion, ginger, egg white, rice wine, sesame oil and salt. Squeeze the mixture through your fingers until thoroughly amalgamated and sticky. Divide into 14 portions and roll each into a ball, then press flat to about the size of the bean curd slices.
❈ Place one piece of filling between two squares of bean curd to make sandwiches and coat lightly with flour. Use the remaining flour and some cold water to make a fairly thick batter for coating.
❈ Heat oil in a wok. Gently fry the bean curd, turning once, until lightly browned on both sides. Lift out and place on a serving plate.

❈ Drain the wok, retaining about 2 tablespoons of the oil. Mix the sauce ingredients together and pour into the wok. Simmer, stirring, until the sauce thickens, then pour over the bean curd.
❈ In a clean wok or saucepan heat the peanut oil until smoking. Add the sliced red onion and cook until lightly browned. Use a slotted spoon to remove the onion, drain well and reserve as a garnish for another dish. Pour a portion of the onion oil over the finished dish and serve at once.

Beijing 北京

"SILVER FISH" WRAPPED IN SNOW

This unusual and economical vegetarian dish goes well with wine. It is simply cooked macaroni dipped into an egg-white batter and fried. The long whitish pieces look like whitebait or minnows dipped into snow.

1½ oz (45 g) dry macaroni
1 teaspoon salt
2 egg whites
½ cup (2 oz) cornstarch
2 tablespoons all purpose flour
oil for deep-frying
1 tablespoon five-spice salt*

Place the macaroni in a saucepan and add half the salt. Cover with plenty of boiling water, stir well and cook until the macaroni is tender, then drain well and let cool.
❈ Whip the egg whites until firm and fluffy. Fold in the cornstarch, the remaining salt and the flour and add just enough cold water to make a thick batter.
❈ Heat the oil in a wok to the smoking point, then lower the heat slightly. Dip the macaroni into the batter and deep-fry until crisp and puffy, but without turning golden. Remove and drain well.
❈ Arrange the fried "silver fish" on a serving plate and serve with the five-spice salt in a small dish.

To make the five-spice salt, heat 1½ tablespoons fine table salt in a wok until it begins to crackle. Add 1 teaspoon Chinese five-spice powder, remove from the heat, stir and cool.

Guangzhou 广州

SILVER NEEDLE NOODLES WITH ASSORTED MEAT SHREDS

Guangdong has a long history of making noodles from dried rice. In one of the oldest methods, cooked rice is dried in the sun, ground to a powder, mixed with boiling water and rubbed into short noodles, sharp at both ends, like needles. A better result, however, is achieved by making the noodles from wheat starch.

3 oz (90 g) lean pork
3 oz (90 g) boneless chicken meat
3 oz (90 g) cleaned squid
3 oz (90 g) fresh prawn or shrimp meat
3-4 dried black mushrooms, soaked for 25 minutes
1 egg
1 oz (30 g) fresh bean sprouts
1 small leek, white part only
1 small slice salted ham
cilantro
lard or oil for frying

SEASONING

1 tablespoon light soy sauce
2 teaspoons rice wine or dry sherry
1½ teaspoons sugar
1 teaspoon sesame oil
1 teaspoon salt

SILVER NEEDLE NOODLES

1 cup (4 oz) wheat starch (gluten-free wheat flour)*
2 tablespoons cornstarch
½-⅔ cup (4-5 oz) boiling water
1 teaspoon lard

Prepare the noodles first. Sift the wheat starch and cornstarch into a mixing bowl, make a well in the center, pour the boiling water in and add the lard. Mix in quickly, working with a wooden spoon, then cover and leave for 5-6 minutes for the wheat starch to soften. Working with oiled hands on a lightly oiled work surface, break off small pieces of the dough and roll into a ball, then rub across the surface with the palm of your hand to form thin noodles, pointed at each end. Use up all the dough and set the noodles aside.

Finely shred the pork, chicken and squid; cut the prawns into small pieces. Drain the mushrooms, remove the stems and cut the caps into shreds. Beat the egg lightly and set aside. Rinse the bean sprouts and drain well. Shred the leek and ham, rinse the cilantro and drain.

Heat a wok, wipe out with an oiled cloth and pour in the egg, tilting and turning the wok so that the egg flows into a wide omelet. Cook until set, then turn and cook the other side. Lift out and spread on a cloth to cool.

Add 2-3 tablespoons of lard or oil to the wok and stir-fry the noodles over high heat for 1 minute, then reduce the heat and continue to stir-fry for another 2 minutes. Remove to a serving plate and set aside.

Add the shredded meats, except the ham, to the wok and stir-fry together until cooked, then add the mushrooms, bean sprouts and leek and stir-fry briefly.

Add the seasoning/sauce ingredients and toss together thoroughly over high heat. Spoon the cooked ingredients over the noodles.

Cut the egg into fine shreds and use together with the ham and cilantro to garnish the dish. Or alternatively, stir these in with the noodles and other ingredients.

*If wheat starch is unobtainable, all purpose flour can be used; the noodles will be heavier and more chewy.

SILVER NEEDLE NOODLES WITH ASSORTED MEAT SHREDS

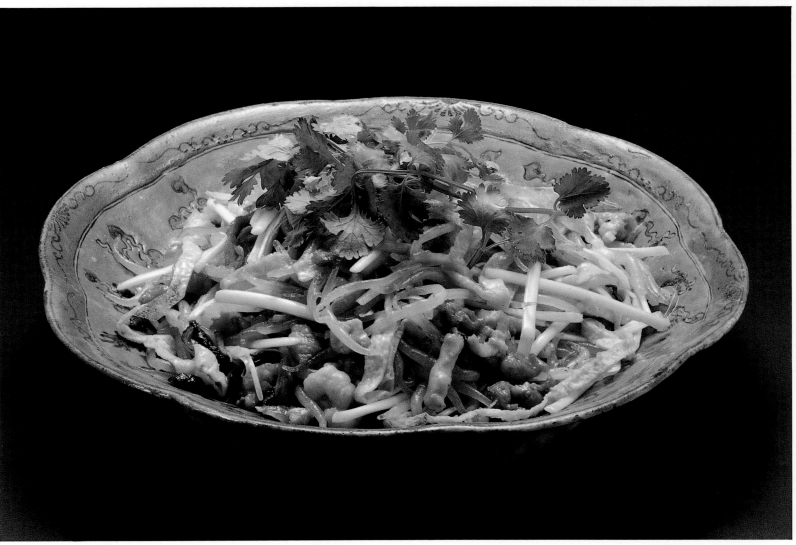

SHA HE NOODLES WITH LEEKS AND SHREDDED PORK

Guangzhou 广州

SHA HE NOODLES WITH LEEKS AND SHREDDED PORK

The Sha He Restaurant in Guangzhou is well known both at home and abroad for the special flavor of its sha he noodles. More than thirty dishes are offered featuring these tender noodles made from rice flour and water from the Nine Dragon Spring, which gives them their unique flavor.

10 oz (315 g) fresh rice ribbon noodles (sha he noodles)
lard or vegetable oil
salt
4 oz (125 g) lean pork, shredded
8 oz (90 g) silver sprouts*
2 young leeks, shredded

SAUCE

2/3 cup (5 oz) Superior Stock (*see page 124*) or chicken stock
1½ tablespoons light soy sauce
1½ teaspoons cornstarch
1 teaspoon rice wine or dry sherry
½ teaspoon sugar
½ teaspoon sesame oil
⅓ teaspoon salt
pinch of white pepper

Stir-fry the noodles in the lard until soft and very slightly crisp on the edges. Lift onto a serving plate, sprinkle with salt and set aside.

❊ Wipe out the wok, add a little more lard and stir-fry the pork until it changes color. Remove, then stir-fry the silver sprouts and leeks until the leeks are tender and wilted. Add the pre-mixed sauce ingredients, return the pork and simmer, stirring, until the sauce thickens. Pour over the noodles and serve at once.

Fresh mung bean sprouts from which the yellow seed pods and long tapering roots have been removed, leaving a slender silver-colored sprout.

Sichuan 四川

STEAMED DRAGON'S EYE ROLLS

12 oz (375 g) unsmoked bacon*
1 tablespoon granulated sugar
½ cup sweetened red bean paste
18 glacé cherries
1 cup (5 oz) glutinous long-grain rice
1 teaspoon salt
2 tablespoons firmly packed brown sugar

STEAMED DRAGON'S EYE ROLLS

Place the pork on a rack, skin upwards, and pour several cups of boiling water over it. Drain, then wipe dry. Melt the granulated sugar in a wok and rub over the pork skin, then use a very sharp knife to cut the pork into long, thin strips like bacon. Roll each strip of pork around a small portion of the sweetened red bean paste and top each with half a cherry. Place cherry-down in a heatproof bowl and set aside.

❊ Steam or boil the glutinous rice with plenty of salt until just cooked. Mix with the brown sugar and pile on top of the pork rolls. Place on a rack in a wok or steamer, cover and steam for about 40 minutes. Invert onto a serving plate. The dragon's eyes form a beautiful pattern.

Choose the best quality pork meat near the ribs; it should be in one piece.

Beijing 北京

RICE AND DUCK MEAT IN LOTUS LEAVES

3 fresh or dried lotus or bamboo leaves
oil for brushing leaves
10 oz (315 g) duck breast meat
3/4 cup (4 oz) glutinous rice
3/4 cup (4 oz) long-grain white rice
1 whole star anise
1 teaspoon Sichuan peppercorns (Fagara or Sansho)
2 teaspoons sesame oil

SEASONING

2 tablespoons finely chopped green onion
1 tablespoon light soy sauce
2½ teaspoons rice wine or dry sherry
1 teaspoon grated fresh ginger
3/4 teaspoon salt

Blanch the fresh leaves or soak the dried ones until softened, then squeeze out the water and brush the underside with oil.

❊ Cut the duck into small strips, place in a dish with the seasoning ingredients, mix well and set aside.

❊ Finely grind the glutinous and the long-grain rice together with the star anise and Sichuan peppercorns. Mix with the duck meat and sesame oil, adding just a little water to moisten.

❊ Divide the lotus leaves into quarters, place a portion of the rice mixture onto each and fold the leaves, ribbed side inwards, around the rice to make little loose parcels.

❊ Arrange side by side on a heatproof plate, set on a rack in a wok or in a steamer, cover and steam over gently simmering water for about 1 hour. Serve immediately.

RICE AND DUCK MEAT IN LOTUS LEAVES

COCONUT BUNS

Guangzhou 广州

Coconut Buns

2½ cups (10 oz) all purpose flour
1¾ teaspoons baking powder
3 tablespoons sugar
2 egg yolks
½ cup (4 oz) lukewarm milk
3 tablespoons lard or butter
1 egg, beaten

FILLING

1½ oz (45 g) fatty bacon
1 tablespoon sugar
1½ tablespoons pine nuts
½ cup (4 oz) peanut oil
¾ cup (1½ oz) shredded coconut
2 tablespoons sugar
1 small egg, well beaten

Sift the flour and baking powder into a mixing bowl, make a well in the center and add the sugar, egg yolks and milk. Cut the lard or butter into small cubes, add to the mixture and work in well. Transfer to a lightly floured board and knead lightly until the dough is smooth and soft. Cover and set aside.

To prepare the filling, finely chop the bacon and fry gently with 1 tablespoon sugar until the fat is almost transparent, then set aside. Deep-fry the pine nuts in the peanut oil until lightly colored. Mix with the bacon, shredded coconut, sugar and egg and set aside.

Divide the dough into about 12 portions and flatten each into a round shape. Place a portion of the filling in the center of each, pull the dough up around the filling and pinch the edges together to completely enclose it.

Place the buns, joined edges downwards, on a lightly oiled baking sheet, brush the tops with beaten egg and set aside until it feels dry, then brush a second time.

Bake in a preheated 400°F (200°C) oven for 20 minutes, or until crisp and golden on the surface.

Beijing 北京

Sesame Cakes with Minced Pork

Sesame cakes can be made with sweet or savory fillings. They were a specialty of the imperial kitchen of the Qing Dynasty (1644-1911 AD), and a story is told about the Empress Dowager Cixi having a dream in which she was eating some sesame cakes. To her astonishment the next morning she was served sesame cakes for breakfast. She rewarded the chef of the imperial kitchen with peacock feathers and twenty pieces of silver. Thus the dish became famous.

½ cup (4 oz) vegetable oil
7 cups (1¾ lb) all purpose flour
1½ cups (12 oz) boiling water
½ cup (4 oz) cold water
3 teaspoons salt
extra water or sugar water for brushing cakes
½ cup (2 oz) white sesame seeds
oil for deep-frying (optional)

FILLING

12 oz (375 g) lean pork
oil for frying
1 tablespoon dark soy sauce
pinch each of salt and pepper
1 tablespoon rice wine or dry sherry
2 teaspoons sugar
chopped fresh cilantro or diced pickled vegetables

Gently heat the vegetable oil in a wok and add 1½ cups (6 oz) of the flour. Mix into a thick paste and continue to cook very gently, stirring constantly until mixture forms a light golden, smooth, soft ball. Remove and let cool.

Sift the remaining flour into a bowl and make a well in the center. Pour in the boiling water and quickly work into the flour, then add the cold water and 1 teaspoon of the salt and work in thoroughly. Transfer to a board and knead until smooth and elastic.

Divide into 36 portions, rolling each into a ball, then roll or press them out flat. Spread a portion of the flour-and-oil dough over half of them and sprinkle with the remaining salt. Press the remaining single pieces of dough on top and pinch the edges together to seal tightly.

Brush one side of each cake with water or a mixture of sugar and water and coat thickly with sesame seeds.

Bake in a preheated oven, 400°F (200°C), until puffed, golden, firm and dry on the surface, or deep-fry in hot oil until cooked through. Set aside, keeping warm.

Very finely chop or grind the pork and sauté in 2-3 tablespoons oil until lightly colored. Add the soy sauce, salt and pepper, rice wine and sugar and continue to stir-fry until there is no liquid left in the bottom of the wok.

Serve the pork with the warm buns, adding chopped fresh cilantro or finely diced pickled vegetables.

SESAME CAKES WITH MINCED PORK

CRISP DOUGH COATED WITH SUGAR AND POWDERED CANDIED ROSE

Sichuan 四川

CRISP DOUGH COATED WITH SUGAR AND POWDERED CANDIED ROSE

3 eggs
¾ cup (3 oz) all purpose flour
3 tablespoons water
¾ cup (6 oz) sugar
cornstarch
oil for deep-frying
1 tablespoon finely chopped candied rose petals*

Beat the eggs in a mixing bowl and add the flour and water. Stir until the batter is smooth, then pour into a lightly greased, heated wok and cook gently, stirring constantly, until the batter forms a soft ball. Lift out and press out on an oiled plate to about ½ in (1.25 cm) thickness. Let cool.

❋ Pour the sugar into a saucepan, add about 3 tablespoons cold water and set aside.

❋ Cut the cooled batter into strips. Cover a plate thickly with cornstarch and press the strips into this, coating them evenly.

❋ Heat the oil in a wok to the smoking point, then reduce the heat slightly. Deep-fry the strips several at a time until puffed and golden, turning once. Lift out and drain well.

❋ Bring the syrup to a slow boil and simmer for 2-3 minutes. When all of the wafers have been fried and well drained, dip them one by one into the syrup and pile on a serving plate. Sprinkle on the candied rose and serve at once.

If candied rose petals are unobtainable add 1 teaspoon rose water to the sugar syrup.

Guangzhou 广州

STEAMED MILK BUNS

MAKES ABOUT 24

DOUGH STARTER

1 teaspoon dry yeast
3 tablespoons warm water
¾ cup (3 oz) all purpose flour

2 cups (8 oz) all purpose flour
½ cup (4 oz) warm water
¾ cup (6 oz) lukewarm milk
3 tablespoons sugar
2 tablespoons softened lard
pinch of baking soda
2 cups (8 oz) all purpose flour
1½ cups (6 oz) wheat starch (gluten-free wheat flour)*
1½ tablespoons baking powder

To make the dough starter, sprinkle the dry yeast into the warm water and stir until completely dissolved, then sift on the flour and work into a soft dough, kneading lightly. Set aside in a warm place for about 10 hours.

❋ Mix the water with 2 cups (8 oz) flour, add the dough starter and work together to a soft dough, cover again and leave a further 8-10 hours until it has at least tripled its bulk.

❋ Pour the milk into a bowl and add the sugar and softened lard. Mix the baking soda with a little water and add to the above, then stir in the remaining flour, the wheat starch and baking powder and mix into the risen dough. Knead together until smooth and elastic.

❋ Divide the mixture into about 24 balls and press a small piece of paper onto the back of each. Set in a bamboo steamer basket, cover and steam for about 10 minutes or until firm textured, springy and well risen. Serve at once.

❋ An assortment of fillings can be used inside steamed milk buns. Try barbecued pork lightly sautéed with green onions and flavored with oyster sauce, or sweetened lotus seed, or red bean paste, or mashed dates.

If wheat starch is unobtainable, all purpose flour can be used; the buns will be slightly heavier and more chewy.

Guangzhou 广州

FLAKY TARTS STUFFED WITH SHREDDED COCONUT

MAKES 24

PASTRY A

2½ cups (10 oz) all purpose flour
½-⅔ cup (4-5 oz) water
3 oz (90 g) lard, melted

PASTRY B

1½ cups (6 oz) all purpose flour
4 oz (125 g) lard, melted

FILLING

¾ cup (6 oz) sugar
½ cup (4 oz) water
1½ tablespoons butter
1½ cups shredded coconut
2 eggs, beaten
1 tablespoon lukewarm milk
½ teaspoon baking powder
½ teaspoon vanilla

Sift the flour for pastry A into a mixing bowl and make a well in the center. Add the water and lard and work into a soft dough. Transfer to a board and knead until smooth and pliable.

❋ Sift the flour for pastry B onto a board, make a well in the center and work in the lard with your fingertips until the dough is smooth, adding just a few teaspoons of water to make the mixture hold together.

❋ Cover the doughs and set aside.

❋ Heat the sugar and water together in a saucepan for about 4 minutes, then add the butter and pour into a mixing bowl. Add the coconut, mix well and let cool. Add the remaining ingredients, working in well.

❋ Roll out each pastry dough and cut with a fluted round cutter into 24 rounds each. Alternatively, the two doughs can be stacked, rolled and cut together.

❋ Fit one type of pastry in a muffin or tartlet pan and top with the other, pressing them lightly together. Place a portion of the filling in the center of each.

❋ Bake in a preheated 400°F (200°C) oven for about 20 minutes or until the filling is puffed and golden and feels dry to the touch, and the pastry is crisp and dry. Serve with tea.

Shanghai 上海

STEAMED SMALL MEAT BUNS

These tasty little meat buns are the specialty of Nan Xiang, a suburb of Shanghai. Their special feature is their perfectly symmetrical shape, resembling a water chestnut, or sometimes a pagoda.

When crab is in season it may be used as the stuffing instead of the pork and cabbage described in the following recipe. The crab buns are shaped so that the opening at the top is in the shape of a carp's mouth, and after steaming the orange-colored crab oil can be seen through the opening.

Although this type of savory snack is very popular, it is rarely made at home. It is served with traditional dips of shredded young ginger and rice vinegar.

WRAPPERS

2 cups (8 oz) all purpose flour
1 egg, beaten
¾ cup (6 oz) water
1 teaspoon baking powder
¾ teaspoon salt

FILLING

6 oz (185 g) lean pork
2-3 cabbage leaves
1½ tablespoons peanut oil
1 green onion, finely chopped
1 clove garlic, finely chopped
1 slice fresh ginger, finely chopped

SEASONING

2 tablespoons chicken stock
1 tablespoon light soy sauce
2 teaspoons rice wine or dry sherry
2 teaspoons sugar
2 teaspoons cornstarch
½ teaspoon sesame oil
pinch of white pepper

Make the wrappers first by sifting the flour into a mixing bowl and pouring the egg into the center. Mix in lightly, then add the water, baking powder and salt and mix together thoroughly. Knead until smooth, then set aside and cover with a damp cloth for 5-6 minutes to activate the baking powder.

✼ Finely grind the pork and finely chop the cabbage leaves. Heat the peanut oil in a wok and sauté the pork, cabbage leaves, green onion, garlic and ginger until the pork turns white, then add the pre-mixed seasoning ingredients and stir-fry together until there is no liquid in the bottom of the wok.

✼ Roll the dough out into a long sausage shape and cut into about 24 pieces. Roll out each piece into a thin round and place a spoonful of the filling in the center of each.

✼ Gather up the edges, pleating them together, then bring to a point, pinch together and twist. Flatten the bases so that they will stand upright, then stand in a lightly oiled steaming basket or on a rack in a wok. Cover and steam for about 14 minutes over high heat until done. The dumplings can be placed on cabbage leaves in the steamer to give them extra flavor and prevent them from sinking through the slats in the steaming basket.

BEAN FLOUR CAKES OR DONKEY ROLLING CAKES

Beijing 北京

BEAN FLOUR CAKES OR DONKEY ROLLING CAKES

Bean flour cakes make a delicious snack or dessert. In Beijing they used to be sold by hawkers, pushing their carts along the road and loudly announcing their products. The elderly people of Beijing remember these cakes as Donkey Rolling Cakes, because the hawkers often sprinkled a layer of dry bean flour over the cakes before giving them to the customers – reminding them of a donkey rolling in the sand and raising a cloud of dust.

½ cup (4 oz) sugar
1 cup (10 oz) red bean paste
3 cups (12 oz) glutinous rice flour
1 cup (8 oz) boiling water
½ cup (2 oz) white sesame seeds
1 cup (6 oz) yellow lentils

Mix the sugar and red bean paste together in a saucepan or wok, stirring over gentle heat until dissolved, then remove and let cool completely.

✼ Sift the glutinous rice flour into a mixing bowl, make a well in the center and pour in the water. Work the mixture into a smooth dough, adding a little extra water if needed, then cover and let stand for a few minutes until the flour softens.

✼ Dry-fry the sesame seeds until golden and beginning to pop, then remove and grind to a powder. Dry-fry the lentils until golden brown and very crisp. Grind to a fine powder and mix with the sesame seed powder.

✼ Spread the dough over a work surface in a large rectangle about ⅓ in (1 cm) thick. Cover with the bean paste, leaving a border at the top. Roll up from the bottom to form a thick roll, then place on a rack in a wok or steamer, cover and steam for about 8 minutes, or until cooked through.

✼ Roll in the sesame and lentil powder, coating thickly, then cut into thick slices and serve.

STEAMED PRAWNS WITH STUFFING

Guangzhou 广州

STEAMED PRAWNS WITH STUFFING

Color, flavor, aroma and shape are important elements in Guangdong snacks. Color is particularly highly regarded. There is a saying that "the color is encountered before the flavor is sampled." In some snacks, artificial coloring is used to achieve the desired effect, but more often it is accomplished by the use and blending of naturally colored ingredients.

6 large river prawns (freshwater shrimp)
4 oz (125 g) chicken breast
1 thin slice Yunnan, Virginia or other well-salted ham
6 small sprigs fresh cilantro
½ recipe Wheat Starch Wrappers (*see page 209*), using all purpose flour
light soy sauce or vinegar

SEASONING

1 teaspoon rice wine or dry sherry
½ teaspoon sugar
pinch each of salt and white pepper

Peel the prawns, leaving the last section and the tail intact. Cut the chicken into 6 strips, about the size of the peeled parts of the prawns, or grind finely. Place the chicken in a dish and add the seasoning ingredients. Cut the ham into 6 strips.

Cut the prawns along the underside without cutting through them completely. Devein and flatten each prawn out. Place a chicken strip or a portion of ground chicken, a ham strip and a cilantro sprig on each prawn and fold up.

Make the wrappers and roll out 6 large enough to enclose the filled prawns. Wrap up each prawn, leaving the tails exposed. Pinch the wrappers together underneath. Arrange on a lightly oiled heatproof plate and place on a rack in a wok or steamer over simmering water. Cover tightly and steam for about 12 minutes or until the prawns are bright pink, the chicken meat white and the wrappers transparent.

Serve with soy sauce or a vinegar dip.

Sichuan 四川

GLUTINOUS RICE DUMPLINGS

The pyramid-shaped delicacies described in this recipe have a long history. They were originally made as an offering to the spirit of the great Chinese poet-statesman Qu Yuan, who died in the third century BC. Although a loyal patriot, he was dismissed from the emperor's service because he complained about the corruption in the imperial court. Disappointed about his failure to save the country, he later committed suicide by jumping into the Mi Luo River in Hunan Province.

To commemorate his death and appease his spirit, every year on the fifth day of the fifth month, when the "Duan Wu" festival is celebrated, the locals fill sections of hollow bamboo with rice and throw them into the river.

Legend has it that the rice was originally thrown by people who went out in a boat to search for his body. They hoped the rice would lure the fish away and prevent them from devouring the body.

In later years bamboo leaves, reeds or rushes were used to wrap the glutinous rice into dumplings, and fillings of sweetened red bean paste, mashed dates or savory ground meat were added; and these specialties are now eaten during the festival.

DUMPLINGS

1 cup (4 oz) glutinous rice flour
¼ cup boiling water
2-3 tablespoons cold water
12 dried bamboo leaves, soaked to soften
oil for brushing leaves

SWEET FILLINGS

6 tablespoons canned sweetened red bean paste
or
6 tablespoons sweetened date paste*

SAVORY FILLING

4 oz (125 g) ground lean pork
2 cloves garlic, crushed
2 tablespoons lard
2 tablespoons light soy sauce
½ teaspoon pepper
1 teaspoon sugar
pinch of salt

Place the rice flour in a mixing bowl and make a well in the center. Add the boiling water and 2 tablespoons of the cold water and mix quickly into a pliable dough, adding the remaining cold water if needed. Knead until smooth, then roll out into a sausage shape and cut into 12 pieces.

Drain the bamboo leaves, dry thoroughly and brush with the oil.

To cook the savory filling, stir-fry the pork and garlic in the lard until white, then add the remaining ingredients and continue frying until the liquid has been absorbed. Cool before using.

Flatten the dough pieces and place half a tablespoon of the chosen filling in the center. Pull the dough up around the filling, pinching the edges together to seal it smoothly.

Place near the lower end of the bamboo leaf and wrap the leaf around it to make a pyramid shape. Set the dumplings on a rack in a wok or steamer, cover and steam over high heat for about 15 minutes or until cooked through. Serve hot or cold. They can be dipped into sugar before eating.

Dates simmered in water until tender, then sweetened with sugar, softened with a little lard and simmered until all of the liquid has evaporated, leaving a thick paste.

Guangzhou 广州

STEAMED SHAO MAI TOPPED WITH CRAB ROE

The Steamed Shao Mai, or dumpling, of Guangdong is an adaptation of the northern xiao long shao mai. In Beijing there is a well-known shao mai shop, the Dou Yi Chu, which opened for business over 200 years ago during the reign of Emperor Qian Long. It is said that when returning to the capital from a journey, the Emperor passed a small restaurant without a signboard. He entered, ordered the xiao long shao mai and found it unusually delicious. Full of praise, he named the shop the Dou Yi Chu ("the one and only"), and through this royal patronage both the shop and shao mai became nationally famous.

6 oz (185 g) fatty pork
4 oz (125 g) fresh prawn or shrimp meat
3 dried black mushrooms, soaked for 25 minutes
24 wonton wrappers*
2-3 tablespoons fresh crab roe, or tiny carrot cubes
   or green peas
chili sauce
hot mustard
light soy sauce

SEASONING
1 egg white
2 teaspoons light soy sauce
2 teaspoons cornstarch
1 teaspoon sugar
½ teaspoon salt
⅓ teaspoon sesame oil
pinch of white pepper

Finely chop the pork, prawn meat and drained mushrooms and mix with the seasoning ingredients.

❊ Use a round cutter to cut wonton wrappers into circles about 3 in (7 cm) in diameter. To fill, place a single wrapper over the thumb and curled forefinger of the left hand and press a spoonful of filling onto the wrapper, forcing the dumpling between thumb and finger into the cupped hand. Squeeze gently, then tap on the work surface to flatten the bottom. The finished dumpling should be cup-shaped and filled right up to the edge of the pastry, the top left open to expose the filling. Place a few grains of crab roe on top of each dumpling.

❊ Set in a lightly greased steamer, cover and steam over simmering water for about 12 minutes or until cooked through. Serve with chili sauce, hot mustard and soy sauce.

*Available commercially, fresh or frozen.

Guangzhou 广州

SISTER ER'S DUMPLINGS

FILLING

4 oz (125 g) lean pork
2½ oz (75 g) fresh prawn or shrimp meat
3 dried black mushrooms, soaked for 25 minutes
1 fresh or canned winter bamboo shoot, about 2½ oz (75 g)
24 cilantro leaves or pieces of green onion tops
oil for frying

SEASONING

2 teaspoons light soy sauce
1 teaspoon rice wine or dry sherry
½ teaspoon sesame oil
½ teaspoon salt
¾ teaspoon sugar
pinch of white pepper

WRAPPERS

1 cup (4 oz) wheat starch (gluten-free wheat flour)*
2 teaspoons cornstarch
½-⅔ cup (4-5 oz) boiling water
½ teaspoon softened lard

Prepare the filling first and let cool while preparing the wrappers. Very finely dice the pork, prawn meat, drained mushrooms and bamboo shoot. In about 1 tablespoon of oil, stir-fry the pork until it whitens. Add the remaining ingredients, except the cilantro, and stir-fry for 30-40 seconds. Add the seasoning ingredients and stir-fry a further 30-40 seconds. Transfer to a dish to cool.

❈ Pour the flour into a mixing bowl, add the cornstarch and make a well in the center. Add the water and, using the handle of a wooden spoon, very quickly work the hot liquid into the flour. When all is incorporated, cover with a cloth and let stand for 5-6 minutes for the flour to soften. Rub the lard into the dough, kneading lightly for 1-2 minutes.

❈ If wheat starch has been used the wrappers can be prepared in the traditional way. Roll the dough into a long sausage shape and cut into 24 pieces. Keep it covered while rolling each piece. Place a piece on a clean board and use a blunt-bladed cleaver (these are especially made for the purpose) to spread the dough into a circle about 3½ in (9 cm) in diameter. Turn over and place a spoonful of filling in the center, top with a single cilantro leaf, fold in half and pinch the edges together. Keep the board and the cleaver very lightly greased with lard.

❈ Plain flour dough can simply be rolled into very thin circles with a rolling pin.

❈ Place the dumplings side by side in a lightly greased steamer, cover and steam over briskly boiling water for about 15 minutes or until the wrappers are translucent.

❈ Serve with soy sauce.

If wheat starch is unobtainable, all purpose flour can be used, although the dumplings will be less transparent and the wrappers slightly more chewy.

THIN PASTRY DIM SUM STUFFED WITH FRESH PRAWNS – HAW GOW

Guangzhou 广州

THIN PASTRY DIM SUM STUFFED WITH FRESH PRAWNS – HAW GOW

Thin Pastry Dim Sum are a famous Guangdong snack said to have been created in a small teahouse in the Wu Chu village of Guangzhou city. Wu Chu used to be a scenic trading center and the teahouse owner would often buy his prawns from the fishing boats of the area. But his original dumpling had a thick skin, and subsequent chefs replaced the original rice flour with wheat starch to produce the thin-skinned perfect snack known as Haw Gow.

5 oz (155 g) fresh prawn or shrimp meat
1½ oz (45 g) pork fat
1½ oz (45 g) bamboo shoots, canned or cooked fresh
1 green onion, white part only
1 recipe Wheat Starch Wrappers (see Sister Er's Dumplings)
hot mustard
light soy sauce

SEASONING

1 teaspoon cornstarch
¾ teaspoon salt
½ teaspoon sugar
¼ teaspoon sesame oil

Coarsely chop the prawn meat and finely chop the pork fat, bamboo shoots and green onion. Mix with the seasoning ingredients, using your fingers to make a smooth and slightly sticky mass. Set aside while the wrappers are prepared.

❈ As each wrapper is done, turn it over and place a spoonful of the filling in the center. Fold the wrapper in half to enclose the filling and pinch the edges together firmly, at the same time pleating the edge of the dumplings so the smooth fold becomes the wider, curved side of the crescent shape (see photograph above).

❈ Arrange on a lightly oiled rack in a wok or steamer, cover and steam over simmering water for about 7 minutes or until the dumplings are as clear as crystal with the prawns showing pink inside.

❈ Serve with hot mustard and soy sauce.

STEAMED SHAO MAI TOPPED WITH CRAB ROE
SISTER ER'S DUMPLINGS

STEAMED RICE WRAPPED IN LOTUS LEAVES

Guangzhou 广州

STEAMED RICE WRAPPED IN LOTUS LEAVES

"Ten miles around Ban Tang are many lotus ponds/Sisters are busy picking lotus/They do not pick lotus flowers but only pick the leaves/Rice in lotus leaves is more fragrant than the flowers."

This is one of the songs from the Zhu Zi Ci collection composed during the final years of the Qing Dynasty (1644-1911 AD). Today, steamed rice wrapped in lotus leaves remains a popular dish.

6 dried lotus or bamboo leaves
2 cups (10 oz) raw long-grain white rice
4 oz (125 g) fresh prawn or shrimp meat
4 oz (125 g) Chinese barbecued pork
3 oz (90 g) roast duck meat
4 oz (125 g) lean pork
4 dried black mushrooms, soaked for 25 minutes
2 eggs
2 tablespoons lard

SEASONING

1 tablespoon oyster sauce
1 tablespoon light soy sauce
2 teaspoons rice wine or dry sherry
1½ teaspoons salt
1 teaspoon sugar
½ teaspoon sesame oil
¼ teaspoon white pepper

Soak the lotus leaves to soften them; drain well. Partially cook the rice until it is tender but still slightly chewy; drain and set aside.

Dice finely the prawn meat, barbecued pork, duck, pork and drained mushrooms. Beat the eggs lightly in a small dish.

Heat the wok, add the lard and heat to smoking point, then pour in the eggs. Cook quickly, stirring until set, then lift out with a slotted spoon and set aside. Add the diced ingredients and stir-fry for 2-3 minutes. Add the seasoning ingredients and mix well. Stir this into the rice.

Place one-sixth of the rice mixture on the underside of each lotus leaf and fold into a square package to completely enclose the filling. Arrange the parcels side by side on a rack in a wok or steamer, cover and steam over simmering water for about 20 minutes. Use scissors to cut a cross in the top of each parcel to expose the contents before serving. The fragrance of the lotus leaf will thoroughly penetrate the rice, giving it a unique and tantalizing taste.

Guangzhou 广州

RADISH PUDDING

Radish pudding is a traditional Guangdong snack; it is made in most households in early winter, when radishes appear in the markets. It is always enjoyed during the Chinese New Year celebrations.

8 oz (250 g) rice flour
1¾ lb (875 g) giant white radish (Japanese daikon or icicle radish)
1½ tablespoons sugar
½ teaspoon white pepper
2 Chinese sausages, steamed for 5 minutes
3-4 dried black mushrooms, soaked for 25 minutes
3 tablespoons dried shrimp, soaked for 25 minutes
1 slice Yunnan or other well-salted ham
3 green onions
2 tablespoons chopped cilantro
2 tablespoons lard
light soy sauce

Place the rice flour in a large mixing bowl and add enough cold water to make the flour evenly damp. Grate the radish and add to the rice flour paste with the sugar and pepper.
❀ Finely dice the remaining ingredients, except the cilantro and lard. Stir-fry in hot lard for 2-3 minutes, then add to the radish paste with the cilantro. Mix well.
❀ Line a deep 10-in (25-cm) square or round cake pan with a piece of waxed paper. Thickly grease the paper and the sides of the tin with lard. Pour in the radish mixture and smooth the top. Place on a rack in a large covered wok or steamer, cover and steam for about 1½ hours or until the pudding feels firm on top and a chopstick inserted into the center comes out clean.
❀ Invert the pudding onto a plate, but do not remove the pan until almost cool. Cut into slices and then into large squares when cold.
❀ Cook on a hot griddle with a very little oil or lard until slightly crisp and golden on the surface. Serve with soy sauce.

RADISH PUDDING

SWEET AND SOUR FISH WITH NOODLES

Beijing 北京

SWEET AND SOUR FISH WITH NOODLES

The story behind this dish concerns the Empress Dowager Cixi, who was fleeing from a foreign aggressor and took refuge in Xian. On her return to Beijing she passed through the Kai Feng Fu, one of China's ancient capitals in Henan Province.

Realizing that the Empress was fond of sweet and sour dishes, a local cook prepared sweet and sour fish with noodles for her. The Empress thought the dish delicious; it became popular and was handed down through the generations.

1 1¼-lb (625-g) carp or other meaty white fish
1 cup (4 oz) cornstarch
oil for deep-frying

SWEET AND SOUR SAUCE

2 tablespoons vegetable oil
½ cup (4 oz) sugar
¾ cup (6 oz) chicken stock
½ cup (4 oz) brown vinegar
3 tablespoons light soy sauce
1 tablespoon dark soy sauce
4 cloves garlic, chopped
1-2 pickled or fresh red chilies, chopped
1 green onion, finely chopped
2½ teaspoons cornstarch

NOODLES*

2 small eggs
2 tablespoons cold water
3 cups (12 oz) all purpose flour

To make the noodles, break the eggs into a large bowl and beat well. Add the water and one-quarter of the flour and beat this mixture until very smooth.

❀ Gradually work in the remaining flour, kneading it with your hands, then turn out onto a lightly floured surface and continue to knead until the dough feels elastic and is very smooth. Cover with a damp cloth and let stand for 20 minutes.

❀ Roll out as thinly as possible, then roll the sheet up into a cylinder and cut into very narrow strips. Toss in flour and set aside.

❀ Scale, clean and fillet the fish. Cut each fillet in half lengthwise to make four long strips. Mix the cornstarch with cold water to make a thick batter and coat the fish.

❀ Heat the oil in a wok to the smoking point, then reduce the heat slightly. Deep-fry the fish, two pieces at a time, until cooked through and lightly browned on the surface. Lift out and keep warm on a serving plate.

❀ Reheat the oil to the smoking point, reduce the heat and deep-fry the noodles in several batches until crisp and golden. Lift out and arrange on another serving dish.

❀ In another wok heat the oil for the sauce and add the sugar. Cook until it caramelizes, then add the remaining pre-mixed sauce ingredients, boiling until the sauce thickens and clears. Pour over the fish and serve.

*2-3 cakes of purchased egg noodles can be used in place of these homemade noodles. They should be softened in water first, then drained well and allowed to partially dry before deep-frying.

Beijing 北京

RICE WITH PINEAPPLE AND ASSORTED FRUIT

2 cups (12 oz) raw short-grain white rice
3 rings fresh pineapple
½ apple
1 Chinese pear or firm, unripe pear
2 tablespoons lard
2 tablespoons chopped walnuts
2 tablespoons raisins
2 tablespoons chopped candied citron
2 tablespoons chopped glacé cherries
3 tablespoons sugar

Cook the rice with 3 cups (24 oz) water over very gentle heat until the rice is tender and the liquid completely absorbed.

❀ Cut the pineapple into small fan shapes. Peel, core and dice the apple and pear.

❀ Heat a wok with the lard and stir-fry the rice until each grain is coated with the fat. Add the nuts and fruit, except the pineapple, and continue to stir-fry for another minute. Sprinkle with sugar and stir-fry a further 2 minutes or until the ingredients are tender and well mixed.

❀ Arrange the pineapple around the edge of a serving plate and pile the rice in the center.

RICE WITH PINEAPPLE AND ASSORTED FRUIT

Guangzhou 广州

GOLDEN RICE WITH PIGEON EGGS

In China there are many rice dishes, but this one is unique and was originally known as Palace Golden Rice. In feudal China, imperial chefs continually had to create new dishes to satisfy demanding empresses. One chef, Fang Shi, was said to have had the ability to turn things into gold; as this recipe demonstrates, in the hands of a capable chef plain white rice can, in fact, be transformed into "gold fragments."

4 cups (16 oz) freshly cooked white rice (about 1½ cups [8 oz] raw rice)
3 cloves garlic
3 oz (90 g) prawn or shrimp meat
2 chicken livers
5 medium eggs
1 tablespoon water
pinch of salt
½ cup (4 oz) vegetable oil
6 pigeon or quail eggs
1 teaspoon sesame oil
6 stalks choy sum or other Chinese green vegetable
½ cup (4 oz) water

SEASONING
2 tablespoons light soy sauce
1 teaspoon salt
1 teaspoon sugar
⅓ teaspoon white pepper

Spread the cooked rice on a tray to cool. Very finely chop the garlic, then dice the prawn meat and chicken livers. Beat the medium eggs lightly in a small bowl, adding 1 tablespoon water and a pinch of salt.

Heat half the vegetable oil in a wok and stir-fry the garlic for 30 seconds. Add the prawns and chicken livers and stir-fry until they change color and are beginning to firm up. Add the rice and stir-fry until warmed through. Add the seasoning ingredients and mix in well. Pour in the beaten eggs and continue to stir-fry over low heat until the eggs have mixed well with the rice. The eggs should still be quite moist and only half cooked.

Pile onto a heatproof plate and shape into a flat mound. Make six small depressions in the top and break a pigeon egg into each.

Heat the remaining vegetable oil in the wok and add the sesame oil. Put in the choy sum and stir-fry briefly, then add ½ cup water, cover and cook until the vegetables are almost tender.

Arrange around the rice dish, and place the whole dish in a steamer or on a rack in a wok. Steam over simmering water until the pigeon eggs are just cooked.

云南
Yunnxn

云南
Yunnan
BELOW THE CLOUDS

POSSIBLY the most beautiful corner in all China is the southwest. It is also possibly the least known, a great pity because Yunnan and neighboring Guizhou and western Guangxi are among the most fascinating — as well as the most scenic — areas in the land. The ravines are steep, the mountains are covered in jungle, the rivers rush in turbulence towards the Gulf of Tonkin and the mighty Mekong slashes through Yunnan. Southeast Asia lies over the next hill; Yunnan borders Burma, Laos and Vietnam, and culinary ties are close.

A rich racial stew makes up the people of the three southwesterly provinces; minorities are probably a majority in Yunnan itself, where dozens of different peoples inhabit the valleys. Some of them are tiny remnants of once-mighty tribes: peoples like the Achang, who now count themselves as only twenty thousand; the fifty-eight thousand Bulong and their cousins, the four thousand remaining Dulong; ten thousand Jinuo people and twenty-three thousand Nu. But there are also sizeable communities like the Bai (over a million); the Hani and the Yao (one million each) and hundreds of thousands of Tibetans. A million Miao live in Guizhou. Thais, too, who stayed behind when their forefathers left to form Thailand, remain in the hills. Five million Yi and fourteen million Zhuang are scattered through all three provinces. Every one of these races has its own culture and cuisine. All are mixed in with what is generally considered to be Chinese cooking to give a gastronomic treat that can be found nowhere else.

Yunnan means Below the Clouds, and the name signifies the remoteness of the land. The clouds referred to are those that eternally shroud the mountains fringing Sichuan. In the past nobody knew what lay on the far side of the forbidding mountains that marked the limits of Chinese civilization, so they just referred to it as "Below the Clouds." This lack of knowledge bred legends and myths of a fabulous land, a kind of Chinese El Dorado. Although the Yuan Dynasty deposed the

CROSSING THE RICE PADDIES

LEO MEIER

(previous page)

AUTUMNAL FIELDS IN NORTHERN YUNNAN

GREGORY HEISLER

A BAI GRANDMOTHER IN HER KITCHEN

GREGORY HEISLER

WATER BUFFALOES, ESSENTIAL TO TRADITIONAL FARMING LIFE

GREGORY HEISLER

Thai kings of Yunnan in the thirteenth century, the province still lay outside the pale of knowledge, wracked by ceaseless Muslim uprisings that were put down by successive dynasties with a bloodthirstiness outstanding even for the Manchus. Then, in the early years of the twentieth century, the great mineral wealth of Yunnan was discovered, and the myth of an El Dorado in the misty hills turned out to be true.

The many races of the southwest provinces have borrowed freely from each others' kitchens. The culinary result is a splendid smorgasbord from hill tribes and hunters, farmers and fishermen, and the sophisticated gastronomy of Nanning, the capital of Guangxi and a city which can boast of a long and unique cuisine of its own. Kunming, Yunnan's capital, claims China's most perfect climate and is known as the city of perpetual spring. Its restaurants also have a well-deserved reputation for exotic dishes which carry the tangy flavor of Vietnamese herbs, steamed carp and perch from the cool waters of the high-country lakes, and noodles served with green peppers. The red peppers of Sichuan make guest appearances in many Yunnan dishes, and one of the gifts of the Kunming kitchen is steamed chicken in a Yunnan pot, which is the Chinese version of a French pot-au-feu.

Into the regional cooking pot go many influences. The various minorities who make up the colorful anthropological map of the southwest make their contribution. The largest recognized minority in China are the Zhuang, who live in their own sprawling, autonomous region occupying half of southern Guangxi Province. A happy, amiable people, the Zhuang have developed a rich and nutritious diet based on the abundance of the fertile southern coast and mountains. One specialty that features in their feasts is a giant pyramid-shaped dumpling stuffed with rice and ground pork. These dumplings are said to be the biggest in China and cook for many hours in sealed pottery jars over the embers of a slow fire.

PUPILS AT THE LI JIANG NATIONAL SCHOOL, YUNNAN PROVINCE

GREGORY HEISLER

China also has minorities within minorities, adding further colorful confusion to its gastronomic map. During the Yuan Dynasty (1206-1368 AD), the Mongols determined to bring the entire country under their central rule. The best way to do so was to establish colonies in the outer reaches of the empire. This they did, but as in later years their empire in China shriveled the outposts were abandoned, leaving racial enclaves like the one on the shores of Lake Lugu, which lies like a spectacular pearl in the highlands on the Yunnan-Sichuan border. There today, Mosuo minority people still proudly claim Mongol origin and on feast days celebrate with dishes like stewed lamb. The descendants of the Mongols in Yunnan – Muslim colonists transplanted to take Yuan rule to the area – are the only sizeable group in south China who today appreciate lamb.

Other ingredients and ideas come from the bordering lands. Indian culture, including Buddhism, seeped into China through Yunnan and has left an underlying influence, and the Han Chinese have brought with them their own many cuisines. The results are a many-splendored table: one dinner can include tribal, Islamic, Vietnamese, Sichuan and other dishes.

The cooking of Guizhou likewise reflects trends from neighboring provinces – the red pepper of Hunan is a notable feature. For generations Guizhou was the poor,

YOUNG BUDDHIST ACOLYTES   LEONG KA TAI

EVERY FERTILE PIECE OF ARABLE LAND IS UTILIZED

MARY ELLEN MARK

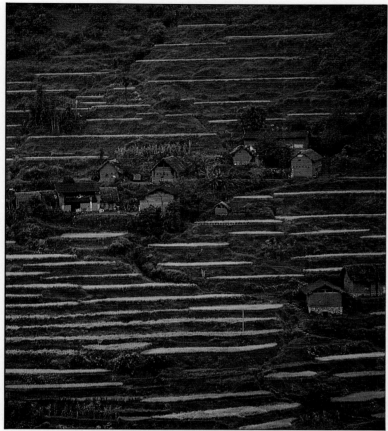

backward relation of southern China. It was said there was not one piece of flat land in the entire province, an exaggerated claim unhappily based on fact. The rice grows vertically in Guizhou, it is said, and seeing the terraces that have been adzed with agony out of the steep hillsides, each as small as a garden and built with enormous labor, one is prepared to believe it. But the rivers are rich, the woods provide game and the province has a selection of mushrooms and fungi second to none.

For generations landlocked, poor Guizhou was also desperately short of salt. There was none to be mined as in other inland provinces, and most people were too poor to buy the salt imported from the distant ports of the South China Sea. Salt was a luxury, and when it could be afforded a block of salt took pride of place in the center of the table. Family and important guests would gather, take a piece of meat or vegetable in their chopsticks and rub it over the salt before eating the morsel. The exotic taste of salt was a rare and valued treat. Other provinces may cook sweet and sour, but Guizhou is known for its unique contribution of salt and sour cooking. Such a recipe calls for a fish to be rubbed inside and out with salt, then to be stuffed with strongly salted pickle and fried. When it is served it comes with yet more salt and pepper. Guizhou diners of today are making up for the salt their forebears could not afford.

A VILLAGE NESTLES AMIDST CAREFULLY TENDED TERRACES   GREGORY HEISLER

A VILLAGE COOK

GREGORY HEISLER

THE RICH FIELDS AND DRAMATIC LANDSCAPE OF NORTHWESTERN YUNNAN

GREGORY HEISLER

蔬果
Vegetables & Fruit

Vegetables & Fruit

FRUIT AND VEGETABLE SELLERS AT SHIMIAN MARKET, SICHUAN PROVINCE

THE daily food of the Chinese is among the healthiest in the world, due mainly to the preponderance of vegetables. Although no longer the incredible luxury it once was, the rarity of meat for most of the population over many centuries has helped to make a tradition in which vegetables play a vital culinary role at the center of the gastronomic stage.

In any city or hamlet, seasonal vegetables can be seen for sale in busy street markets. Like a culinary kaleidoscope ceaselessly in motion, the colors, variety and types of vegetables on sale change with the locality and the season as new crops are harvested and reach the marketplace. Foreigners will recognize many familiar vegetables on sale, because for thousands of years the Chinese farmer has enthusiastically adopted plants brought back by returning traders and adventurers, and chefs have just as keenly adapted these newcomers to existing recipes. Vegetables from every continent grow in China today, but so do many others which have seldom made the gastronomic trip abroad.

With the economic reorganization of recent years, under which China's eight hundred million peasants have been encouraged to grow and sell their own private crops after meeting state quotas, the range of vegetables on sale has notably increased. Nowhere is this more evident than in the verdant south, where a subtropical climate helps the diligent market gardeners coax a fresh vegetable crop from their tiny plots every two months. It is a very different story in the north. Any autumn visitor to Beijing can see loads of Tianjin cabbages – the big, elongated vegetables known as Chinese cabbages – trucked into the city from the state farms of Hebei Province. The cabbage is stored in every home to eke out the chill winter months when fresh vegetables do not grow, and ones that are on sale are expensive imports to the capital from more temperate zones. The hardy cabbages keep for months in the cold winters, and although the outer layers may become yellowish and dry, the inside remains tender and juicy until spring returns. Along with turnips and a vast variety of pickles, the humble cabbage plays a vital role in the daily diet of many millions of northern Chinese for six months of the year.

One of the gastronomic tragedies of China's culinary history is that so many of the delightful regional specialties are unknown elsewhere. The blue turnip of Tianjin, for example, is still unknown to most people outside Hebei and Shandong. Similarly, some of the crunchy and deliciously fresh winter-garden crops of the south never make it to the northern markets, where they would bring joy to the monotony of Manchurian tables in the long winter months. With the exception of the wealthy and the privileged, people have always had to make do with what is produced close at hand. This is, however, slowly changing with improvements in transport.

The Chinese chef in every regional kitchen insists, wherever possible, on the freshest vegetables — preferably straight from the garden, but if that is impossible, certainly direct from the market. This fastidiousness can be seen in any Chinese market, where buyers prod, poke and peer at the goods on display to ensure they have not passed their peak. Many newcomers to a Chinese table may think they are eating some exotic new plant when they are merely enjoying an unfamiliar part of an old favorite. The leaves of the pea plant, for example, are generally discarded in the West, but are a prized delight in Guangzhou. Another example is the spinach root, usually unknown in Europe, but as eagerly cooked and eaten in China as the green leaves. For the uninitiated, China has a vast, baffling array of vegetables. This is because over the centuries China has borrowed with willing enthusiasm from every continent to add to its own rich garden heritage, and a nation of gardeners lets no small corner of ground go to waste – gourds, squashes and melons grow on vines covering storehouses in the fields; the bamboos that line village lanes provide food as well as building materials; seaweed gives a free, mineral-rich crop, while inland the prized water chestnut and valuable lotus grow in ponds which are home for duck and carp alike.

Vegetables in the Chinese cuisine have played an important role for four major reasons: religion, poverty, health and farm economics. Those who follow Buddhist teachings choose to avoid eating meat (though not necessarily fish), and vegetable dishes have been raised to glorious heights to provide a vibrant, exciting meatless cuisine. On the other hand, millions of peasants have traditionally been unable to afford meat – famine, in-

vasion, immigration or political instability have often caused culinary chaos making meat and fish too expensive for any but the wealthy or privileged.

Even in the good times there have been many cooks in the kitchens of China who prefer the healthy vitality of vegetables. Ancient herbalists have long recognized (although not always aware of the scientific and dietary reasons) that vegetables play a vital part in maintaining good health, and insisted that a variety of fresh garden foods should be on the menu at every meal. The growth of China's huge population has put immense pressure on the patient, ancient agricultural practices, and simple economics has dictated the intensive farming practices in use today; one field of carefully tended vegetables can keep many more people alive than if the same area were used to graze two sheep or a cow. Hence the absence of grazing stock in most parts of the country: plants are more efficient people-feeders than animals.

A STRIKING SELECTION OF CHINESE VEGETABLES

SHUFUNOTOMO

Guangzhou 广州

STUFFED WINTER MELON SOUP

This is a traditional banquet delicacy to serve during summer and autumn. The melon takes on a jade color, appears crystal-like and is translucent, the ingredients within the melon being half visible.

2 lb (1 kg) rounded end of a winter melon*
1 chicken carcass
4 oz (125 g) prawn or shrimp meat
4 oz (125 g) frog or chicken meat
4 oz (125 g) duck meat
4 oz (125 g) lean pork
4 oz (125 g) lean ham
4 oz (125 g) fresh or canned straw mushrooms
4 oz (125 g) luffa or stalks of broccoli or kale
6 cups (1 l) Superior Stock (*see page 124*) or chicken stock
cilantro leaves (garnish)

SEASONING

2 teaspoons salt
1 teaspoon sesame oil
1 teaspoon sugar
1/3 teaspoon white pepper

Thinly skin the end of the melon, then scoop out the seeds and fibrous center. Place in a large pot with the chicken carcass inside and add boiling water to cover. Simmer gently for about 20 minutes. Discard the chicken bones and the water and set the melon aside.

Cut the meat and vegetables into small dice. Place in a large casserole and add the seasoning ingredients. Carefully turn over the melon so that it covers the diced ingredients, forming a dome in the casserole. Pour the stock into the casserole, then set it on a rack in a wok or steamer, cover and simmer over gentle heat for about 1 hour or until the diced ingredients and the melon are completely tender and full of flavor. Garnish the melon top with cilantro leaves or designs cut from melon or cucumber skin. Skilled chefs often cut the design directly onto the melon before cooking.

If unobtainable, substitute a hollowed watermelon shell and add chopped chayote as a vegetable.

Sichuan 四川

STUFFED PEA SPROUT SOUP

Pea sprouts, in actual fact, are not sprouts at all but the tender round leaves of the sweet pea plant. They are bright green and have a delicate taste. Served as a vegetable accompaniment, pea sprouts are simply stir-fried, but in this interesting and unusual recipe, small balls of finely ground chicken are pressed onto the pea leaves to make a delicious and subtly flavored soup. Giving the impression of a bouquet of white flowers, this dish is a favorite at springtime banquets.

4 oz (125 g) chicken breasts
1 small egg white
2-3 teaspoons cornstarch
1 lb (500 g) pea leaves
5 cups (1 1/4 l) clear chicken stock
1 tomato
salt

Very finely grind the chicken breasts with a cleaver or in a food processor. Add the lightly beaten egg white and the cornstarch and mix to a paste.

Rinse the pea leaves in cold water, sorting out any tough stems and discolored leaves. Drain well and wipe the larger leaves with a cloth to dry. Press a small ball of the chicken paste onto as many leaves as possible.

Bring the stock to boil, then reduce the heat and add the pea leaves. Simmer for about 5 minutes, or until the vegetable is tender and the chicken white, then add salt to taste. Do not overcook, or the leaves will turn yellow and become bitter.

Drop the tomato into a saucepan of boiling water, remove and peel. Cut it into wedges, then trim away the pulp and seeds leaving petal shapes. Arrange these on top of the soup and serve at once.

Guangzhou 广州

HAINAN COCONUT POTAGE

Coconut trees are abundant in tropical China, particularly on Hainan Island, where this dish originated. There are many stories about coconuts; one concerns Emperor Cheng Di who, in about 20 BC, chose Zhao Feiyan as his Empress. Her sister wove a mat with coconut leaves and sent it to her as a present to congratulate her, wishing her to be a mother to many sons, just like the fruitful coconut tree.

2 coconuts
1 oz (30 g) fresh mushrooms
4 oz (125 g) chicken breast meat
2 oz (60 g) lean ham
coconut or peanut oil
½ cup (4 oz) coconut cream
3 cups (24 oz) water or chicken stock
¾ teaspoon salt
cilantro

Saw the tops off the coconuts and use the liquid as a refreshing drink.

🌼 Cut the mushrooms, chicken and ham into small dice. Sauté briefly in a wok with a little coconut or peanut oil and place in a saucepan with the coconut cream, water and salt. Bring to boil and simmer for about 5 minutes; then divide the soup between the two coconut shells, place the tops of the shells in position and set on a rack in a wok or steamer. Cover and steam for about 30 minutes or until the soup has thoroughly absorbed the flavor of the coconut.

🌼 Garnish with chopped cilantro and serve.

HAINAN COCONUT POTAGE

THICK JADEITE SOUP

Beijing 北京

THICK JADEITE SOUP

There is a touching story behind the creation of this dish, concerning a beautiful young girl who was about to be married to a handsome prince when their tribe was invaded by foreigners. Before he departed to lead his army into battle, the prince gave the girl a piece of jade as a token of his love.

The girl gazed at the piece of jade night and day, thinking of her prince, and could not eat or sleep. Her worried mother made this nutritious soup, in which the bright green of spinach contrasted with the white of the chicken to represent the piece of jade she so prized. She ate, regained her health and married the triumphant prince.

SPINACH SOUP

8 oz (250 g) fresh spinach leaves, finely chopped
1 teaspoon rice wine or dry sherry
1 teaspoon sugar
1½ tablespoons lard or vegetable oil
1½ cups (12 oz) chicken stock
1 tablespoon cornstarch

CHICKEN SOUP

9 oz (280 g) chicken breast meat
1 teaspoon rice wine or dry sherry
½ teaspoon sugar
¾ teaspoon salt
2 teaspoons ginger juice
3 egg whites
1½ cups (12 oz) chicken stock
1 tablespoon cornstarch
1 tablespoon lard or vegetable oil
cherry tomatoes (garnish)

Stir-fry the spinach in a wok with the rice wine, sugar and lard until softened, then add the stock and cover. Simmer gently for about 7 minutes until the spinach is tender. Mix the cornstarch with a little cold water or stock, stir into the soup and simmer, stirring, until thickened.

🌼 To prepare the chicken soup, very finely grind the chicken meat and season with the rice wine, sugar, salt and ginger juice. Beat in the egg whites, stirring until the mixture is very thick and smooth. Add the chicken stock and cornstarch and beat again thoroughly.

🌼 Heat the wok and add the lard. Pour in the chicken mixture and simmer, stirring, for about 6 minutes over moderate heat or until the chicken has cooked through and is very white.

🌼 Pour the chicken soup into a deep serving dish, keeping it as much to one side of the dish as possible. Reheat the spinach soup and carefully pour into the other side of the dish, using a wide spatula to push the chicken soup to the side, so that the two colors are clearly separated. Garnish with cherry tomatoes and serve.

Beijing 北京

WINTER MELON CUP WITH LOTUS SEEDS

The giant white winter melon is a common Chinese vegetable, very juicy and rich in vitamins though rather plain in taste. It is said to clean the system, reduce swelling, stop pain and make the skin smooth, soft and moist. In this recipe the soup ingredients are simmered in the scooped-out melon skin.

1 8-lb (4-kg) winter melon*
chicken stock
1 oz (30 g) dried lotus seeds, soaked for 1 hour
3 oz (90 g) duck breast meat
2 dried black mushrooms, soaked for 25 minutes
3 oz (90 g) lean ham
3 oz (90 g) lean pork
1 dried scallop, soaked for 25 minutes
1 tablespoon rice wine or dry sherry
2 slices fresh ginger
1 egg white, well beaten
1 tablespoon cornstarch
1½ oz (45 g) fresh or canned crabmeat

Select the more attractive end of the melon, wipe it with a damp cloth and scoop out the seeds and the fibrous center. Carve a decorative motif on the skin around the sides and use a sharp knife to make zig-zag cuts around the rim.

※ Fill the melon with boiling stock and add a large pinch of salt. Stand upright in a heatproof dish and place on a rack in a wok or steamer. Cover and steam over briskly boiling water for about 20 minutes.

※ Skin the lotus seeds and use a toothpick to push out the bitter center core. Finely dice the duck meat, mushroom caps, ham and pork, and shred the scallop. Place in a saucepan, adding the lotus seeds and wine. Ladle the stock from the melon over the ingredients and bring to boil. Cook until the lotus seeds are tender, then return to the melon.

※ Add the ginger, egg white and cornstarch mixed with a little cold water and return to the steamer. Steam for 30-35 minutes, then remove the ginger and stir in the crabmeat just before serving.

*If unobtainable, substitute a hollowed watermelon shell and add chopped chayote as a vegetable.

GREEN BEANS WITH CHICKEN OIL

BROAD BEANS WITH CHICKEN OIL

Shanghai 上海

GREEN BEANS WITH CHICKEN OIL

Rendered chicken fat is used to add a gloss and a deliciously rich flavor to many dishes, particularly fresh vegetables. It is sometimes used as cooking oil, but is usually heated up and poured over the finished dish.

10 oz (315 g) fresh green beans
1 tablespoon vegetable oil
3/4 teaspoon salt
1/2 cup (4 oz) chicken stock
1 teaspoon cornstarch
2 teaspoons rendered chicken fat, melted

Rinse the beans, drain well, and cut off both ends.
✿ Heat the oil in a wok and stir-fry the beans for 2 minutes. Add about 1 tablespoon of water, cover and cook for another minute or until tender but still crisp. Add the salt and the chicken stock mixed with cornstarch and simmer, stirring, until the sauce thickens. Stir in the chicken fat before serving.

Shanghai 上海

BROAD BEANS WITH CHICKEN OIL

10 oz (315 g) fresh broad beans, shelled
1 teaspoon salt
2 cups (16 oz) chicken stock
2 teaspoons cornstarch
1 tablespoon rendered chicken fat, melted

Shell the beans, scald in boiling water, then drain and immerse in cold water until cool. This brightens the color. Drain and peel off the outer skin. Place the beans, salt and chicken stock in a wok, bring to boil and simmer until the beans are tender. Remove with a slotted spoon and set aside.
✿ Boil the liquid briskly until reduced to about 1/2 cup (4 oz). Mix the cornstarch with a little cold water and stir into the sauce to thicken; return the beans and stir until warmed through. Mix in the chicken fat and serve.

Sichuan 四川

"CHICKEN" AND DRIED LILY FLOWERS

"Golden needles" are the dried flower buds of the tiger lily. These lilies grow in the south and north of China, but are especially abundant in Sichuan. The flower is picked while still in bud, and usually sold in the dried form, the best quality being bright yellow. Nutritious and delicious, dried lily buds impart a subtle muskiness to a dish. In this recipe they are artistically presented in small knotted bundles with cubes of vegetarian chicken.

2 oz (60 g) dried lily buds (golden needles)
12 oz (375 g) vegetarian chicken*
1 whole bamboo shoot, canned or cooked fresh
3 tablespoons oil for frying
1 teaspoon sesame oil

SEASONING/SAUCE

1 1/2 cups (12 oz) chicken stock
1 tablespoon rice wine or dry sherry
1 tablespoon light soy sauce
3-4 slices fresh ginger
1 teaspoon sugar
3/4 teaspoon salt
pinch of white pepper
2-3 teaspoons cornstarch

Soak the lily buds in hot water for about 30 minutes to soften. Cut off the hard ends and tie together in pairs, knotting in the center. Drain and squeeze out excess water.
✿ Cut the "chicken" into bite-size pieces. Cut the bamboo shoot into thin slices, using only the open-structured point of the shoot. Heat the oil in a wok, stir-fry the lily buds briefly and push to one side. Add the "chicken" and bamboo shoot and stir-fry until they are crisp and lightly colored.
✿ Add the pre-mixed seasoning/sauce ingredients, except the cornstarch, and bring to boil. Simmer, covered, over gentle heat for about 30 minutes or until the "chicken" is tender and the lily buds have imparted their unique flavor to the dish.
✿ Mix the cornstarch with a little cold water and stir into the sauce, simmering until thickened. Add the sesame oil and serve at once.

Vegetarian chicken is made from layers of bean curd skins seasoned with soy sauce, compressed to a rectangular shape and steamed. It can sometimes be purchased from Chinese food stores. Chicken breasts can be used as a substitute and cooked in the same way.

SPRING BAMBOO SHOOTS WITH SALTED VEGETABLES

Shanghai 上海

SPRING BAMBOO SHOOTS WITH SALTED VEGETABLES

Bamboo grows abundantly south of the Yellow River in China. The shoots are a valued ingredient in Chinese cooking and differ according to the time of harvest. Spring bamboo shoots have a faint scent and a clear color. Winter bamboo shoots are plump, short and crisp, with a distinct taste, and can be easily stored for use throughout the year. Bamboo shoots gathered in the summer and autumn are called whip bamboo shoots and only the tender parts at the top are eaten.

1 lb (500 g) fresh or canned spring bamboo shoots
1 oz (30 g) salted mustard greens, shredded*
1 teaspoon cornstarch
½ teaspoon sesame oil

SEASONING/STOCK

1 cup (8 oz) chicken stock
2 tablespoons lard
1 teaspoon salt
½ teaspoon sugar

Trim the bamboo shoots and cut them into wedge-shaped slices about 1-in (2.5-cm) long.

❉ In a wok heat the seasoning/stock ingredients to the boiling point, add the bamboo shoots and cover. Simmer until tender but still crisp, about 6 minutes. Add the mustard greens and stir in evenly, then add the cornstarch mixed with a little cold water and stir until the sauce thickens. Adjust the seasoning and stir in the sesame oil before serving.

Available as a preserve in Chinese food stores.

Sichuan 四川

SICHUAN PICKLED VEGETABLES

Pickled vegetables are very popular in Sichuan and are prepared by almost every family in the towns and villages. They refresh the palate, removing greasiness and helping fats break down in the system. Their stimulating saltiness, coupled with the sharp taste of vinegar and chili, has a warming effect on the body. Pickling preserves vegetables, making them available at all seasons – even during midwinter, when fresh vegetables are in limited supply in China.

Pickles are served and used in many ways. They may be eaten uncooked as a side dish, stir-fried in different dishes or added to braises and soups to heighten flavor.

Pickles are made throughout the year as the vegetables come into season. Typical Sichuan pickled vegetables include cabbage, kale, turnip, giant white radish, carrot, gourd, chili, bell pepper, long beans, celery, young ginger and the local long, thin cucumbers similar to those used in Japanese cooking.

The method used and the degree of saltiness or hotness required – a matter of personal choice – will dictate the fermenting time. Pickled vegetables, usually packed in large stone jars, last for many months and generally do not require refrigeration.

Family recipes for pickles, and those created by restaurant chefs, are usually closely guarded secrets. The seasoning ingredients comprise salt, dried chilies, rice wine and other liquors, and brown sugar. But other spices and condiments, including those that make up the famed Chinese five-spice mixture (cassia, fennel, pepper, licorice or anise, and cinnamon) are often used for flavor and aroma.

SICHUAN PICKLED VEGETABLES

SWEET AND SOUR VEGETARIAN SPARERIBS

BAMBOO SHOOTS STUFFED WITH PRAWNS

Beijing 北京

SWEET AND SOUR VEGETARIAN SPARERIBS

This tasty vegetarian dish was created by a famous Beijing chef who fashioned typical vegetarian ingredients – yam and winter bamboo shoots – into the shape of spareribs. Crisp outside and tender inside, this dish is well known and much appreciated among the many Chinese vegetarians who hold the yam to have important nutritional and medicinal value.

3 lb (1½ kg) yams or taro
1 teaspoon salt
½ cup (2 oz) cornstarch
7 oz (220 g) fresh or canned winter bamboo shoots
2 teaspoons sesame oil
3 tablespoons peanut oil

SAUCE

1 tablespoon sesame oil
1 tablespoon finely chopped fresh ginger
½ cup (4 oz) chicken stock
1 tablespoon dark soy sauce
1 tablespoon sugar
2½ teaspoons cornstarch
2 teaspoons brown vinegar
salt and pepper

Peel the yams and cut into cubes. Place on a rack in a wok or steamer, cover and steam until very tender, then mash while still warm, adding the salt and cornstarch. Mix until smooth and set aside.

🦐 Peel the fresh bamboo shoots and cut off the tough bases. Cut shoots lengthwise into quarters about 2 in (5 cm) long. Cut away the corrugated inner part of each piece to produce a smooth strip resembling a sparerib bone.

🦐 Press a portion of the mashed yam around each "bone" to give the appearance of a sparerib, leaving both ends of the "bone" exposed.

🦐 In a large wok heat the 2 teaspoons of sesame oil and the peanut oil until very hot. Carefully fry the "spareribs" in several batches until golden brown. Drain and pile on a serving plate.

🦐 Rinse the wok, add 1 tablespoon of sesame oil and stir-fry the chopped ginger for about 30 seconds. Mix the remaining sauce ingredients in a dish and pour into the wok. Bring to the boil and simmer, stirring, until thickened. Return the "spareribs" and stir gently in the sauce until well coated. Remove and sprinkle with a little extra sesame oil before serving.

Shanghai 上海

BAMBOO SHOOTS STUFFED WITH PRAWNS

3 oz (90 g) peeled fresh prawns or shrimp
3 oz (90 g) white fish fillet
3 oz (90 g) pork fat
1 lb (500 g) fresh or canned spring bamboo shoots
2 egg whites, beaten
1 cup (4 oz) cornstarch
1 lb (500 g) lard
1 tablespoon rendered chicken fat, melted

SAUCE

¾ cup (6 oz) chicken stock
2 teaspoons rice wine or dry sherry
1½ teaspoons cornstarch
½ teaspoon salt

Grind the prawns, fish and pork fat until smooth and mix together thoroughly.

🦐 Simmer the fresh bamboo shoots until partially cooked, and drain well. Make two lengthwise slits from the center to the tip and fill with the stuffing, squeezing the bamboo shoots back into their conical shape. Dip into the egg white and coat with cornstarch.

🦐 Heat the lard in a wok and fry the stuffed bamboo shoots over moderate heat for about 3 minutes, then remove and drain well.

🦐 Mix the sauce ingredients together, bring to boil, return the bamboo shoots and cook quickly over high heat for 2-3 minutes. Sprinkle with the chicken fat and serve at once.

STIR-FRIED PEAS WITH BROWN BEAN SAUCE

Beijing 北京

STIR-FRIED PEAS WITH BROWN BEAN SAUCE

4 oz (125 g) lean pork
8 oz (250 g) fresh peas, shelled
2 tablespoons lard
2 green onions, chopped
3 slices fresh ginger, chopped
1 tablespoon brown bean sauce
2 teaspoons light soy sauce
1 teaspoon rice wine or dry sherry
2 tablespoons chicken stock
½ teaspoon sesame oil

Dice the pork to the size of peas. Boil the peas until just tender and drain well, then cover with cold water and set aside.
※ Stir-fry the diced pork in the lard in a wok over high heat until it turns white, then add the green onions, ginger and brown bean sauce. Stir-fry for about 1 minute or until fragrant. Add the peas with the rice wine, stock and sesame oil, stir-fry together briefly and serve.

Beijing 北京

STIR-FRIED CUCUMBER

4 oz (125 g) lean pork
1 large cucumber
1 teaspoon salt
1 tablespoon lard
1 green onion, chopped
3 slices fresh ginger, chopped
1 tablespoon brown bean sauce
2 teaspoons light soy sauce
1 teaspoon rice wine or dry sherry
1½ tablespoons chicken stock
½ teaspoon sesame oil

Cut the pork into small dice. Peel and dice the cucumber, discarding the seed cores. Sprinkle with salt and let stand for 10 minutes. Rinse well in cold water and drain thoroughly.
※ Stir-fry the pork in the lard in a wok over high heat until it turns white. Add the green onion, ginger and brown bean sauce and stir-fry for about 1 minute or until fragrant. Add the cucumber, soy sauce, wine and stock and stir-fry together for another minute, then add the sesame oil and serve.

STIR-FRIED CUCUMBER

Guangzhou 广州

DEEP-FRIED MASHED POTATO IN PEAR SHAPES

The imitation of a pear is almost perfect in this innovative dish. The flavor is delicate, soft and smooth. After tasting several other courses and some wine at a banquet, the Chinese like to serve an imitation dish to match the cheerful atmosphere.

1½ lb (750 g) peeled potatoes
2 tablespoons cornstarch
1 small slice ham
2 eggs, well beaten
1 cup dry breadcrumbs

FILLING

1½ oz (45 g) chicken hearts
1½ oz (45 g) lean pork
1 oz (30 g) fresh prawn or shrimp meat
3 fresh or dried mushrooms, soaked for 25 minutes
1 tablespoon lard

SEASONING

1 teaspoon rice wine or dry sherry
½ teaspoon sugar
½ teaspoon salt
⅓ teaspoon sesame oil
pinch of white pepper

Cut the potatoes into cubes and boil in salted water until very tender. Drain thoroughly and leave to dry for about 1 hour. Mash smoothly, adding the cornstarch, and set aside.
※ To prepare the filling, finely dice the chicken hearts, pork, prawns and mushrooms and mix with the seasoning ingredients. Heat the lard in a wok and sauté the filling for about 2 minutes over moderate heat until cooked. Remove and let cool.
※ Divide the potato mixture into 10 portions and form each into a flat round. Place a spoonful of the filling in the center of each and, working with well oiled hands, form each into a pear shape, ensuring that the filling is totally enclosed. Cut the ham into slivers and use as the "stems."
※ Heat the oil in a wok over moderate heat, coat each potato "pear" with beaten egg and breadcrumbs and deep-fry until golden. Lift out carefully, drain well and serve at once.

DEEP-FRIED MASHED POTATO IN PEAR SHAPES

STIR-FRIED HAZELNUTS WITH PORK AND BROWN BEAN SAUCE

BROAD BEANS AND BAMBOO SHOOTS

Beijing 北京

STIR-FRIED HAZELNUTS WITH PORK AND BROWN BEAN SAUCE

3 oz (90 g) lean pork
4 oz (125 g) hazelnuts
2 cups (16 oz) peanut oil
2 green onions, chopped
2 slices fresh ginger, shredded
1 tablespoon brown bean sauce
1 teaspoon light soy sauce
1 teaspoon rice wine or dry sherry
2 tablespoons chicken stock
½ teaspoon sesame oil

Cut the pork into small dice. Toast the hazelnuts or blanch in boiling water until the skins loosen, then rub off.

❋ Heat the peanut oil in a wok and fry the hazelnuts until lightly colored; remove and set aside.

❋ Pour off all but 2 tablespoons of the oil and stir-fry the pork until it turns white. Add the green onion, ginger and brown bean sauce and stir-fry together for 1½ minutes.

❋ Add the hazelnuts, soy sauce, rice wine and stock. Simmer for 2 minutes, then sprinkle with the sesame oil and serve at once.

Sichuan 四川

BROAD BEANS AND BAMBOO SHOOTS

4 oz (125 g) fresh or frozen broad beans
1 tablespoon lard
6 oz (185 g) fresh spring bamboo tips, or sliced canned
    bamboo shoots
1 cup (8 oz) chicken stock
1 teaspoon salt
1 teaspoon soy flour or cornstarch
1 tablespoon rendered chicken fat, melted

Drop the broad beans into boiling water and simmer briefly until the skins loosen, then drain and peel off the skins to reveal the jade green beans.

❋ Heat the lard in a wok and stir-fry the broad beans and bamboo shoots together over moderate heat for about 1½ minutes. Pour in the stock, reserving a little to mix with the thickening agent, and add the salt. Cover and simmer until tender but still crisp. Mix the soy flour or cornstarch with the

reserved stock, pour into the wok and simmer gently, stirring, until thickened.

❋ Spoon onto a serving plate and carefully stir in the chicken fat. Serve hot or cold.

Shanghai 上海

GREEN VEGETABLE HEARTS WITH CREAM SAUCE

1½ lb (750 g) green vegetable hearts, or young bok choy or
    broccoli
2 tablespoons oil for frying
2 teaspoons cornstarch
1 tablespoon cream

SEASONING/SAUCE

½ cup (4 oz) chicken stock
1 teaspoon salt
½ teaspoon pepper

Remove the outer leaves of the vegetables, wash thoroughly and drain well. Scald in boiling water for a few seconds, drain and rinse in cold water to retain the bright green of the leaves.

❋ Heat the oil in a wok and stir-fry the vegetables quickly until partially cooked, then add the seasoning/sauce ingredients, cover and simmer until the vegetables are tender.

❋ Stir the cornstarch into the cream and pour into the wok, stirring until the sauce thickens. If the sauce in the wok has evaporated, add a splash of cold water to give a good quantity of creamy sauce.

❋ Check the seasoning, then turn out onto a serving plate and serve at once.

GREEN VEGETABLE HEARTS WITH CREAM SAUCE

TOMATOES STUFFED WITH EIGHT DELICACIES

Beijing 北京

Tomatoes Stuffed with Eight Delicacies

The number eight is considered to be lucky in China. The old city of Beijing, for example, is said to have been built like the body of an eight-armed warrior, for it had eight gates. The lucky number eight also features in Chinese cooking, where eight different ingredients are often used in a stuffing, as in this dish.

6 large ripe tomatoes
hard-cooked eggs (garnish)
button mushrooms (garnish)

FILLING

2 oz (60 g) white fish fillet
2 oz (60 g) chicken breast meat
4 fresh or canned button mushrooms
4 fresh or canned straw mushrooms
4 dried black mushrooms, soaked for 25 minutes
2 small stalks Chinese kale (gai larn) or broccoli
1½ oz (45 g) fresh or canned bamboo shoots
1 2-in (5-cm) piece cucumber

SEASONING

1 tablespoon rendered chicken fat, melted
2 teaspoons rice wine or dry sherry
¾ teaspoon salt
1 slice fresh ginger, finely chopped

SAUCE

¾ cup (6 oz) chicken stock
1½ teaspoons cornstarch
1 teaspoon rice wine or dry sherry
½ teaspoon salt

Drop the tomatoes into a pot of boiling water for about 8 seconds, then remove and peel carefully. Slice the tops off and reserve, then scoop out the seeds and soft inner flesh and set aside.

To prepare the filling, place the fish and chicken with the fresh and the dried black mushrooms on a rack in a wok or steamer, cover and steam until tender. Boil the vegetable stalks to soften. Chop all the filling ingredients into very small dice, add the seasoning ingredients and mix well. Stuff the tomatoes with this filling and put the lids in place.

Arrange in a heatproof dish and steam for about 15 minutes, then drain off the liquid that has accumulated in the dish. Garnish with hard-cooked eggs and button mushrooms.

Boil the sauce ingredients in the wok, stirring until thickened, and pour over the tomatoes before serving.

MUSHROOMS AND STUFFED BOK CHOY HEARTS

Beijing 北京

Mushrooms and Stuffed Bok Choy Hearts

12 young bok choy hearts
3 oz (90 g) white fish fillet
cornstarch
1 teaspoon dried shrimp eggs or 1 small carrot
24 small fresh or canned button mushrooms
½ cup (4 oz) chicken stock
salt
1 tablespoon rendered chicken fat, melted

SEASONING

1 egg white, well beaten
1 tablespoon finely chopped green onion
2 teaspoons rice wine or dry sherry
2 teaspoons melted lard
1 teaspoon ginger juice
⅓ teaspoon salt

Wash the bok choy hearts and cut in halves lengthwise, then trim the root section so that the leaves are just holding together at the bottom. Scald in boiling water, then rinse in cold water to retain the color. Drain well, coat the root section on the inside with cornstarch and set aside.

Grind the fish very finely and mix with the seasoning ingredients. Beat the mixture until it is smooth and white and place a spoonful of it into the root section of each piece of vegetable.

Finely shred the carrot, if used, and sprinkle over the fish stuffing, or add a few shrimp eggs.

Turn each mushroom cap between your fingers and, using a sharp knife held at an angle to the cap, make a series of curving cuts following the natural shape of the cap from center top to the edge. Remove narrow strips of mushroom flesh so that the finished cap has a pinwheel effect when viewed from the top. Sprinkle with salt and arrange in the center of a heatproof plate.

Place the stuffed bok choy hearts around the edge of the dish, filling outwards, and set on a rack in a wok or steamer. Cover and steam for about 15 minutes or until the vegetables and mushrooms are both tender.

Pour the chicken stock into a wok with the liquid from the plate, add ½ teaspoon salt and bring to boil. Simmer until slightly reduced, then add the chicken fat and pour over the vegetables before serving.

GREEN PEPPERS WITH PRAWN FILLING

DRY STEWED WINTER BAMBOO SHOOTS WITH MUSHROOMS

Guangzhou 广州

GREEN PEPPERS WITH PRAWN FILLING

Green bell peppers originated in the South American tropics and were introduced into China during the Ming Dynasty (1368-1644 AD). The Guangdong variety have rounded, ridged shapes resembling lanterns and are called either lantern or bell peppers.

6 green bell peppers
6 oz (185 g) fatty pork
6 oz (185 g) fresh prawn or shrimp meat
3 tablespoons cornstarch
oil for frying

SEASONING

½ teaspoon salt
½ teaspoon sugar
pinch of baking soda
pinch of white pepper

SAUCE

1 tablespoon fermented black beans
2 green onions
1 teaspoon grated fresh ginger
1 teaspoon finely chopped garlic
½ cup (4 oz) chicken stock
2 teaspoons rice wine or dry sherry
2 teaspoons light soy sauce
⅓ teaspoon sesame oil
1 teaspoon sugar
pinch each of salt and pepper

Cut the peppers into quarters, trimming away the stems, seeds and internal ribs. Coarsely grind the pork and prawn meat and mix to a paste with the seasoning ingredients. Dust the inside of the peppers with cornstarch, then fill each with a portion of filling, smoothing the top. Coat the filling lightly with cornstarch.

❀ Heat the oil and fry the stuffed peppers, filling side down, for about 2 minutes, then turn and fry the other side for a further 2-3 minutes. The peppers should soften but retain a certain crispness. Drain and arrange on a serving plate.

❀ Finely chop the black beans and the white parts of the green onions. Drain off the oil from the wok and return about 1½ tablespoons. Stir-fry the black beans, green onions, ginger and garlic for 1½ minutes, add the remaining sauce ingredients and bring to boil. Simmer for about 1 minute, then add a little cornstarch mixed with cold water to thicken. Pour over the peppers just before serving.

Beijing 北京

DRY STEWED WINTER BAMBOO SHOOTS WITH MUSHROOMS

This recipe involves two cooking methods – stewing and deep-frying. The former tenderizes and flavors, the latter gives a crisp finish.

6 oz (185 g) fresh or canned winter bamboo shoots
    (peeled weight)
4 oz (125 g) fresh or canned button mushrooms
1 cup (8 oz) chicken stock
2 tablespoons light soy sauce
1½ teaspoons sugar
oil for deep-frying
1 tablespoon rice wine or dry sherry
1 teaspoon sesame oil
1 teaspoon sugar (optional)

Wash the bamboo shoots and slice lengthwise into narrow strips. Use a sharp knife to cut a cross in the top of each mushroom cap. Place the bamboo shoots and mushrooms in a saucepan and cover with boiling water. Simmer for 6 minutes, then drain well.

❀ Transfer to a pottery casserole and add the stock, soy sauce and sugar. Bring to boil, then reduce heat and simmer gently, uncovered, until the liquid has evaporated. Stir from time to time so the ingredients are evenly cooked and absorb the seasoning.

❀ Heat the oil in a wok until smoking. Dry the bamboo shoots and mushrooms on paper towels and deep-fry in a frying-basket for 1-1½ minutes or until thoroughly crisp on the surface, but do not overcook or they will taste dry and bitter.

❀ In another wok, stir-fry the bamboo shoots and mushrooms with the rice wine and sesame oil. If desired, sprinkle with sugar before serving.

FRIED "YELLOW CROAKER"

One may be astonished to find yellow croaker fish featuring on the menu of a Chinese vegetarian restaurant, but although the dish looks almost exactly like its aquatic counterpart, it is in fact made from only vegetarian ingredients, wrapped in bean curd skin and molded into a fish shape. A garnish of colorful and tasty ingredients gives it an attractive appearance as well as a salty, hot and sweet taste.

3 dried black mushrooms, soaked for 25 minutes
8 oz (250 g) cooked or canned winter bamboo shoots, chopped
2 teaspoons rice wine or dry sherry
½ teaspoon salt
4 oz (125 g) peeled yam or taro
2 tablespoons peanut oil
2 dried bean curd skins
1 tablespoon all purpose flour
2 teaspoons cornstarch
oil for frying

SAUCE

¼ red bell pepper
¼ green bell pepper
1 oz (30 g) canned bamboo shoots
2 green onions
2 dried red chilies, finely chopped, or 1 tablespoon hot bean sauce
½ teaspoon finely chopped fresh ginger
1 tablespoon light soy sauce
1 tablespoon red vinegar
2 teaspoons rice wine or dry sherry
1 tablespoon sugar
½ cup (4 oz) chicken or vegetable stock
1 teaspoon sesame oil

Drain the mushrooms and squeeze out as much water as possible. Remove stalks and dice the caps finely. Mix with the bamboo shoots and season with wine and salt, then set aside.

Cube the yam and steam over briskly simmering water until tender, then drain and mash while still warm. Heat the peanut oil in a wok and stir-fry the bamboo shoots and mushrooms for 1 minute, then mix in the yam and set aside.

Wipe the bean curd skins with a wet cloth to soften. Place one on top of the other and spoon the filling along the center of the top one. Wrap the top skin around the filling in a narrow rectangular shape, then wrap the other skin around this, working it into the shape of a fish.

Mix the flour and cornstarch with a little cold water and brush thickly over the "fish."

Shallow-fry the "fish" in a wok on both sides until golden brown. Lift out carefully, using two spatulas, and place on a serving plate. Keep warm.

To prepare the sauce, dice the peppers finely, discarding inner ribs, seeds and stem. Dice the bamboo shoots and green onions. Heat 3 tablespoons of the frying oil and stir-fry the vegetables for 1½ minutes or until softened. Add the chilies or hot bean sauce and fry briefly, then add the remaining sauce ingredients and bring to boil. Simmer briskly until the sauce has reduced slightly and pour over the "fish." Serve immediately.

FRIED "YELLOW CROAKER"

VEGETABLE AND CHICKEN ROLLS

Beijing 北京

VEGETABLE AND CHICKEN ROLLS

6 oz (185 g) chicken breast meat
18 bok choy hearts, or hearts of other fresh young Chinese
   green vegetable
2 fresh red chilies or ½ red bell pepper
2 egg whites
3 tablespoons cornstarch
large pinch of salt
3 tablespoons lard or vegetable oil

SEASONING/SAUCE

¾ cup (6 oz) chicken stock
1 green onion, finely chopped
2 slices fresh ginger, shredded
2 teaspoons rice wine or dry sherry
½ teaspoon salt
1½ teaspoons cornstarch

Cut the chicken meat into 18 long, thin slices and set aside. Trim and thoroughly wash the vegetable hearts and drain well. Cook in boiling water until half done, then drain. Cut the chili or pepper into thin slivers.

🌸 Mix the egg whites with cornstarch and salt to a paste. Spread some of this paste over each piece of chicken and wrap around the center of each vegetable heart. Spread the remaining cornstarch paste over the top of the chicken and tie a strip of red chili or pepper around the center of each to hold the bundles in place.

🌸 Heat the lard or vegetable oil in a wok and gently fry half the vegetable rolls, turning several times carefully, until the chicken is white and the vegetable is cooked through. Remove, cook the remaining rolls and set aside.

🌸 Reheat the wok, pour in the pre-mixed sauce ingredients and bring to boil. Carefully slide in the rolls and turn in the sauce until evenly coated. Lift onto a serving plate and serve immediately.

STEWED MUSHROOM SOUP

Guangzhou 广州

STEWED MUSHROOM SOUP

Several types of mushrooms grow in different seasons in Guangdong. Gill fungus, which grows during periods of excessive rainfall, is of poorer quality and slightly inferior fragrance than the large winter mushrooms with a thick cap and strong scent. This type is called "dong gu," and the variegated ones are the most outstanding, with a cracked surface and excellent color and fragrance.

This kind of mushroom soup is traditionally simmered in a clay or "sandy" pot covered with a piece of tissue paper tied on with string.

24 dried black mushrooms, soaked for 25 minutes
6 slices fresh ginger
2 green onions
6 cups (1½ l) Superior Stock (*see page 124*)
2 tablespoons rendered chicken fat (optional)

SEASONING

2 teaspoons rice wine or dry sherry
1¾ teaspoons salt
1 teaspoon sugar

Drain the mushrooms and trim the stems close to the caps. Place in a saucepan with half the ginger and green onions, add a pinch of salt and cover with cold water. Bring to boil, simmer for 3 minutes and drain.

🌸 Return the mushrooms to the saucepan, adding the remaining ginger and green onions, the seasoning ingredients, stock, and chicken fat, if used. Bring just to boil, cover and simmer very gently for about 30 minutes. The liquid should be kept just below the boil so that the soup remains clear. Skim off the chicken fat and serve.

Beijing 北京

BRAISED BAMBOO SHOOTS

12 oz (375 g) fresh or canned bamboo shoots
½ cup (2 oz) cornstarch
2 cups (16 oz) oil for frying
3 slices fresh ginger
¼ small red bell pepper
¼ small green bell pepper
½ teaspoon sesame oil

SEASONING/SAUCE

¾ cup (6 oz) clear stock*
1 tablespoon dark soy sauce
1 teaspoon rice wine or dry sherry
1 teaspoon sugar

Wash fresh bamboo shoots and boil for about 8 minutes or until half cooked; drain canned bamboo shoots. Cut into long

BRAISED BAMBOO SHOOTS

STIR-FRIED DICED CARROTS

slices, make a short slit along the center of each slice and pull one end through the center slit so that the slice of bamboo shoot forms a curl. Coat with cornstarch and fry in hot oil until the coating is lightly colored. Lift out and drain.

In another wok heat 1½ tablespoons oil and fry the ginger slices for 30 seconds, then discard. Add the bamboo shoots and pour in the seasoning/sauce ingredients. Simmer until the bamboo shoots are tender.

Shred the pepper finely and add to the pan. Heat until softened, then sprinkle with the sesame oil and serve.

To prepare the clear stock, stir-fry a handful of bean sprouts in a wok, then add 2 cups (16 oz) water and simmer briefly until reduced by half. Use the sprouts for other purposes.

Beijing 北京

STIR-FRIED DICED CARROTS

This side dish originated in the days of the Manchurian invasion. During the battle the soldiers had no time to cook, so they would just roast over an open fire whatever meat or vegetables they could find, then add some brown bean sauce to enhance the flavor. Even after the establishment of the Qing Dynasty (1644-1911 AD) this style of cooking remained popular, although the imperial chefs improved the flavor by stir-frying and these dishes became daily side dishes at the imperial court.

4 oz (125 g) lean pork
8 oz (250 g) young carrots
1 tablespoon sesame oil
2 cubes dried bean curd, soaked for 10 minutes
1 tablespoon dried shrimp, soaked for 25 minutes
2 tablespoons lard
2 green onions, chopped
2 slices fresh ginger, chopped
1 tablespoon brown bean sauce
1 tablespoon light soy sauce
2 teaspoons rice wine or dry sherry
⅓ cup (2½ oz) chicken stock
1 teaspoon cornstarch

Dice the pork and carrots and sauté the carrots in the sesame oil in a wok for about 2 minutes or until they turn red, then set aside. Squeeze the water from the dried bean curd and cut into small dice. Drain the shrimp.

In a wok, stir-fry the pork in the lard over high heat until it turns white, then add the green onions, ginger and brown bean sauce and stir-fry for another minute.

Add the carrots, bean curd and dried shrimp and continue to stir-fry until the carrot is tender. Add the soy sauce and rice wine and fry again briefly, then add the stock mixed with the cornstarch and stir-fry together until the sauce thickens. Add about 1 teaspoon of the sesame oil used to stir-fry the carrots, and serve at once.

Beijing 北京

FRIED WINTER BAMBOO SHOOTS

Winter bamboo shoots are the very young shoots of a particular type of hairy bamboo. They have a distinct flavor and are considered to be tastier than other winter vegetables. In this dish they are combined with crisply fried lobe-leaf seaweed.

1 lb (500 g) fresh or canned winter bamboo shoots
¾ teaspoon salt
2 tablespoons rice wine or dry sherry
1 oz (30 g) lobe-leaf seaweed (wakame)
oil for deep-frying

Peel the coarse outer leaves from the fresh bamboo shoots and cut off their tough bases. Cut each shoot lengthwise into quarters, place in a dish and season with the salt and wine.

Soak the seaweed in warm water to soften, then drain well and cut out the hard spine and any tough ribs. Rinse again in cold water, cut into small pieces and drain.

Heat the wok and add about ½ cup (4 oz) oil. When very hot, stir-fry the bamboo shoots until the edges are crisp, then remove with a slotted spoon and set aside.

Add another cup (8 oz) oil and heat to the smoking point. Deep-fry the seaweed until crisp and bright green. Do not overcook or it will turn brown and taste bitter. Remove from the oil, mix with the bamboo shoots and serve immediately.

FRIED WINTER BAMBOO SHOOTS

TWO KINDS OF MUSHROOMS WITH GREEN VEGETABLES

MUSHROOM AND PORK PATTIES

Shanghai 上海

TWO KINDS OF MUSHROOMS WITH GREEN VEGETABLES

2 hearts of young Chinese cabbage (bok choy)
peanut or vegetable oil
8 oz (250 g) fresh button mushrooms
12 dried black mushrooms, soaked for 25 minutes

SAUCE A

1 cup (8 oz) liquid from the soaked dried mushrooms
1 tablespoon dark soy sauce
1 teaspoon sugar
1 teaspoon cornstarch

SAUCE B

½ cup (4 oz) chicken stock
1 tablespoon milk or cream
1 teaspoon cornstarch
½ teaspoon sugar
½ teaspoon sesame oil
¼ teaspoon salt

Cut the vegetable hearts in half lengthwise, remove the ends of the stems and discard any wilting or loose leaves. Rinse well in cold water, then shake out as much water as possible.
✿ Stir-fry the cabbage in a wok with 1 tablespoon oil for 1 minute. Add 3 tablespoons water, cover and braise until tender. Lift out, drain and keep warm.
✿ Trim the fresh button mushrooms and rinse with cold water, then dry well. Drain the black mushrooms, squeeze the water out and cut off the stems.
✿ Heat about 2 tablespoons oil in a wok and stir-fry the black mushrooms for 1 minute. Mix the sauce A ingredients together and pour into the wok. Simmer for about 3 minutes or until the liquid is well reduced and the mushrooms are tender. Spoon onto one end of an oval serving plate and arrange the green vegetables across the center.
✿ Rinse out the wok and heat 2 tablespoons oil. Stir-fry the button mushrooms quickly, add the sauce B ingredients and simmer until softened. Check the seasoning, dish out onto the other end of the serving plate and serve at once.

Beijing 北京

MUSHROOM AND PORK PATTIES

Black mushrooms are considered to be the queen of the mushrooms, not only because of their exceptional taste but also because of their high nutritional and medicinal value. People who work with black mushrooms are said never to suffer from influenza because they are constantly inhaling the powder from the dried mushrooms.

24 medium-size dried black mushrooms
6 oz (185 g) lean pork, preferably fillet/tenderloin
1 tablespoon cornstarch
1 cup (8 oz) oil or lard for frying
3-4 slices canned or fresh and cooked bamboo shoot (garnish)

SEASONING

2 teaspoons ginger juice
1 egg white
½ teaspoon salt

SAUCE

¾ cup (6 oz) reserved mushroom liquid or chicken stock
1 tablespoon rice wine or dry sherry
1 tablespoon light soy sauce
1½ teaspoons sugar
1-2 teaspoons oyster sauce
2½ teaspoons cornstarch

Place the mushrooms in a heatproof dish and cover with warm water. Let soak for at least 25 minutes until softened, then place the dish on a rack in a wok or steamer, cover and steam for 10 minutes. Remove and drain well, then cut off the stems, squeeze the excess liquid from the caps and set aside.
✿ Very finely grind the pork, add the seasoning ingredients and stir the mixture in one direction only until smooth. Dust the inside of the mushroom caps lightly with cornstarch and fill with a portion of the pork paste, smoothing the tops with a wet spoon.
✿ Heat the oil or lard in a wok and fry the mushrooms, filling downwards, for about 1½ minutes. Remove and drain well.
✿ Pour off the oil, add the pre-mixed sauce ingredients except the cornstarch to the wok and bring to boil. Slide in the mushrooms and simmer for about 4 minutes, then transfer to a serving plate and garnish with the bamboo slices.
✿ Mix the cornstarch with a little cold water and stir into the sauce. Stir over moderate heat until thickened, then pour over the mushroom patties and serve at once.

Guangzhou 广州

STUFFED MUSHROOMS

10 dried black mushrooms, soaked for 25 minutes
½ teaspoon salt
2 tablespoons cornstarch
6 oz (185 g) chicken breast meat
1 tablespoon chicken stock or water
1 teaspoon rice wine or dry sherry
1 egg white
1½ teaspoons lard
pinch each of salt and pepper
½ slice Yunnan or other well-salted ham
10 cilantro leaves
1 tablespoon rendered chicken fat, melted (optional)

SAUCE

½ cup (4 oz) chicken stock
1 teaspoon rice wine or dry sherry
1 teaspoon cornstarch
pinch each of salt and pepper

Drain and rinse the mushrooms in boiling water and add the salt. Drain again, then squeeze to remove excess liquid. Trim the stems close to the caps and dust inside each cap with cornstarch.

Very finely grind the chicken meat in a food processor. Add the stock, wine, egg white, lard, salt and pepper, and mix in one direction only until the filling is smooth and sticky. Use a wet spoon to mound it into the mushroom caps, smoothing the tops.

Lightly oil a wide, flat, heatproof plate and arrange the mushrooms on this with the filling up. Chop the ham very finely, sprinkle a little over each mushroom and add a cilantro leaf.

Set the plate on a rack in a wok or steamer, cover and steam for about 15 minutes or until the mushrooms are tender and the filling is cooked through.

Mix the sauce ingredients together in another wok and simmer until thickened. Pour the sauce over the mushrooms and sprinkle with the chicken fat, if used, before serving.

STUFFED MUSHROOMS

Beijing 北京

SNOWFLAKE WALNUT PASTE

Walnuts are good for the skin, hair (making it more black and shiny), lungs and kidneys, and are said to stimulate the appetite. This rich combination of ground walnuts and dried fruits makes a dessert suitable to serve after a banquet or important dinner.

4 slices white or whole-grain bread
3 oz (90 g) halved walnuts
1½ cups (12 oz) vegetable oil
1½ oz (45 g) pitted dates
1 oz (30 g) raisins
1 oz (30 g) dried apricots
1 oz (30 g) candied citron, mango, papaya or pineapple
3 eggs, separated
1½ tablespoons lard
3 tablespoons sugar
strips of dried fruit and peel

Remove the crusts from the bread, tear into pieces and soak in a dish with water until softened, then drain and squeeze out as much water as possible.

Drop the walnuts into a saucepan of boiling water, leave for 3 minutes, then drain and carefully peel off all the skin. This is time consuming, but the skin must be removed or the dish will have a bitter aftertaste.

Heat the oil in a wok and fry the peeled walnuts for about 3 minutes over moderate heat or until lightly colored. Remove and drain well, then chop very finely and mix with the bread.

Finely chop the dried and candied fruit and stir into the nut and bread mixture, adding the egg yolks.

Heat the wok, add the lard and gently fry the mixture over moderate to low heat for about 5 minutes, then add the sugar and continue cooking until it forms a glossy ball. Pile into an attractively shaped dish and press down firmly, then unmold onto a serving plate.

Beat the egg whites until stiff and pour into a lightly oiled shallow heatproof dish. Decorate with strips of dried fruit and peel and place on a rack in a wok or steamer. Cover and steam for about 6 minutes or until firmly set, then slide on top of the walnut paste and serve at once.

Shanghai 上海

FRESH FRUITS IN WATERMELON

Long ago, folk artists south of the Yangtze River developed the "watermelon lamp" by carving historical and legendary scenes into the skin of a watermelon, scooping out the flesh and placing a lighted candle inside the melon to illuminate the illustrations.

This carving art is used in modern cuisine and melons are decorated with traditional designs of flora and fauna with suitable calligraphy.

1 round watermelon, plus 1 watermelon end
4 lb (2 kg) diced fresh fruit, including orange and tangerine segments, pear, apple and pineapple
glacé or maraschino cherries

Wash the round melon and cut off the top to form a lid. Decorate the edge of the melon and lid with a scalloped or zig-zag design.

Scoop out the flesh, pick out the seeds and cut half of the flesh into cubes. Mix with the diced fresh fruit and glacé cherries and set aside.

Carve the desired design into the rind of the melon, then shape the extra watermelon end to use as a base.

Stand the base on a serving platter and position the carved melon shell on top. Fill with the prepared fruit. Place the lid in position and serve.

CANDIED APPLE

Beijing 北京

CANDIED APPLE

This northern-style dessert has become popular in Beijing restaurants around the world, and consists of slivers of apple coated with piping-hot sugar toffee. They are dipped into a dish of ice water before eating so that the outer coating of toffee is crisp, while the apple is tender and sweet inside.

3-4 ripe apples
½ cup (2 oz) all purpose flour
3 tablespoons cornstarch
1 egg white, lightly beaten
oil for deep-frying
1-2 teaspoons sesame oil
ice water

TOFFEE

½ cup (4 oz) sugar
2 tablespoons water
1 tablespoon lard

Peel and core the apples, then cut into wedges. Place the flour in a plastic bag, add the apple wedges, close the top and shake vigorously to coat the apple evenly with flour. Remove the apple and mix the remaining flour with the cornstarch and egg white to make a thick batter, adding a little cold water as needed.

❋ Heat the oil in a wok until almost smoking and add the sesame oil. Dip each piece of apple into the batter and deep-fry in several batches until golden, turning once or twice. Drain well.

❋ Spread a little sesame oil over a serving plate and pour the ice water into a bowl.

❋ Drain the wok and add the toffee ingredients. Cook over moderate heat without stirring until the sugar has turned a caramel color, then quickly turn off the heat.

❋ Dip each piece of apple into the toffee using wooden chopsticks and place on the oiled plate. Serve immediately, dipping into the ice water before eating.

STUFFED PEARS

Sichuan 四川

STUFFED PEARS

The snow pear from Sichuan has a crisp, firm texture, is very sweet and juicy, and is thought to be beneficial for the lungs and throat. The unique dish described in this recipe is often served as dessert at winter banquets.

8 Chinese "snow pears" or other ripe fresh pears
1 tablespoon glutinous rice
1 tablespoon pearl barley
8 lotus seeds, fresh, dried or canned
8 fox nuts (optional)
4 dates
16 glacé cherries
1½ tablespoons chopped candied citron or pineapple
½ cup (4 oz) crushed rock candy
1 tablespoon water

Peel, core and stem the pears. Rinse the rice, barley, lotus seeds and fox nuts, place in a heatproof dish on a rack in a wok or steamer, cover and steam until cooked.

※ Pit the dates and chop them with 8 glacé cherries and the citron. Add to the cooked ingredients and stuff the filling into the prepared pears.

※ Stand the pears upright on a heatproof plate and steam for about 15 minutes or until tender. Decorate each with a glacé cherry.

※ Melt the rock candy in a wok, adding 1 tablespoon water. Cook gently until golden, then pour over the pears and serve.

Sichuan 四川

LOQUAT JELLY

The serving of dried and fresh fruits at banquets goes back some two thousand years in China. We can find such terms as "Bian Shi" in ancient books. "Bian" indicates a kind of food basket made of split bamboo, which was used to hold fruit or dried meat at banquets and when offering sacrifices to gods or ancestors.

Although actual desserts made a late appearance in Chinese menus, many varieties of jellied fruit desserts became popular once the gelatinous seaweed extract agar agar became available. This recipe can be adapted for seasonal availability of fruits, loquats being a refreshing summer dessert.

24 fresh loquats, or apricots
½ oz (15 g) agar agar strips or powder*
3 cups (24 oz) cold water
½ cup sugar
glacé cherries

Skin the loquats and remove the seeds, then place one each in the bottom of 24 Chinese teacups or other small dishes.

※ Place the agar agar in a wok or saucepan, add the water and slowly bring to boil, stirring constantly. Simmer for 2-3 minutes, then add the sugar and stir slowly until dissolved. Simmer for another 2-3 minutes.

※ Strain through a fine mesh strainer over the loquats. Allow to cool, then chill in the refrigerator.

※ Unmold the jellies onto a serving plate and decorate the dish with glacé cherries. Serve cold.

Strip agar agar may require more time to dissolve than powdered types. Jellies made with agar agar do not require refrigeration once they have set.

LOQUAT JELLY

Glossary

ABALONE The king of the mollusks in Chinese cuisine. It is widely available canned or dried, but, like most other ingredients in any Chinese recipe, fresh is better.

AGAR AGAR Sheets of dried, pressed seaweed that feature in some Chinese and Manchurian dishes. It is used like gelatin, which can act as a substitute. Can also be bought in powdered form.

BALSAM PEAR (CHINESE BITTER MELON) A small, wrinkled, cucumber-like vegetable with soft flesh and a central seed core. It adds a tart taste to stews and braised dishes, and is sold fresh or canned. Cucumber is a pleasant alternative.

BAMBOO SHOOTS These look like the horn of a small water buffalo. Different species vary in size, texture and taste. Originally the shoot was used in northern and western cuisines, but in recent years it has also appeared on the Guangdong table. They can be bought in cans in Chinese stores; celery hearts make a passable substitute.

BEAN CURD The processed extract of the soybean, available as a jelly or custard, or in dried, fried, hard or soft cakes of all shapes and sizes. Takes on the taste and aroma of whatever it is cooked with.

Bean curd sheets come in dry layers and are used to wrap other ingredients, usually for stews. When slowly cooked, the sheets dissolve to produce a rich soy milk broth. Soak or dampen before use.

Preserved or *fermented bean curd* comes in tough-skinned squares in a pickle of chili and brine. Known as Chinese cheese, the taste often seems offensive to Western palates, just as dairy cheeses are often unpleasant in taste and odor to the Chinese.

BEAN PASTE There are many varieties, made from different ingredients added to a basic fermented paste usually made from soybeans. Pastes can be found in cans and jars in every Chinese food shop. Even if the colorful labels are in Chinese only, the pictures give a good indication of what the contents will taste like.

Hot bean paste is served with every Sichuan and Hunan meal. It is made from the basic soy paste with hot red peppers crushed and fried in oil. Salty and palate-jarringly hot, it gives Sichuan food its distinctive taste.

Hot black bean paste is one of the most flavorful of all the seasonings; it is a marvelous accompaniment to crab. This fermented sauce comes in many brands and styles. All are delicious.

Sweet bean paste is a rich, salty, sweet sauce made from soybeans fermented with salt, sugar and seasonings. Used in marinades, as a seasoning and as a dip.

Yellow bean paste comes from the yellow soybean and is very salty. Used sparingly it is delicious, but too much can kill rather than complement other tastes.

BEAN PASTE, SWEETENED RED This is a thick, sweet mixture made from red beans. Used as a filling for cakes, dumplings and buns.

BEAN SAUCES *Brown bean sauce* is a more liquid version of the fermented bean paste, being quite salty in taste but mildly flavored. *Hot bean sauce* is a mixture of fermented soybean and chili preserved in salt.

BEAN SPROUTS Available fresh or canned. The fresh ones will keep for at least a week in a sealed plastic bag or box, and are vastly superior to the canned variety.

To grow them at home, soak a half cup of dried soy or mung beans overnight. Line a colander with dampened cheesecloth, place the beans on top, put another layer of cloth over them and pour on a cup of warm water. Suspend the colander in a large saucepan and place in a warm cupboard. Give the beans another soaking through the cloth four times a day for five days, by which time you should have a nice crop of sprouts ready for the pot or wok.

BEAN THREAD NOODLES Made from mung bean starch. The light, translucent threads are used to thicken stews and hot pots or as the base for a vegetarian meal.

BITTER MELON *See* **BALSAM PEAR**.

BOK CHOY Choy means "vegetables" in Chinese and bok means "white." The chef in the Chinese kitchen has an enormous range from which to choose. Generally, the generous southern gardens provide the widest selection of fresh greens; the further north one goes, the narrower the range. The Chinese "white cabbage" is a small, white-stemmed cabbage with deep-green leaves, a favorite of the Guangdong kitchen and a staple green accompaniment for many a meat or bean curd dish. There are hundreds of different varieties of cabbage, scores of assorted types of bok choy. Some cousins of this family are as small as 4 in (10 cm) long; others grow three times as large. Bok choy should be cooked as swiftly as possible, no more than two or three minutes, and served immediately to keep the succulent taste and goodness of the leaves.

CABBAGE Comes in a great variety from tiny, delicate bok choy to the solid northern Tianjin cabbage. It is an essential and delicious part of many meals. Any cabbage can be used with magnificent effect.

CAMPHOR Woodchips used to smoke poultry, particularly chicken for Jiangsu, Henan and Anhui dishes. Black tea leaves do the job equally well.

CASSIA A variety of cinnamon found in southern China.

CHICKEN FAT The rendered fat of a chicken, melted in a double boiler over rapidly boiling water. Used for stir-frying and to add flavor and shine to sauces and finished dishes. Duck fat is treated in the same way.

CHILI OIL Used in spicy dishes, this is made by heating 1/2 cup (4 oz) of sesame or vegetable oil and adding 2 1/2 tablespoons chili powder, flakes or, best of all, whole chilies. The oil is then cooled and strained. It keeps indefinitely in a storage jar.

CHILI PASTE Can be added to the food during cooking or placed in a side dish for diners' individual use.

CHOY SUM A sparsely leafed green vegetable with small yellow flowerheads and a slightly bitter flavor.

CHRYSANTHEMUM The fresh petals of white chrysanthemum flowers are used as a garnish and for their delicate flavor in some dishes.

CILANTRO Also called coriander or Chinese parsley, this has a much stronger flavor than the Western parsley, which can be used as a poor substitute. Cilantro will grow like a weed in a windowbox or garden, and every serious amateur chef should have some growing.

FEN LIQUOR A strong spirit used mainly in marinades. Vodka, white rum or brandy can be used instead with little cost to taste.

FERMENTED BLACK BEANS Soft, dried, salted black beans used as a flavoring.

FERMENTED GLUTINOUS RICE JUICE The result of cooked glutinous rice being treated with brewer's yeast to produce a fermentation with a strong brewed flavor.

FISH SAUCE More familiar in the Vietnamese kitchen, but originally Chinese and still used in many country recipes. The pale brown, light sauce can be used sparingly for cooking or as a condiment in which to dip vegetables.

FIVE-SPICE POWDER Made from cinnamon, brown Sichuan peppercorns, cloves, fennel and anise. Different chefs call for different proportions of the spices, and trial and error is the best way to find a suitable blend. It is available commercially.

FUNGI Countless varieties of dried fungi are available, including *cloud ear fungus* and *wood ear fungus*. Soak to soften.

GALANGAL The aromatic rootstock of certain plants of the ginger family; also called laos.

GINGER One of the major ingredients in Chinese cuisine. Its taste is as pleasing as the appearance of the knobbly, gnarled root is ugly. With meat, fowl, fish and vegetable dishes, steamed, stir-fried or stewed, finely chopped ginger is indispensable for almost every Chinese meal. It can be stored for weeks in a refrigerator, but use it fresh wherever possible. Make sure all skin is peeled off before use.

GINGER JUICE Made by squeezing slices of fresh ginger in a garlic press.

GINGKO NUTS Small, oval nuts, sometimes called white nuts. Used mainly in vegetarian dishes, stuffings, soups, or as a garnish. Sold fresh, canned or dried, the bitter core must be removed before use.

GLUTINOUS RICE Available as long- or short-grain varieties, it has a cloudy, white appearance, unlike the usual pearly white rice. When cooked it forms a sticky mass, and is often used in sweets and cakes.

GOLDEN NEEDLES The dried flower buds of the tiger lily. Used in simmered winter dishes and stir-fried to both give and take flavor from other ingredients. Usually knotted before being added to the dish.

HOISIN SAUCE Made from soybeans and chilies, with sugar and salt added to give it a sweet but biting taste. A delicious partner for meat and poultry dishes.

LARD Rendered pork fat used for stir-frying and for sweets and pastry making.

LICHEES Justly famed as one of the best ways to finish a feast. The rough red skin peels off to reveal the ripe, plump, juicy pulp. Also available canned.

LOQUATS Look like apricots but taste like peaches.

LOTUS The floating leaves of the lotus, immortalized in Chinese paintings, are only the most obvious part of the plant. The seeds, pale yellow when dried, are used for decorating desserts or for casual nibbling. The root looks like a string of plump, firm sausages, the sweet flesh inside something like a ripe cucumber. The delicacy can be braised, stir-fried or boiled, and at festivals is sold as a candied sweet.

LOTUS SEED PASTE Boiled and mashed with oil and sugar, the seeds make a dry but rich paste.

LUFFA A long, green gourd halfway between a skinny pumpkin and an okra. It can be distinguished in markets by the heavy ridges running along the skin, and is sometimes known as angled luffa because of the angles made by these ridges. The squash-like flesh, with little taste of its own, is usually stir-fried with other vegetables or meat.

MAO TAI A potent (some might say lethal) clear spirit with an overwhelming odor and a memorable aftereffect. Not for nothing is it known as White Lightning. Mao Tai is a common accompaniment for a Chinese banquet, along with rice wines and some of China's excellent beers. Newcomers to the Chinese table should beware of overindulgence in Mao Tai and similar spirits, such as the equally fearsome Kaoliang.

MELONS Available in all shapes and sizes, but the most commonly used are the globe-shaped, light green *winter melons*. The white, juicy flesh can be cut out and cooked as the main ingredient in the famed Winter Melon Soup, then served in the original gourd which has been carved into a superb decorative shape. Substitute hollowed watermelon for the shell and chayotes for the flesh.

MONOSODIUM GLUTAMATE (MSG) You either swear by it or curse it. Many professional Chinese chefs call MSG "the master" because a handful of the substance allows them to serve just about anything and make it taste good. But in recent years there has been a wide backlash against MSG; many people doubt its culinary value and fear its side effects. Originally made from wheat gluten which had been dried and fermented, MSG has for decades been made chemically. Overuse of it causes various symptoms such as headaches, hot flushes, mouth dryness and tiredness. Many chefs and experienced cooks refuse to use MSG, and in such culinary capitals as Hong Kong there is a move in a number of leading Chinese restaurants to ban its use. Some of these establishments proudly boast that they do not use MSG; the result is that they attract hordes of knowledgeable gourmets who want to savor real tastes instead of chemicals.

MUSHROOMS These come in infinite varieties. Every province has its prize ones, but *dried black mushrooms* are universal. They can be purchased in most Chinese food stores and must be soaked to soften before use. Any type of mushroom makes a palatable and acceptable alternative in home cooking, although European varieties have a foreign flavor. The most common Chinese types are *button mushrooms, yellow straw mushrooms, golden needle mushrooms, black forest mushrooms* and the large *umbrella mushrooms* of Hunan.

MUSTARD The green leaves, which come in a number of forms, mostly dark green and sometimes pickled, are used in stir-fried dishes and some stews. The thick stem/root section needs to be shredded or diced before use.

NOODLES Fat, thin, long, short, broad, slender – take your pick because they come in all shapes and sizes. They can be made of mung bean starch, wheat flour or rice. Home cooks in non-Asian countries can use Italian pastas in place of noodles in most Chinese recipes.

OIL FOR STIR-FRYING Vegetable oil is almost invariably used. It can be flavored with chili (*see* chili oil) or, more rarely, with onion, ginger or five-spice powder.

ORANGE PEEL Is used to add a dash of sweetness to spicy Hunan and Sichuan dishes. You can buy it dried or canned, or cut your own.

OYSTER SAUCE A delicious and classic accompaniment to swiftly stir-fried greens. The rich flavoring comes from steamed oysters judiciously blended with soy sauce and salt.

PEA LEAVES The small, bright green leaves from the sweet pea plant. Young spinach will do instead.

PEPPER The black and white varieties were introduced during the Tang Dynasty (618-907 AD), when pepper was called for in almost every dish at the tables of the wealthy.

PEPPER, SICHUAN The brown peppercorn of western China – the flower pepper of Sichuan – is still favored above the "barbarian" pepper, and the whole peppercorn is often cooked rather than being ground. It is in fact the seed of the prickly ash tree (*Xanthoxylum pipertum*). Also known as Fagara pepper, and sold under the Japanese name Sansho.

PEPPERCORN SALT A mixture of ground Sichuan brown peppercorns and salt. Used as a seasoning and condiment.

PICKLES Served at the start of a meal or to add a pungent, salty flavor to Chinese cooking, they differ depending on the region and the season. There are countless varieties of vegetables and pickling solutions, but among the most popular pickles are cabbages, mustard greens and roots, radishes, turnips and cucumbers. Chilies are often added to the brine to give a spicy taste.

PLUM SAUCE Tart and sweet at the same time, it has a taste that seems heaven-sent to go with roast goose or duck. It also contains apricots, chili and vinegar, which explains the exciting reddish brown tone.

PORK CAUL FAT A large, netlike sheet of pork fat, used to wrap food to form rolls or to prevent dryness. It holds the food together while frying but eventually melts away unless coated with batter or flour, when it makes a crisp crust. Available from Chinese food stores.

PRAWNS or SHRIMP The heads and tails are generally left on to add flavor and color to the dish. To devein, hold with the back curling upwards, push a toothpick into the center back and gently hook out the dark vein. You can also cut along the back with a sharp knife and pull out the vein.

Cooked prawns or shrimp are easily peeled by sliding the shell off. To peel uncooked prawns, cut the shell along the underside between the rows of legs and remove the whole shell.

PRESERVED VEGETABLES Used to give a pungent, salty flavor to Chinese dishes. Sold by weight in Chinese food stores, they are also known as spiced vegetables. Preserved mustard is the most common – either mustard greens or the mustard stem or root, which must be shredded or diced before use.

QUAIL EGGS Readily available hard-cooked in cans. Substitute very small chicken eggs.

RED FERMENTED RICE (WINE LEES) A mash of red rice and wine. Called for in some regional recipes and virtually impossible to obtain in Western countries. Japanese miso paste can be used instead, but should first be diluted with water.

RICE WINE Many varieties are available, but *Shaoxing rice wine* is possibly the most famous in China and essential to many Shanghai and Yangtze Valley recipes. Available in most Chinese food stores worldwide, any shopowner will be delighted to chat about the different wines he stocks. As a drink to accompany food, it should be served warm from a teapot-like container in small cups without handles. Dry sherry can be used as a substitute in cooking.

SCALLION OIL Used to give extra flavor when stir-frying. It is made by frying coarsely chopped green onions (scallions) in oil until light brown. Use 4 green onions to 3 tablespoons of oil, and discard onions with a slotted spoon before using the oil. Peanut oil is preferred by Cantonese cooks, although other vegetable oils are suitable.

SEA CUCUMBER (BÊCHE-DE-MER) Actually a sea slug, this is a delicacy among southern gourmets who prize its rubbery texture. Known also as sea bear (because of its resemblance to bear's paw), it is the basis of expensive specialty dishes in some of the world's top Chinese restaurants. Soak, remove stomach, then pre-cook for one to several hours, depending on cooking time of final dish.

SEAWEEDS Mostly used in conjunction with other vegetables in soups. They must be soaked before use, preferably overnight, and should be rinsed thoroughly before and after soaking.

SESAME OIL Comes from the crushed and roasted seeds of the sesame plant. This treatment gives the oil its rich, nutty taste. It is used mainly as an aromatic garnish, and occasionally for cooking.

SESAME PASTE A thick tan paste made from ground sesame seeds. Peanut butter is a rather poor substitute for the aromatic, thick richness of sesame, but Middle Eastern sesame paste, or tahini, is widely available.

SHARKS' FINS Can be bought from well-stocked Chinese stores, but they are extremely expensive and daunting to prepare.

SHRIMP CHIPS Also called prawn crackers or "krupuk," they are compressed slivers of shrimp and flour paste. They expand into large translucent chips when deep-fried.

SHRIMP PASTE Is sold dried and should be cooked before being eaten. It has an unpleasant smell before cooking, but adds a distinctive flavor to certain dishes. Anchovy paste can be used instead if necessary.

SILVER SPROUTS Mung bean sprouts with the roots and seed pods removed. They are silvery when cooked.

SOY SAUCE Makes a Chinese meal. It is hard to imagine picking up your chopsticks without this familiar friend at your elbow. Salty, pungent, and essential for cooking and as a table-top condiment, it is absolutely indispensable for the enjoyment of Chinese food. *Light soy sauce* is thinner and lighter in flavor than *black soy sauce*, which is used mainly in stews. *Sweet soy sauce* is thick, black and sweet.

STAR ANISE   Comes from a shrub that is cousin to the magnolia. It gets its name from the star-like splay of its pod. Western anise, although not from the same botanical family, can be used as a substitute.

STOCKS   Vary from region to region, and are made by boiling meat, bones, poultry or vegetables in water for hours, then skimming and filtering. Bouillon cubes are a poor substitute. Clear stock is made by simply frying a handful of bean sprouts and then boiling them in 1 or 2 cups (8-16 oz) of water.

VERMICELLI   Usually a transparent bean thread noodle made from mung bean starch; can also be made from rice flour. Sold dried, in bundles. Both types can be deep-fried or used in soups and stews.

VINEGAR   Plays an important, often overlooked role in every regional kitchen. Each province prides itself on the quality and clarity of its vinegar. *Rice vinegar,* light and clear with a sharp taste, is the most common. Any good-quality vinegar is an acceptable alternative.

Several other types of vinegar are used in Chinese cooking. Distilled from fermented rice, the range includes *red vinegar,* which is mildly flavored and used in sauces and dips; *brown* or *black vinegar,* stronger in taste and color, and with a slight sweetness and fine aroma; *sweet black vinegar* is an especially sweetened dark rice vinegar used only occasionally.

WATER CHESTNUTS   Really the bulb of wild rushes. Very expensive and a lot of trouble to prepare when fresh, but available in cans. The powdered flour called for in some Chinese recipes is also available in Oriental markets.

WHITE RADISH   A popular cold starter, sliced thinly and eaten either raw with chili or pickled; also called daikon. Its sharp taste turns sweet when cooked. Sweet white turnip can be substituted in cooked dishes.

YUNNAN HAM   Reputedly the finest in China. There is nothing quite the same, but a dried Westphalian or Smithfield ham comes close.

WAGUO INN, NEAR SHIMIAN VILLAGE, SICHUAN PROVINCE

HARALD SUND

Index

POULTRY

SEAFOOD

ACKNOWLEDGMENTS

The author and publisher would like to thank the proprietors and staff of the following restaurants for their co-operation and assistance in the production of *China the Beautiful Cookbook*. In particular we would like to thank the chefs who shared the original recipe for each dish with us.

BEIJING

Quanjude Roast Beijing Duck Restaurant, Pianyifang Roast Beijing Duck Restaurant, Donglaishun Restaurant, Kaorouji Restaurant, Kangle Restaurant, Douyichu Shaomai Restaurant, Nanlaishun Xiaochi Restaurant, Tongheju Restaurant, Henan Restaurant, Jinyang Restaurant, Hongbinlou Restaurant, Yanbinlou Restaurant, Chunyanlou Restaurant, Fangshan Restaurant, Tingliguan Restaurant, Fengzeyuan Restaurant, Cuihualou Restaurant, Shaguoji Restaurant, Beijing Vegetarian Restaurant, Beijing Hotel, Xinqiao Hotel.

SHANGHAI

Shanghai Old Restaurant, Laozhengxing Restaurant, Renmin Restaurant, Dafugui Restaurant, Yangzhou Restaurant, Yufoshi Vegetarian Restaurant, Lüyangcun Restaurant, Dongfeng Restaurant, Lübolang Restaurant, Zhiweiguan Hangzhou-style Restaurant, Ningbo Restaurant, Dahongyun Restaurant, Meilongzhen Restaurant, Xinya Cantonese-style Restaurant, Meiweizai Restaurant, Chenghuangmiao Food Centre, Qiaojiazha Dianxin House, Qiaojiazha Restaurant, Wufangzai Dianxin House, Dahuchun Dianxin House, Experimental Restaurant of Shanghai Food and Beverage School, Dianxin House of 1st Food and Beverage Corporation of Huangbu in Shanghai.

GUANGDONG

Panxi Restaurant, Nanyuan Restaurant, Likoufu Sea Food Restaurant, Dasanyuan Restaurant, Dongjiang Restaurant, Snake Restaurant, Shahe Restaurant, Beiyuan Restaurant, Guangzhou Restaurant, Datong Restaurant, Beixiu Restaurant, Daijiang Caotang Restaurant, Quanwailou Restaurant, Shaocheng Restaurant, Tianfu Restaurant.

SICHUAN

Chengdu Restaurant, Furong Restaurant, Xiaodongtian Restaurant, Chen Mapo Bean Curd House, Gongcun Restaurant, Xingfu Restaurant, Yudong Restaurant, Huixian Restaurant, Rongleyuan Restaurant, Laosichuan Restaurant, Jingchengyuan Restaurant, Shangqingsi Restaurant, Yuyuan Restaurant, Yeweixiang Restaurant, Caigengxiang Vegetarian Restaurant.

錦

銀杏黃平青

水煮香瓜術

拙拙麵

銀耳枝花蓮